Essential Social Work Skills

Essential Social Work Skills
A Practical Guide

Glen Hong

California State University, Los Angeles

cognella® | ACADEMIC PUBLISHING

Bassim Hamadeh, CEO and Publisher
Amy Smith, Project Editor
Abbey Hastings, Associate Production Editor
Emely Villavicencio, Senior Graphic Designer
Sara Schennum, Licensing Associate
Natalie Piccotti, Director of Marketing
Kassie Graves, Vice President of Editorial
Jamie Giganti, Director of Academic Publishing

Cover: Copyright © 2017 iStockphoto LP/Cecilie_Arcurs.
Cover: Copyright © 2017 iStockphoto LP/7io.
Cover: Copyright © 2017 iStockphoto LP/Nongkran_ch.
Cover: Copyright © 2018 iStockphoto LP/Asiseeit.

Printed in the United States of America.

ISBN: 978-1-5165-8002-6 (pbk) / 978-1-5165-8003-3 (al)

Brief Contents

Detailed Contents

PREFACE

M any of my colleagues who graduated with their master's degree and are working out in the field would often say to me, "Very little of what I have learned in school is helping me right now." The statements would go on even further as I heard, "I do not know how to diagnose properly, nor do I feel comfortable giving case presentations, and I feel ill prepared for my licensing exam." I have not only heard this from cohorts, but I have experienced this in my past when I graduated with my MSW. Upon graduation with my emphasis on macro practice, I went directly into the field of mental health, and I was honestly not prepared for what was required of me. When I began working, I realized that my graduate program covered a lot of information in several areas, but the application and the ability to master information that I needed was not available to me.

That is why I chose to write this book. This book is a practical guide that covers what social work is, and how it is used on the various levels which include:

- the micro level
- the mezzo level
- the macro level

What makes this book different is that it includes how to implement interventions in a very detailed manner, as well as being able to integrate the various levels and lenses that a social worker must use to solve complex problems. I really emphasized the use of micro-level interventions in this text, which includes diagnosing and treatment planning, use of individual therapy models and family therapy models because often social workers are the least prepared when it comes to these areas. The other reason I emphasized micro-level interventions is because it is necessary for a social worker to be competent in this area to pass the current licensing exam. Mental health is a growing field and, as social workers, knowledge on all levels, especially the micro level, is needed.

The text will come from the standpoint of addressing current and future issues that graduate level students are facing now. The CSWE (The Council on Social Work Education) and the BBS (The Board of Behavioral Sciences) have emphasized in having MSW programs go through a conversion into a more medically based clinical curriculum. This text will not only comply with the Accreditation standards for the MSW program, but it will also prepare students for the ethics and clinical licensing exams that students will need to take after graduation.

I will be using many case examples from my own experience as well as having the student actually incorporate therapeutic interventions in this text. For example in relation to CBT, students are often taught the unhealthy coping skill of mind reading where the client assumes that people are thinking negative thoughts about him/her. This text will take it a step further and actually give the student the follow-up questions and implementation to properly reframe an irrational thought for the client.

EXAMPLE: UNHEALTHY COPING: MIND READING

Therapist:	"How did you know that they hated you? Did they tell you that they hated you?"
Ct:	"No, but I know that they hated me because I could just feel it coming from them." (Mind Reading)
Therapist:	"That means that you would be able to read minds if they did not say anything about disliking you. If you can read minds, what number from 1–100 am I thinking of right now?" (Logic Question)
Ct:	"I don't know, 51?"
Therapist:	"No, it was 10. That means that you cannot read minds. Is it possible that those negative feelings were coming from within you? (Transition Question)

Another aspect that I incorporate is actually using clinical licensing test examples. Through the use of this book, I will demonstrate how what is being learned in this text will benefit students down the road. Below is an example of what graduates and future licensed clinicians will need to know to pass their clinical exam:

LCSW CLINICAL EXAM VIGNETTE

A client John, aged 30, comes in to see you at your clinic. The client states that he hears voices and that he believes that his neighbor is out to get him. He shares that "he puts flowers in a way that I do not like, and there are billboards that prove that my mind is being read." John adds that he has not slept for one week just thinking about it and that he has stopped using cocaine several months ago. John adds that he has had thoughts of suicide and "I get really sad about my future." John's mother is crying as she shares, "We have had so much mental illness in my family and he gets the ups and downs just like me."

What are the diagnostic considerations for this client?

    A. schizophrenia bipolar disorder
         schizoaffective disorder
         major depression
    B. substance-induced psychotic disorder
         major depression
         bipolar disorder
         schizophrenia
    C. bipolar disorder
         psychotic disorder unspecified
         major depression
         r/o schizoaffective disorder
    D. substance abuse
         bipolar disorder
         major depression
         schizophrenia

To answer this question, it would require a social worker to know how to differentially diagnose, as well as have common knowledge of the medical components that are involved with this client. If a person is not properly trained, the common answer to pick is D. This is considered one of the harder clinical questions on the exam, and students who use this text will know exactly how to address and answer this question because of the foundational knowledge they will learn. The answer for this vignette is C.

Fast forward to now as I have had seventeen years working in the field of mental health, I have been teaching clinical courses for the MSW program for over seven years and as the MSW program has gone through a curriculum transition that is more reflective of the current licensing examination format, I have been able to help benefit future practitioners to be prepared for the challenges that they will face. Now, I am getting responses from my students who are graduating that are vastly different than me and my colleagues when we graduated. Students who have taken my clinical courses are saying, "I feel like I am so ahead of the game and I have already registered to take my licensing exam." I am also hearing "You have made complicated information so easy to understand that my supervisor during clinical supervision appears embarrassed because I appear to know more than him." I take so much pride and satisfaction from hearing from students two to three years later after graduation, and being told how they passed their licensing exam the first time around. Being able to take my setbacks, use it as motivation to learn and grow in my career, and to now be able to pass this knowledge on to current students is such a rewarding feeling.

I feel like I have used the past seven years as a professor to properly hone and develop a curriculum format that is tailored for today's social worker. This text also effectively incorporates the various levels of social work into a more integrative form, being true to the person-in-environment model. The text will come with the following materials for instructors which include:

- a master syllabus
- weekly PowerPoint lectures
- flashcards
- test bank questions

ACKNOWLEDGMENTS

I have so many people to thank for this book. First of all, thank you to Kassie Graves, Vice President of Acquisitions, for giving me a chance and believing in this project. I will always be grateful to you and look forward to collaborating more with you in the future. I would also like to thank Amy Smith, Project Editor, for keeping me on track and holding me accountable for making this book the best that it could be. The same thank you goes to Alia Bales, Production Editor, for being integral in making this project happen. And thank you to Jamie Giganti, Director of Academic Publishing, who worked tirelessly in getting this book published. I would also like to thank all of the individuals who reviewed this book and provided the feedback that was incorporated into the final revision of this text. A special thanks to Sheila Gillespie Roth from Carlow University and Ronald Toseland from the University at Albany. I would like to thank my wife Aki for supporting me throughout this endeavor, as well as thanking my sister Diane for giving me the push and direction to begin this project. I would also like to thank all of my close family and friends who are too many to name for all of their support as well. And lastly, I would like to thank all of the students who helped motivate me to see this project through.

CHAPTER 1

The Clinical Social Worker

What does it mean to be a social worker? The joke that my former supervisor would always make is that, "Social work is the discipline of doing everything!" There is definitely truth to that as social work involves putting on so many hats and advocating for the underserved community on many levels. Social work is the discipline that looks at a person in their environment, and utilizing a strengths perspective, conducts an analysis from an ecological perspective. As a social worker, you are looking at an individual in their environment and viewing their interactions through multiple lenses. Let's take a look at some core concepts of social work.

SOCIAL WORKS STARTS WITH MASLOW'S PYRAMID

When assessing individuals, it is important to take into account their needs related to Maslow's hierarchy and address basic needs first. If as social workers we went onto the streets and offered individuals who were homeless free therapy, their first response would be to ask for food or shelter because insight-oriented therapy would be the last thing on their minds. Once their basic needs were secured, then assistance in the form of mobile mental health services including counseling and medications would be initiated. This is an example of a deficit need (food, clothing) taking precedence over growth needs (mental health). When it comes to seeing a client, we as social workers are looking at prioritizing the first three tiers of Maslow's pyramid over the top two tiers. Nasir (2014) points out how, when providing homeless outreach in Pakistan to those on the street, their basic needs had to be addressed first before anything else.

Maslow's (Nasir, 2014) hierarchy of needs is a motivational theory in social work and psychology comprising a five-tier model of human needs using hierarchical levels within a pyramid. Maslow stated that people are motivated to achieve certain needs and that some needs take precedence over others. Our most basic need is for physical survival, and this will be the first thing that motivates our behavior. Once that level is fulfilled, the next level up is what motivates a person to continue to move up the pyramid. Maslow's five-stage model can be divided into deficiency needs and growth needs. The first four levels are often referred to as deficiency needs, and the top level is known as growth needs. The deficiency needs are said to motivate people when they are unmet. Also, the need to fulfill such needs will become stronger the longer the duration they are denied. For example, the longer a person goes without food, the hungrier he/she will become and the more motivated that person will be to obtain food.

One must satisfy lower-level deficit needs before progressing on to meet higher-level growth needs. When a deficit need has been satisfied, it will go away, and our activities become goal-directed towards meeting the next set of needs that we have yet to satisfy. However, growth needs continue to be felt and may even become stronger once they have been engaged. Once these growth needs have been reasonably satisfied, one may be able to reach the highest level called self-actualization. Below are the five stages of Maslow's hierarchy (1943):

1. Biological and physiological needs—air, food, drink, shelter, warmth, sex, sleep
2. Safety needs—protection from elements, security, order, law, stability, freedom from fear
3. Love and belongingness needs—friendship, intimacy, trust and acceptance, receiving and giving affection and love. Affiliating, being part of a group (family, friends, work)

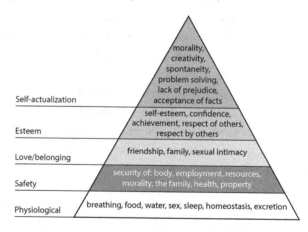

FIGURE 1.1 An Interpretation of Maslow's Hierarchy of Needs

4. Esteem needs—achievement, mastery, independence, status, dominance, prestige, self-respect, respect from others
5. Self-actualization needs—realizing personal potential, self-fulfillment, seeking personal growth and peak experiences

SOCIAL WORK INVOLVES CRITICAL THINKING

Critical thinking is the intellectually disciplined process of actively and skillfully conceptualizing, applying, analyzing, synthesizing, and/or evaluating information gathered from or generated by observation, experience, reflection, reasoning, or communication as a guide to belief and action (Scriven and Paul, 1987). Critical thinking is one of the most important components of social work. Critical thinking is crucial to the process of moving students from merely acquiring and displaying knowledge to critically examining and engaging with the issues of social work as a discipline and a profession (Gibbins, 2004). Moreover, it is understanding that as a social worker you may have a particular point of view of what you believe is going on with a client, but you put that aside and do your best to see from the perspective of the client. At the same time, it is up to the social worker to identify a theoretical lens that will work best for the client. It is very important as a social worker to not take information at face value but to really look into it without judgment and bias. This leads to the four elements of critical thinking which are:

1. Curiosity
    a. Ask questions
2. Realism
    a. See with all of your senses
3. Skepticism
    a. Have healthy doubt
    b. Do not take things for granted
4. Using a social justice lens
    a. Bring a complex and social justice lens to our understanding related to the clients, groups, and communities that we work with

From there, it is important to come up with a theory about why what you are addressing is taking place. *Theories* are a set of ideas intended to explain a certain phenomena regarding individuals and behaviors (Rogers, 2013). Using theories helps us in three ways:

1. It helps us understand our clients in relation to their circumstances.
2. It allows us to explain problems that arise at different stages of life.
3. It guides us toward deciding what *theoretical lens* we are going to use.

For example let's say a young couple who are 24 years of age came in for couples counseling and they are pondering divorce. They share that they have lived together since they were 18 years old, and after getting married this past year they have been fighting constantly and do not understand why this is happening. Their rationale was that they have lived together for five years and barely fought and so the step of marriage would be a smooth transition. One of them shared that they believed, "The longer they lived together before marriage, the lower the chance of them divorcing." Given that this statement is a strong belief that the couple holds, as a social worker, it would be important to research and find pertinent information that could assist this couple. In doing so, we would need to gather data regarding this statement and find out if this is true or not. Once the information has been gathered, the next step is to take a look at what you have and to begin the process of examining the information accumulated. Critical thinking involves five concepts (Holmes, 2015):

1. analyzing—methodically examining in detail the constitution of your acquired information
2. evaluating—assessing to determine the quality of your information and give a value to it
3. reasoning—the process of forming conclusions, judgments, or inferences from facts or premises
4. decision-making—the act of making a decision about the information received
5. problem-solving—the process of finding solutions to difficult or complex problems

If we take a look at statistics regarding living together and divorce rates, we can find out if this statement is true. Based on statistical research (Kuperberg, 2014), it is found that couples who live together before marriage have a 49% chance of divorcing within the first five years of marriage. Conversely, it is found that couples who do not live together before marriage have a 20% rate of divorce within the same five years.

So given the rationale of the couple, what they believed to be true would be false. If this is truly the case, the question then becomes why that is the case, and in finding this information, we can identify how to best treat this couple. In terms of starting to think critically, the following components are needed:

1. Take an interest in the unknown.
2. Challenge appearances.
3. Push/Prod/Poke to make it all add up.
4. Accept the results.

If we took the original statement at face value, it would logically make a lot of sense: If a couple lives together before marriage, both individuals know what they are getting into and essentially have a practice run at marriage. So after the couple gets married, they would have far fewer problems than a couple who had never lived with each other. However, for this couple this was not the case. As a social worker it is important to use critical thinking, because this will help us look at theoretical models to help explain what is actually taking place. In relation to critical thinking, social work is based on theories. We would need to look at theoretical models that would help explain the dynamic with the couple that is being seen.

Going back and trying to understand the research behind divorce rates and cohabitation, it has long been accepted that living together is a precursor for divorce. However, research performed by Kuperberg (2014) on cohabiting and marriage found that it is not the cohabitation before marriage that is the cause for the increase in divorce rates, but rather it is the age when couples choose to live together. This couple began living together at the age of 18 and committed to a very mature relationship at a stage of life when individuals are trying to figure out their own individuality and who they are as a person. Erickson describes this stage as *identity versus role confusion*, where individuals ask questions about themselves like, "Who am I?" and "What can I become?" Given that both are in the identity versus role confusion life stage, it appears that not having the experience to explore this stage more may be a strong contributing factor in their marital problems. This western-based theoretical model would be a good starting point to help validate and eliminate the confusion and disappointment that the couple is feeling. Through her research, Kuperberg (2014) dispelled the notion of cohabitation being the cause of divorce at all, and was able to pinpoint youth and stage of development as factors for higher divorce rates. Kuperberg used her critical thinking skills and helped to explain the phenomena of divorce from a different lens.

EVIDENCE-BASED PRACTICES

It is important to note that as social workers, it is imperative that we are up to date with research and *evidence-based practices*, which are scientifically based theories that have been proven to be effective in treating individuals and explaining human phenomena. Along the same lines, it is also important as social workers to be proficient in the ability to implement the practice-based interventions. So if that young couple did come in to see you for counseling and carried the belief that cohabitation lead to divorce, you would be able to provide up-to-date research information as well as scientifically proven therapeutic interventions to best treat them as a couple. Also, it would be important to look at other factors related to that couple, including ethnicity, religious beliefs, and various other ecological factors. In closing, social workers need to wear many hats and have to have the ability to practice the concept of *systematic eclecticism*, which is the ability to practice multiple theoretical modalities while treating a client to maximize improvement in the client. This process involves utilizing critical thinking skills and being able to effectively implement multiple theoretical models.

SOCIAL WORK USES THE ECOLOGICAL MODEL

The ecological model comes from Urie Bronfenbrenner, and the premise examines human development by studying how human beings create the specific environments in which they live. More specifically, human beings develop according to their environment and there are overarching influences that affect the development of an individual. This views behavior and development as an interactive relationship, which is also known as the "bioecological" model. Bronfenbrenner postulated that in order to understand human development, the entire ecological system in which growth occurs needs to be taken into account (Tudge, 2011). This system is composed of five socially organized subsystems that support and guide human development. Each system depends on the context of the person's life and offers an ever-growing diversity of options and sources of expansion. Furthermore, within and between each system are direct and indirect influences. This construct of direct and indirect influences needs to be examined to see if the individual has the proper conditions to expand and succeed in his/her life. Below are the various systems of the ecological model.

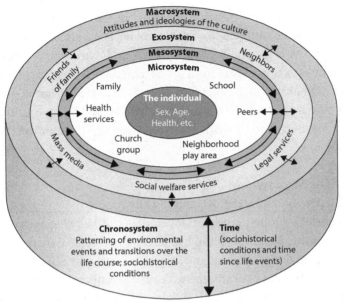

FIGURE 1.2 Bronfenbrenner's Ecological Theory

The McGraw Hill Companies, Inc, https://image.slidesharecdn.com/santrocktls5pptch012-110105133127-phpapp01/95/
dev-psychch1keynote-35-728.jpg?cb=1294241034. Copyright © 2010 by The McGraw-Hill Companies, Inc.

1. The Micro System

The micro system's setting is the direct environment that the individual lives in. Your family, friends, classmates, teachers, neighbors, and other people who have direct contact with you are included in your micro system. The micro system is the setting in which we have direct social interactions with others. In the micro system, an individual is not a mere recipient of the experiences when socializing with those in the micro system, but is also a significant contributor to the construction of the surrounding environment.

2. The Mesosystem

The mesosystem involves the multiple relationships between the microsystems in one's life and how that can affect the individual. This means that an individual's family experience may be directly related to a child's school experience. For example, if a child is experiencing neglect and turmoil at home, this could directly result in the child performing poorly at school both academically and socially. It is important to look at the multiple microsystem interactions to see if one environment is hindering the ability to excel in another direct environment.

3. **The Exosystem**

The exosystem is the broader environment that is having a direct effect on the individual's immediate environment. For example, let's say there is a father who is having difficulty at work and is constantly under stress because he is taking orders from an unreasonable boss. Even though the father's job has nothing directly to do with the child at home, the father begins to act out and yell at the child. This would be an example of an exosystem influence of work affecting the micro system of the home environment.

4. **The Macrosystem**

The macrosystem is the overarching environmental influences such as cultural beliefs, economic conditions, and political ideologies that affect an individual's life. More specifically, in a larger perspective there are aspects of life that are out of the control of the individual that can either enhance or diminish the opportunity to succeed. The effects of larger principles defined by the macrosystem have a significant influence throughout the interactions of all other layers of the ecological model. The macrosystem influences what, how, when, and where we carry out our relations. For example, if a child is born into a marginalized community with minimal rights for and extreme racism is prevalent, that will have a cascading effect on every level of that child's various systems.

5. **The Chronosystem**

The chronosystem involves the environmental events that occur over an individual's lifespan and impacts the individual because of circumstance and developmental stage. This may also involve the socio-historical contexts that may influence a person. One example of a chronosystem is a country going through an economic collapse. This would affect individuals on all levels from the country, to the states, down to the cities, communities, and the families. This would be a major life transition on all levels regardless of who you are.

SOCIAL WORK UTILIZES THE PERSON-IN-ENVIRONMENT MODEL

Social work looks into the interaction that takes place between the individual and the environment. Social work believes in conducting an environmental analysis when assessing the client and believes in the premise that an individual who lives in a rich and prosperous environment will thrive, and an individual who lives in a poor and limited environment will decline in functioning. The person-in-environment model combines the concepts of Maslow's pyramid and the ecological model and identifies the individual on three basic levels. It is important to note that the individual is looked at from a system's perspective looking at the three areas of interaction that influence one another:

1. micro: individual
2. mezzo: family, neighborhoods, schools
3. macro: larger social forces or policies

On the micro level, the social worker is looking at trying to understand human behavior by measuring a person's interrelated biological, psychological, and social functioning and how this is affecting the client medically. This is what is known as the biopsychoscial assessment. The biological component includes:

- overall health
- weight
- physical abilities
- medications
- substance use
- genetics
- family medical history
- neuro-developmental functioning and history

From a psychological standpoint, as a social worker, we want to look at:

- mental health
- self-esteem
- personality
- cognitive and emotional stages of development

And finally from a social perspective, we want to look at:

- relationship with family, peers and community
- social perspective which includes:
  ▸ How does a person identify?
  ▸ How have forces of privilege or oppression impacted the person?
- job security and stability for adults
- school environment for children

Let's take a look at the vignette below:

Mrs. H. has immigrated to the United States with her 10-year-old and her husband. She is living with her cousin in a house in Arcadia with her cousin's husband and their five children. Mrs. H. has been told by her cousin that she can only stay there for three months. Mrs. H. is unable to work due to her physical disability and she states that she has been having dizzy spells and has passed out a few times during the past two weeks. Her son is failing school and her husband is not working due to his own physical ailments. Mrs. H. comes to your mental health clinic and states, "I am feeling really depressed and unhappy right now. I am also beginning to hear voices telling me that someone is watching me and I have not slept for one week. Sometimes I feel like ending it all." She is also a recovering drug addict from her home country and states, "I have feelings of wanting to use cocaine again." Mrs. H. is crying in your office, asking you for help.

From a micro level, let's take a look at what is taking place with Mrs. H.:

- suicidal
- mental health symptoms
- medical issues
- substance abuse issues
- family issues
- unemployed
- residential issues

On the mezzo level for Mrs. H.:

- the living area for the family is too small
- only 3 months to live there
- financial problems
- the son is having problems in school
- the husband is unable to work due to his own physical problems

In terms of the macro level:

- immigration
- documentation status
- access to resources that can assist the family
- cultural issues

- economics
- possible racism and xenophobia

SYSTEMS THEORY

Regarding the client (micro) and its other interacting components that include the mezzo and macro levels, this is where the concept of systems theory comes into play. Here we are looking at the micro, mezzo, and macro interaction and defining the system as a combined entity. In relation to **systems theory**, it is defined as the maintained mutual interactions of its components and proposes that the actions can best be understood by studying them in their context (Minuchin, 1974). Systems theory concepts include:

- roles—expected behaviors and tasks of individuals
  - socially expected roles vary by factors such as class, age, race, gender, and education
- boundaries—patterns of behavior that define a system's or a sub-system's roles
  - a person straying out of the boundary may disrupt the system
  - will adapt to bring the system back in balance
  - may seek services of social worker to bring system back in balance more effectively
- entropy—a system's movement toward disorganization and death
- negative entropy—a system's movement toward growth and development
- input—energy, ideas, and information received by one system from another
- output—result or change that occurs as a result of input
- feedback—input provided to a system informing it about its strengths, weaknesses, and ability to perform specific tasks
- homeostasis—state of balance and internal stability that systems work to acquire and maintain

If we look at the roles that Mrs. H. has below, it is very telling.

- immigrant
- mother
- wife
- cousin
- guest
- homeless person
- mental health patient
- recovering addict
- medical patient

Given all of the roles that she has, it is no wonder she is suffering so much. It is also important from a treatment plan perspective to identify roles, because once roles are identified, you as the social worker can see if resources are needed in that area for the client. For example, given the fact that she is a mental health patient, she will need to be linked to mental health services. Also given the fact that she is facing a loss of housing, she will also need housing and shelter care.

In terms of summarizing and understanding social work in relation to the individual and their environment, it is important to know the following:

- It is imperative to understand human development through the interaction between the individual and his or her environment.
- The way people react to life events shapes how they approach their world.
- Clients don't live in a vacuum; they have positive and negative interactions with others.
- People receive and expend energy from surrounding systems.
- Humans are adaptable and can change.

On the last point stated, this concept comes from the Strengths Perspective (Weick et al., 1989), which states that all human beings have strengths, talents, and abilities as well as the capacity for growth, development, and adaptation. The strength perspective believes that clients are (Weick et al., 1989):

- experts on their situations
- insightful about their problem-solving approaches
- resilient and resourceful
- partners with social workers in the change process
- able to grow and become competent at solving complex dilemmas

What are some of the strengths that Mrs. H. is displaying given her situation?

- survivor
- resilient
- dedicated mother and wife
- hard-working
- multi-tasker
- responsible
- self-sufficient

It is very important as a social worker to empower individuals by identifying the strengths that the individual is already displaying. In terms of Mrs. H., it is imperative to provide her the resources and environmental support that matches her inner determination and strength that she is already displaying.

SOCIAL WORK USES THE GENERALIST PERSPECTIVE

A review of summary data from the Council on Social Work Education (CSWE) reveals that advanced generalist practice is the fastest growing area of concentration for Master of Social Work (MSW) programs in the United States (CSWE, 2006). Its growth is a testament given that advanced generalist practice is traditionally associated with rural regions; however, this construct of defining the whole individual that started with the working poor is now becoming standardized, regardless of socioeconomic status. It was long assumed that rural settings, with their limited resources and access to opportunity, would benefit from a generalist practitioner, a social worker who wore many hats and could change them often in response to competing client and community needs (Campbell, 1990). There are three defined characteristics of a generalist social worker:

1. The generalist is often the first professional to see clients as they enter the social welfare system.
2. The worker must therefore be competent to assess clients' needs and to identify their strengths, stress points, and problems.
3. The worker must draw on a variety of skills and methods in serving clients.

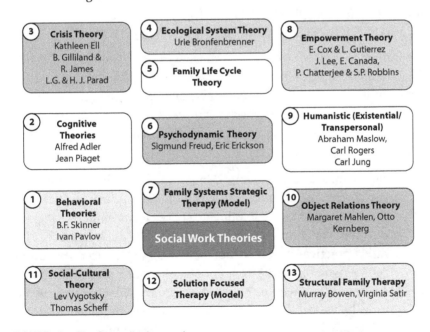

FIGURE 1.3 The Generalist Approach

Source: http://image.slidesharecdn.com/theoriesofsocialwork-100813071026-phpapp02/95/slide-22-728.g?1323753458.

While urban and metropolitan settings may be better resourced than rural settings, the struggle with shortages of personnel and services still exists. Given the rapidly changing social service environment and the competition for limited resources, the same arguments that placed advanced generalists in small towns also support their fit within urban settings (Barber, 1995). Whether responding to directives even with a lack of resources or justifying the need for services to policymakers, direct practitioners must be able to work on all levels to be of service with often beyond their identified clients.

The future of social work requires that students are prepared for the unique and complex situations that arise when assisting clients. Social workers must be able to provide a framework for advanced practice using a conceptual lens through which they can identify and promote innovative solutions while remaining ethical through professional practice. Advanced practice requires multiple skills that include providing a sound foundation to implement various models and the creativity to address complex practice issues when problems do not fit nicely into a box. Overall, social work seeks improvement of societal well-being, which is the premise of the discipline, and expertise and mastery on multiple levels is required. Generalist practice is a multi-system focus, meaning that solutions need to be addressed on micro, mezzo, and macro levels.

MACRO PRACTICE VERSUS DIRECT PRACTICE VERSUS CLINICAL PRACTICE

The various roles and practices of social work can be confusing. For example, clinical social workers sit down one-on-one with patients and offer mental health treatment to help an individual improve the quality of their life. This may sound like providing direct services, but there are distinctions regarding the scope of what a social worker does. There are three types of social work:

1. **macro practice** (indirect)—Macro social workers work indirectly with clients but at the level of programs, institutions, and government policy. The indirect services focus on improving the environment of the individual so that all individuals can succeed.
2. **direct practice**—Direct service social workers connect people and services working on the front lines. They perform intakes and initial screenings and help to determine program eligibility, all the while providing targeted case management services referring individuals and families to necessary services out in the community.

3. **clinical practice**—Clinical social workers provide direct services to individuals who have psychiatric disorders (mental and emotional health problems) through conducting initial assessments, diagnosing clients, providing intensive treatment plans and providing interventions. In a medical setting, clinical social workers are often part of a multidisciplinary team, with colleagues in various disciplines that include psychiatry and nursing.

WHAT DOES IT MEAN TO BE A LICENSED CLINICAL SOCIAL WORKER (LCSW)?

The licensed clinical social worker, or LCSW, is a subsector within the field of social work. LCSWs work with clients in order to help deal with issues involving mental and emotional health. There are a wide variety of specializations the licensed clinical social worker can focus on. These include specialties such as working with mental health issues, substance abuse, public health, school social work, medical social work, marriage counseling, children, and family therapy. Some may choose to work purely in a research, policy-making, or administrative capacity. The possible career paths as a licensed clinical social worker are many and varied. The LCSW services society in a wide variety of ways. The most common career path is becoming a mental health counselor. With the help of the LCSW, the client can gain tremendous insight into their emotional makeup and find healing from past traumas. A marriage and family counseling specialist might aid a family in working through their issues, facilitating dialogue, and ensuring that everyone's needs are met. This can result in marriages being strengthened that might otherwise end in divorce. The school counseling aspect of the LCSW can help students to be properly assessed so their unique needs are met, which in turn allows them to excel within the academic setting. There are so many ways in which a licensed clinical social worker can service humanity and impact lives on individual, family, and societal levels.

These are just a handful of the ways a licensed clinical social worker can have an immense impact on the quality of life for families. Regarding obtaining your LCSW, it is important to note that there is a much greater emphasis on the use of the medical model and being able to properly implement the beginning stages of treatment effectively. Regardless of where you choose to channel your energies (micro, mezzo, or macro) in terms of how you choose to impact humanity, it is vital that you are well-prepared for the licensing exam that you will take in the future. Below is some basic information as well as a sample question from the LCSW exam.

HOW TO GET YOUR LCSW

Here is the process of how to get your LCSW from the Board of Behavioral Sciences (2017)

1. Get your qualifying master's degree.
2. Register with the BBS as an ASW registrant and begin earning post degree experience.
3. Apply to take your state's Law and Ethics examination.
4. When you have earned the total 3,200 hours and passed your state's Law and Ethics exam, apply for the clinical examination.
5. Pass the clinical examination.
6. Apply for initial licensure.
7. Get your official LCSW license.

The scope of being a LCSW is wide and vast, but regarding the clinical licensing exam, it is important to stress that the beginning stage of treatment, which includes differential diagnosing and treatment planning, is essential to master. This will be covered in the later chapters, however below is an example of a clinical vignette question from the LCSW exam:

VIGNETTE

A client John, aged 30, comes in to see you at your clinic. The client states that he hears voices and that he believes his neighbor is out to get him. He shares that his neighbor puts flowers in a way that John does not like and that there are billboards that prove his mind is being read. John adds that he has not slept for one week just thinking about it and that he has stopped using cocaine for the past several months. John adds that he has had thoughts of suicide and "I get really sad about my future." John's mother is crying as she shares, "We have had so much mental illness in my family, and he gets the ups and downs just like me."

What are the diagnostic considerations for this client?

A. schizophrenia
bipolar disorder
schizoaffective disorder
major depression
B. substance-induced psychotic disorder
major depression

bipolar disorder

schizophrenia

C. bipolar disorder

psychotic disorder unspecified

major depression

r/o schizoaffective disorder

D. substance abuse

bipolar disorder

major depression

schizophrenia

As stated earlier, to answer this question, it would require a social worker to know how to differentially diagnose and to have common knowledge of the medical components that are involved with this client. If a person is not properly clinically trained, the common answer to pick is D. This is considered one of the hardest clinical questions on the exam, and I promise that as you go through this book, you will know exactly how to address and answer this question because of the foundational knowledge you will acquire. The correct answer for this vignette is C.

Social work involves being a practitioner who wears many hats and looks through various levels to best understand social problems. This begins from the medical model looking through a micro level lens to looking at the family and community environment through a mezzo level lens, as well as identifying macro components involving economics and discrimination. Social work aims to promote social justice and serve the underserved communities by taking into account all aspects of human life. It is also being able to look at the interaction of all the components that make up an individual's life.

REFERENCES

Barber, J. G. (1995). Politically progressive casework. *Families in Society, 76*(1), 30–37.

Board of Behavioral Sciences (2017). Navigating the LCSW Licensing Process. Retrieved from http://www.bbs.ca.gov/app-reg/lcs_presentation.shtml

Campbell, J. A., & Shepard, M. (1990). Social work education for rural practice: The advanced generalist. *Human Services in the Rural Environment, 14*(1), 21–24.

Council on Social Work Education (CSWE) (2006). Statistics on social work education in the United States, 2006: A summary. Alexandria, VA: Author.

Council on Social Work Education (CSWE). (2017). Directory of accredited programs. Retrieved from http://www.cswe.org/default.aspx?id=17491

Gibbins, J., & Gray, M. (2004). Critical Thinking as Integral to Social Work Practice. *Journal of Teaching in Social Work, 24*, 19–38.

Holmes, N. G., Wieman, C. E., & Bonn, D. A. (2015). Teaching critical thinking. *Proceedings of the National Academy of Sciences, 112*(36), 11199–11204.

Kuperberg, A. (2014). Age at coresidence, premarital cohabitation, and marriage dissolution: 1985–2009. *Journal of Marriage and Family, 76*, 352–369. doi: 10.1111/jomf.12092.

Maslow, A. H. (1943). A theory of human motivation. *Psychological Review, 50*(4), 370–396.

Maslow, A. H. (1962). *Toward a psychology of being.* Princeton, NJ: D. Van Nostrand Company.

Minuchin, S. (1974). *Families and family therapy.* Cambridge, MA: Harvard University Press.

Nasir, M., Khalid, A., & Shoukat, A. (2014). Maslow theory of human development and emergence of street children phenomenon in Pakistan. *Pakistan Vision, 15*(2), 98–123.

Rogers, A. T. (2013). *Human behavior in the social environment* (3rd ed.). New York: Routledge Taylor & Francis Group.

Scriven, M., Paul, R. (1987). Defining critical thinking. Retrieved from: https://www.criticalthinking.org/pages/defining-critical-thinking/766

Tudge, J., Mokrova I., Karnik R. B., & Hatfield, B. E. (2011). Uses and misuses of Bronfenbrenner's bioecological theory of human development. *Journal of Family Theory & Review, 1* (4), 198–210.

Weick, A., Rapp, C., Sullivan, W.P., & Kisthardt, W. (1989). A strengths perspective for social work practice. *Social Work, 34*(4), 350–354.

CHAPTER 2

The Code of Ethics

PURPOSE OF THE NASW CODE OF ETHICS

Straight from the preamble of the NASW Code of Ethics (2017), the following is stated regarding the mission of a social worker:

> The primary mission of the social work profession is to enhance human well-being and help meet the basic human needs of all people, with particular attention to the needs and empowerment of people who are vulnerable, oppressed, and living in poverty. A historic and defining feature of social work is the profession's focus on individual well-being in a social context and the well-being of society. Fundamental to social work is attention to the environmental forces that create, contribute to, and address problems in living.
>
> Social workers promote social justice and social change with and on behalf of clients. "Clients" is used inclusively to refer to individuals, families, groups, organizations, and communities. Social workers are sensitive to cultural and ethnic diversity and strive to end discrimination, oppression, poverty, and other forms of social injustice. These activities may be in the form of direct practice, community organizing, supervision, consultation administration, advocacy, social and political action, policy development and implementation, education, and research and evaluation. Social workers seek to enhance the capacity of people to address their own needs. Social workers also seek to promote the responsiveness of organizations, communities, and other social institutions to individuals' needs and social problems.

When it comes to the social work core set of values, this has been embraced by the history of the profession and has been the foundation for the purpose and perspective of social work. The following six core values are:

- service
- social justice
- dignity and worth of the person
- importance of human relationships
- integrity
- competence

As defined by the NASW (2017), the core values serve six purposes:

1. The Code identifies core values on which social work's mission is based.
2. The Code summarizes broad ethical principles that reflect the profession's core values and establishes a set of specific ethical standards that should be used to guide social work practice.
3. The Code is designed to help social workers identify relevant considerations when professional obligations conflict or ethical uncertainties arise.
4. The Code provides ethical standards to which the general public can hold the social work profession accountable.
5. The Code socializes practitioners new to the field to social work's mission, values, ethical principles, and ethical standards.
6. The Code articulates standards that the social work profession itself can use to assess whether social workers have engaged in unethical conduct. NASW has formal procedures to adjudicate ethics complaints filed against its members.* In subscribing to this Code, social workers are required to cooperate in its implementation, participate in NASW adjudication proceedings, and abide by any NASW disciplinary rulings or sanctions based on it.

The Code offers a set of values and principles to guide decision making when ethical issues arise. It is important to note that the Code does not tell social workers what to do in every instance as situations can be complex and fluid. However what it does try to do is to be a guide to making the most ethical decisions possible given circumstances with which social workers will be confronted. The Code of Ethics cannot prevent unethical behavior, but it does set a standard for social workers to act in the best interest of the population being served.

NASW CODE OF ETHICS

The following are the six broad principles of the NASW Code of Ethics. The code is set to establish an ideal for which social workers should aspire (NASW, 2017).

THE FIRST PRINCIPLE IS VALUE

> Social workers' primary goal is to help people in need and to address social problems.
> Social workers elevate service to others above self-interest. Social workers draw on their knowledge, values, and skills to help people in need and to address social problems. Social workers are encouraged to volunteer some portion of their professional skills with no expectation of significant financial return (pro bono service).

I have had the pleasure to work with outstanding social workers who committed their lives to serving their chosen community and making a difference. They took their passion, gathered the proper knowledge, developed their skills, and used their lives to make a difference. One social worker I worked with in the past grew up in the foster care system and suffered from the inadequate resources and mistreatment of children in that environment. He never met his biological parents, nor any of his siblings for that matter, but instead of being bitter and using that as a reason to not succeed in life, he devoted his life to using that pain to make a difference for other foster care kids who are in the system. He put himself through school and, after he obtained his MSW and his LCSW, he opened up his own foster care home that services children and encompasses all aspects and struggles that a child goes through once they are in the system. He is a shining example of a social worker being of value.

THE SECOND PRINCIPLE IS SOCIAL JUSTICE

> Social workers challenge social injustice. Social workers pursue social change, particularly with and on behalf of vulnerable and oppressed individuals and groups of people. Social workers' social change efforts are focused

primarily on issues of poverty, unemployment, discrimination, and other forms of social injustice. These activities seek to promote sensitivity to and knowledge about oppression and cultural and ethnic diversity. Social workers strive to ensure access to needed information, services, and resources; equality of opportunity; and meaningful participation in decision making for all people.

Teaching at a university that is in the heart of Los Angeles, I have met numerous professors who are devoting their lives to social justice. One of the professors in the department of Social Work grew up in South Central which is a predominantly African American community that is struggling with poverty and violence. He has dedicated his life to serving the community that he grew up in, which has been underserved and consistently forgotten. My colleague is working with the community churches, mental health clinics, volunteers, and congressman to help create after school drop-in centers for young teens so that they have a place to be safe and to have a foundation that will lead them to not only graduate high school, but to go to college. He is doing all of this while going for his PhD in social work. He is an example of social justice.

THE THIRD PRINCIPLE IS DIGNITY AND WORTH OF A PERSON

Social workers respect the inherent dignity and worth of the person. Social workers treat each person in a caring and respectful fashion, mindful of individual differences and cultural and ethnic diversity. Social workers promote clients' socially responsible self-determination. Social workers seek to enhance clients' capacity and opportunity to change and to address their own needs. Social workers are cognizant of their dual responsibility to clients and to the broader society. They seek to resolve conflicts between clients' interests and the broader society's interests in a socially responsible manner consistent with the values, ethical principles, and ethical standards of the profession.

I have seen thousands of clients throughout my career and regardless of the therapeutic model that I choose as a social worker, the most important element is building rapport and establishing a relationship with the client. In doing so, this lets the individual that you are working with know that their life matters. Regardless of circumstances, decisions that have been made, and what the client heard that negatively affected his/her life, the dignified message was and always is clear: You are a worthy person.

THE FOURTH PRINCIPLE IS IMPORTANCE
OF HUMAN RELATIONSHIPS

> Social workers recognize the central importance of human relationships. Social workers understand that relationships between and among people are an important vehicle for change. Social workers engage people as partners in the helping process. Social workers seek to strengthen relationships among people in a purposeful effort to promote, restore, maintain, and enhance the well-being of individuals, families, social groups, organizations, and communities.

When I worked for the Transitional Aged Youth program which served at-risk youth, this remains today one of the most fulfilling jobs that I have ever done in the field of social work. My coworker and I provided gang members mental health services at a vocational school, and in-between classes we met with each member and would figure out ways to ensure that they would graduate with a vocational degree. This required collaboration with the school teachers, the school administrators, and the families of the students. It really took a team to get students to graduate as well as following up and ensuring that gainful employment took place. This is the importance of human relationships.

THE FIFTH PRINCIPLE IS INTEGRITY

> Social workers behave in a trustworthy manner. Social workers are continually aware of the profession's mission, values, ethical principles, and ethical standards and practice in a manner consistent with them. Social workers act honestly and responsibly and promote ethical practices on the part of the organizations with which they are affiliated.

Having integrity is crucial when being a social worker. When I was an intern and was placed at a mental health facility for my first year, I was co-facilitating a group for clients with schizophrenia. The facilitator who I was shadowing did not care about the clients at all and during the group, she ended up telling the group, "Do what you want for one hour," and then turned her back while reading a magazine. She ended up telling me, "They cannot tell the difference anyway," and how she used this time to budget her checkbook. She also gave me the advice that, "You only focus on those you can truly help and they are pretty hopeless." Looking back, it was pretty sad how she used her job to fulfill her needs and how she completely neglected her duties to the clients she was supposed to serve. I never forgot about that experience and use her as a reminder to have integrity every day I work as a social worker.

THE SIXTH PRINCIPLE IS COMPETENCE

> Social workers practice within their areas of competence and develop and enhance their professional expertise. Social workers continually strive to increase their professional knowledge and skills and to apply them in practice. Social workers should aspire to contribute to the knowledge base of the profession.

Being competent is doing only what is within your scope of practice, and within that practice doing it well. As a social worker, we have to put on many hats and be competent on so many levels. If you are providing individual therapy, competence is required on the micro level implementing a proper therapeutic intervention. If you are localizing outreach programs on a community level, competence in organizing on a mezzo level will be what is required for success to be achieved. If you are assisting in writing and trying to pass a bill through legislation, competence on a macro level understanding policy will be what is expected of you.

SOCIAL WORKERS' ETHICAL RESPONSIBILITIES IN PRACTICE SETTINGS

Working in the field of social work, I have had the opportunity to work in some really great settings, and at the same time, I have been in some terrible placements. In discussing the ethical responsibilities in a practice setting, I will be discussing both the good and the bad that I have experienced.

SUPERVISION AND CONSULTATION

a. Social workers who provide supervision or consultation should have the necessary knowledge and skill to supervise or consult appropriately and should do so only within their areas of knowledge and competence.
b. Social workers who provide supervision or consultation are responsible for setting clear, appropriate, and culturally sensitive boundaries.
c. Social workers should not engage in any dual or multiple relationships with supervisees in which there is a risk of exploitation of or potential harm to the supervisee.

d. Social workers who provide supervision should evaluate supervisees' performance in a manner that is fair and respectful.

When I began my first job post-graduation, my supervisor was an elderly man who told me on our first meeting, "Supervision is on a need-to-know basis. Other than that, experience will be your guide." When we did have supervision, he wanted to meet at Hooters and discuss cases over beers. I was very naive and just happy to have a job at that time, and also I did not feel like I had any rights due to him being directly responsible for my licensing hours. Also, I actually did not mind having beers with him, and I justified to myself that it could be worse—I could have a really bad supervisor who micromanaged everything that I did. As the two years to accrue my hours were completed, coupled with the lack of proper supervision that I had received, that really set back my career. After I completed and submitted my licensing packet to the board and qualified to take my LCSW exam, I took my test. I failed! The lack of supervision and consultation really hurt me in the end. I had to take initiative and really seek out help outside of my supervisor to be able to pass the exam the second time around. I also realized that I was not as well-equipped as I should have been to serve the clients that I was seeing. In the end, I feel like I provided a disservice to the community and to myself.

EDUCATION AND TRAINING

a. Social workers who function as educators, field instructors for students, or trainers should provide instruction only within their areas of knowledge and competence and should provide instruction based on the most current information and knowledge available in the profession.
b. Social workers who function as educators or field instructors for students should evaluate students' performance in a manner that is fair and respectful.
c. Social workers who function as educators or field instructors for students should take reasonable steps to ensure that clients are routinely informed when services are being provided by students.
d. Social workers who function as educators or field instructors for students should not engage in any dual or multiple relationships with students in which there is a risk of exploitation or potential harm to the student. Social work

educators and field instructors are responsible for setting clear, appropriate, and culturally sensitive boundaries.

As a professor as well as someone who has supervised staff, I take very seriously the need to provide proper education and training to students and those under my supervision. After I failed my licensing exam the first time around, I made a commitment to myself to take my career more seriously. It was then that I ended up taking a seminar training for the licensing exam, and I will never forget what took place at that seminar. There were over two hundred people there, and as the group was going over sample questions that were about differential diagnosing and treatment planning, more than half of the attendees were getting the answers wrong, including me. Eventually one lady raised her hand and angrily shared, "This test is not real life and does not properly go over what a clinician really does when treating a client!" When she shared that I felt so validated and many of the attendees in that crowd were cheering and agreeing with her.

It was then that the trainer responded and shared, "This exam is reflective of the medical model and how to properly diagnose a client, based on evidenced-based practices. With all due respect if you are getting the answers wrong, it is not the test to be angry at, but the lack of proper supervision that you have received." It was then when my heart sank and all of us who were angry sat down quietly. I was humbled because I realized that my knowledge base at that moment was not up to par for what was required for the licensing exam. Also, along with the other attendees in that room that quietly sat down, it appeared that the majority of us were all the product of limited information being passed down from one generation of incompetent social workers to another, and I wanted to break that cycle for myself. I wanted to be a part of the other half of the room who understood and were able to answer the questions that were being asked.

It was at that moment that I had made the decision that no matter who supervised me, I would dictate and decide my career from that moment on. After that, I worked with one of the staff psychiatrists at my workplace who was kind enough to educate me regarding the test, and when I understood what to look for, I was able to pass my exam the second time around. I used that experience so when I became a supervisor, I used that position to properly educate staff that were getting their hours. Also in the university setting, I used that setback to educate students in the classroom early on regarding the medical model and how to differentially diagnose properly. I get a lot of groans and complaints initially from students because they feel they do not need to know it and it is difficult, but at the end of the semester, there is appreciation. During my tenure as a professor, I have and continue to get so much joy and satisfaction when I hear from former students who passed their licensing exams the first time around.

It was also during this time when I was studying for my licensing exam that I was able to work with a wonderful social work administrator for a new county program. The program involved assisting the homeless population and I was able to see the essence of social work. Understanding the medical model is very important, but so is understanding the various levels that can dictate an individual's life. Within this population, there are many who suffer from a multitude of problems including a chronic and severe mental illness, substance abuse issues, medical problems, and an overall lack of basic survival needs. On the micro level, we would outreach and link those with medical or mental health issues to the services that they needed. Along with that, we worked with case managers of food banks and shelters to link those we were assisting to have their basic needs met. This led to mezzo-level interventions that involved outreach and engagement services where we would gather as many resources as possible. Individual meetings with agencies eventually became monthly collaborative meetings with the local food banks, homeless shelter, mental health agencies, and substance abuse programs to ensure the most effective delivery of service. Every entity would work together as well as learn from what each agency was offering in terms of service. This form of collaboration led to more efficient and effective delivery of service to this population. From there, once clients were stabilized they would be linked to employment services and training, along with assistance for clothing and supplies. The monthly collaborative meetings continued to expand, as well as greater communication with the various agencies as a whole. This opened the door for macro-level interventions of legislating for funding for homeless outreach programs. During this time we gathered outcomes measures through what was established and continued to host community forums to gather vital information.

Funding was later provided and various outreach programs have been established to assist this underserved community ever since. The administrator that I worked with was integral in making this happen, and I was so blessed to be able to work and assist on the various levels needed to help those that we could. This time period brought social work concepts to life for me from Maslow's pyramid, the ecological model, critical thinking, and the belief of the generalist social work perspective. I have continued to use this experience to best pass on what social work is, whether in the work or classroom setting. This period for me was the foundation for my social career and I am so blessed to have met both the psychiatrist and the social administrator during that time.

PERFORMANCE EVALUATION

Social workers who have responsibility for evaluating the performance of others should fulfill such responsibility in a fair and considerate manner and on the basis of clearly stated criteria.

Performance evaluations are important and if you are a supervisor, it is vital to make sure that you are doing a fair and impartial job. On the flip side, if you are being supervised and are a subordinate staff, your performance evaluation should reflect your ability to perform the essential job duties of the position. When the supervisor is conducting performance evaluations, I have broken it down into six areas that a supervisor should look at (OCFS, 2018):

1. Translate organizational goals into individual job objectives and requirements.
2. Communicate expectations regarding staff performance clearly.
3. Provide feedback to staff.
4. Coach the staff on how to achieve job objectives and requirements.
5. Identify the staff's relative strengths and weaknesses.
6. Determine a development or corrective action plan for improving job performance.

Also if you are a staff member under a particular supervisor, you deserve the right to ask the following questions (OCFS, 2018, p. 1):

- *What am I expected to do?*
- *How well am I doing?*
- *What are my strengths and weaknesses?*
- *How can I do a better job?*
- *How can I contribute more?*

Some of the reasons performance evaluations fail is because (OCFS, 2018):

1. The supervisor does not know what the worker has done.
2. The supervisor is not skilled in determining the current performance level of the staff.
3. The supervisor fails to set specific objectives for the employee.
4. Self-evaluation by the supervisor is ignored or minimized.
5. The evaluation is only based on historical rather than current developmental levels of the employee.
6. The communication with the employee is a one-way communication that does not benefit the supervised staff.

7. Too much emphasis on filling out forms and not enough on problem solving and creating a corrective action plan.

8. No specific plan for follow-up when the next review occurs.

When I was first hired as a supervisor, I worked at a government facility where staff turnover was very high. The other supervisors would often give bad performance evaluations to really good staff so that they were forced to stay and continue to work for them. This often did not allow staff to transfer from the facility and it also limited their ability to be promoted in the future. It was very disturbing to see this kind of practice, but unfortunately in several settings this was often the case. It made me very sad that when a worker was transferred to me and then applied for a promotion, I would have to have long conversations with the interviewer because of the previous poor evaluations that were given. I had to reassure the interviewer that the worker was truly a victim of circumstance and that their ability to perform their job duties was high. In closing, performance evaluations do not define your worth as a social worker, but if you are in a situation that I am describing above, make plans to ensure that you always have options with your career by knowing your rights.

CLIENT RECORDS

a. Social workers should take reasonable steps to ensure that documentation in records is accurate and reflects the services provided.

b. Social workers should include sufficient and timely documentation in records to facilitate the delivery of services and to ensure continuity of services provided to clients in the future.

c. Social workers' documentation should protect clients' privacy to the extent that is possible and appropriate and should include only information that is directly relevant to the delivery of services.

d. Social workers should store records following the termination of services to ensure reasonable future access. Records should be maintained for the number of years required by relevant laws, agency policies, and contracts.

One of the most important aspects of client records is to protect the private information of your clients. According to U.S. Department of Health and Human Services (2017), here is the information that is to be protected if you are a client:

- information your doctors, nurses, and other health care providers put in your medical record
- conversations your provider has about your care or treatment with other staff
- information about you in your health insurer's computer system
- billing information about you at your clinic
- most other health information about you held by those who must follow these laws

It is vital that client records are treated with care and not treated in a negligent and careless manner as a treating social worker. Social workers must comply with a client's rights to (USDHHS, 2017):

- ask to see and get a copy of health records
- have corrections added to their health information
- receive a notice that tells them how their health information may be used and shared
- decide if they want to give permission before health information can be used or shared for certain purposes, such as for marketing
- get a report on when and why the client's health information was shared for certain purposes
- If the client believes his/her rights are being denied or health information isn't being protected, the client can
  ‣ file a complaint with their provider or health insurer
  ‣ file a complaint with Health and Human Services (HHS)

BILLING

Social workers should establish and maintain billing practices that accurately reflect the nature and extent of services provided and that identify who provided the service in the practice setting.

There should be accurate billing of time and of services that you provide to your clients. There should not be an exaggerated amount of time that you add that has nothing to do with the direct one-to-one contact that you have with your client.

CLIENT TRANSFER

a. When an individual who is receiving services from another agency or colleague contacts a social worker for services, the social worker should carefully consider the client's needs before agreeing to provide services. To minimize possible confusion and conflict, social workers should discuss with potential clients the nature of the client's current relationship with other service providers and the implications, including possible benefits or risks, of entering into a relationship with a new service provider.

b. If a new client has been served by another agency or colleague, social workers should discuss with the client whether consultation with the previous service provider is in the client's best interest.

When it comes to transferring client cases, it is important to follow the basic rule of thumb which is "You only transfer a case because it is for the benefit of the client." Oftentimes a case will be transferred within an agency because one clinician has more expertise in a particular area that the client needs, or maybe because a particular client is more comfortable with a female therapist over a male. Also if a client is moving out of the area, then it is up to you to ensure that the transition for the client is smooth as the relocation process occurs. This would mean providing resources to the client in their new area of relocation, as well as continuing to treat the client up until the transition has been finalized. Regardless, you as the social worker want to ensure the smoothest transition for the client as possible.

ADMINISTRATION

a. Social work administrators should advocate within and outside their agencies for adequate resources to meet clients' needs.

b. Social workers should advocate for resource allocation procedures that are open and fair. When not all clients' needs can be met, an allocation procedure should be developed that is nondiscriminatory and based on appropriate and consistently applied principles.

c. Social workers who are administrators should take reasonable steps to ensure that adequate agency or organizational resources are available to provide appropriate staff supervision.

d. Social work administrators should take reasonable steps to ensure that the working environment for which they are responsible is consistent with and encourages compliance with the NASW Code of Ethics. Social work administrators should take reasonable steps to eliminate any conditions in their organizations that violate, interfere with, or discourage compliance with the Code.

As stated earlier in this section, I have had some really good and some really bad experiences. When it comes to a good administrative team, there is cohesion and clarity as the primary focus is on having a positive work environment where individuals can thrive and excel in their craft. On the other hand, bad administrative teams are chaotic with no clear direction, and even the simplest problems become difficult to solve because of the disarray within the administrative team. In a bad administrative environment, there is a lot of "Do as I say, not as I do" type of leadership, where the administrators lack insight into their own contributions to the work environment and always seek to blame versus seek healthy solutions. Regardless of the scenarios, this will trickle down to the subordinate staff and productivity either will excel or diminish because of it. If a social worker is working in an administrative capacity, it is vital that the individual is a stable presence and a true advocate for the staff that is being supervised.

CONTINUING EDUCATION AND STAFF DEVELOPMENT

Social work administrators and supervisors should take reasonable steps to provide or arrange for continuing education and staff development for all staff for whom they are responsible. Continuing education and staff development should address current knowledge and emerging developments related to social work practice and ethics.

Continuing education is important not only for staying current on information as a social worker, but it is also vital when you are seeking to obtain your LCSW license. Some of the required continuing education that you will need includes classes on child abuse, domestic violence, substance abuse, and elder abuse; however, this can vary from state to state. It is vital that you are compliant with the specified continuing education courses pre-licensure so that there will be no difficulty when you submit your application packet in the future.

COMMITMENTS TO EMPLOYERS

a. Social workers generally should adhere to commitments made to employers and employing organizations.

b. Social workers should work to improve employing agencies' policies and procedures and the efficiency and effectiveness of their services.

c. Social workers should take reasonable steps to ensure that employers are aware of social workers' ethical obligations as set forth in the NASW Code of Ethics and of the implications of those obligations for social work practice.

d. Social workers should not allow an employing organization's policies, procedures, regulations, or administrative orders to interfere with their ethical practice of social work. Social workers should take reasonable steps to ensure that their employing organizations' practices are consistent with the NASW Code of Ethics.

e. Social workers should act to prevent and eliminate discrimination in the employing organization's work assignments and in its employment policies and practices.

f. Social workers should accept employment or arrange student field placements only in organizations that exercise fair personnel practices.

g. Social workers should be diligent stewards of the resources of their employing organizations, wisely conserving funds where appropriate and never misappropriating funds or using them for unintended purposes.

So much of social work is about teamwork and working together to enhance the goals of the agency mission that you are a part of. If there is a good administrative team that is supportive, as well as committed staff who are all on board, communities can experience tremendous change. Ideally, you want to be able to be a part of a team that is committed to each and every staff member, and in return the staff is putting in their best efforts daily to improve the lives of others. Commitment to employers is a natural byproduct of a healthy work environment and loyalty that is established because of the appreciation of the environment provided by the employer.

LABOR-MANAGEMENT DISPUTES

a. Social workers may engage in organized action, including the formation of and participation in labor unions, to improve services to clients and working conditions.

b. The actions of social workers who are involved in labor-management disputes, job actions, or labor strikes should be guided by the profession's values, ethical principles, and ethical standards. Reasonable differences of opinion exist among social workers concerning their primary obligation as professionals during an actual or threatened labor strike or job action. Social workers should carefully examine relevant issues and their possible impact on clients before deciding on a course of action.

If ever you are in a labor dispute, it is important to understand your rights and what you can do to protect those rights. Just as social workers advocate for clients, it is important that you are an advocate for yourself, especially if you are in a hostile work environment. A hostile environment can result from the unwelcome conduct of supervisors, co-workers, customers, contractors, or anyone else with whom the victim interacts on the job, and the unwelcome conduct renders the workplace atmosphere intimidating, hostile, or offensive. From the U.S. Depart of Labor (2017), examples of behaviors that may contribute to an unlawful hostile environment include:

- discussing sexual activities
- telling off-color jokes concerning race, sex, disability, or other protected bases
- unnecessary touching
- commenting on physical attributes
- displaying sexually suggestive or racially insensitive pictures
- using demeaning or inappropriate terms or epithets
- using indecent gestures
- using crude language
- sabotaging the victim's work
- engaging in hostile physical conduct

The labor laws are clear that a violation is occurring if (USDOL, 2017):

1. First, unlawful harassing conduct must be unwelcome and based on the victim's protected status.
2. Second, the conduct must be subjectively abusive to the person affected; and objectively severe and pervasive enough to create a work environment that a reasonable person would find hostile or abusive.

Also it is important to note that if you do believe that you are a victim of harassment, it is important to document by dating and describing the events, as well as keep track of the following factors (USDOL, 2017):

1. the frequency of the unwelcome discriminatory conduct
2. the severity of the conduct
3. whether the conduct was physically threatening or humiliating, or a mere offensive utterance
4. whether the conduct unreasonably interfered with work performance
5. the effect on the your psychological well-being
6. whether the harasser was a superior within the organization

Hopefully, you will never have to be in a situation like this, but if it ever does occur, it is important to be prepared. Before taking any action at your work, please make sure to contact your union or workers representative and provide the written documentation that you do have.

VIGNETTE

Below is an actual vignette that took place with one of my coworkers when I first began working in the field. This vignette will be used again in the next chapter as it encompasses so many ethical issues:

VIGNETTE

You are working at a mental health agency as a social worker and you have been there for four months. One day, your boss tells you that a client has been transferred to you, as the client was complaining about her previous social worker. Upon your initial session with the client, she shares that the previous social worker and herself had sexual relations, as she stated that "he promised me he would get me social security in exchange for going out with him." The client also shares that "I was terminated really quickly by him and there was no real explanation because I thought we were getting serious."

After completing the initial meeting with your new client, you take that information to your boss and he tells you, "That is why I transferred the case to you." You then ask the boss if any action is going to take place against the social worker and he tells you, "That is none of your business and I will take care of it." You then take the issue to your supervisor, and your supervisor tells you, "There is a boys' club here and you do not want to screw around with it. Just leave it alone because you do not want this going on your performance evaluation." As you spend time there, you realize that your boss, the accused social worker, and your supervisor are all friends.

QUESTIONS TO CONSIDER

1. What are the ethical issues in this case that apply to the practice setting?
2. What are the possible repercussions if the social worker decides to follow through with a grievance?
3. What would be the appropriate plan of action if the social worker decided to follow through with her grievance?
4. What was the final outcome?

REFERENCES

NASW (2017) Code of Ethics of the National Association of Social Workers. Retrieved from: https://www.socialworkers.org/About/Ethics/Code-of-Ethics/Code-of-Ethics-English

Office of Child and Family Services New York (2018). Retrieved from: https://ocfs.ny.gov/ohrd/materials/30365.pdf

U.S. Department of Health and Human Services (2017). Health Information Privacy. Retrieved from: https://www.hhs.gov/hipaa/for-individuals/guidance-materials-for-consumers/index.html

U.S. Department of Labor (2017). Workplace Harassment. Retrieved from: https://www.dol.gov/oasam/programs/crc/2012-workplace-harassment.pdf

CHAPTER 3

Ethical Decision-Making

SOCIAL WORKERS' ETHICAL RESPONSIBILITY TO CLIENTS

The NASW Code of Ethics was approved by the NASW in 1996 and revised and delegated upon in 2008. The NASW Code of Ethics is intended to serve as a guide to the everyday professional conduct of social workers (NASW, 2017). This Code includes four sections, with the first section being the Preamble. The Preamble summarizes the social work profession's mission and core values. The second section is the Purpose of the NASW Code of Ethics. This provides an overview of the Code's main functions and a brief guide for dealing with ethical issues or dilemmas in social work practice (NASW, 2017). The third section is the Ethical Principles section. This presents broad ethical principles, based on social work's core values that inform social work practice (NASW, 2017). The final section is Ethical Standards which includes specific ethical standards to help guide social workers' conduct and behavior when practicing the profession. All of the ethical responsibilities to clients are directly taken from the NASW website (NASW, 2017).

COMMITMENT TO CLIENTS

> Social workers' primary responsibility is to promote the well-being of clients. In general, clients' interests are primary. However, social workers' responsibility to the larger society or specific legal obligations may on limited occasions supersede the loyalty owed clients, and clients should be so advised. (Examples include when a social worker is required by law to report that a client has abused a child or has threatened to harm self or others.)

When treating clients, it is important to understand *informed consent*, which states that if a person is a danger to self, danger to others, or gravely disabled, that the client meets criteria for hospitalization and confidentiality can be breached. This is explained at the initial session by the therapist to the client. This also applies if there is an apparent danger to a child and the possibility of elder abuse, where the social worker becomes a *mandated reporter* and must report their suspicions to the proper authorities. In all other cases, confidentiality cannot be breached unless the client is authorizing the release of information to go elsewhere, for example, releasing client information to another therapist because the case has been transferred. It is very important to understand that we are protecting the client's well-being at all costs, which means making the difficult decisions when it appears that the client is unable to do it for him/herself.

SELF-DETERMINATION

> Social workers respect and promote the right of clients to self-determination and assist clients in their efforts to identify and clarify their goals. Social workers may limit clients' right to self-determination when, in the social workers' professional judgment, clients' actions or potential actions pose a serious, foreseeable, and imminent risk to themselves or others.

It is vital to allow clients to determine where and what their therapeutic goals should be. It is a collaborative effort between the client and the therapist, and the client should be involved and assertive throughout the process. Self-determination can become tricky however when dealing with a client who is not always capable of making the best decisions for him/herself. If for example you have a client who is chronically and severely mentally ill, and they are to testify in court and their medical records are being requested because of an issue with their landlord, this is where the client's ability for self-determination may be compromised. In this example, let's say that the client is completely okay with the release of records to the court, but you as their social worker believe that the release of those records may compromise the client regarding this case. You as the social worker can intervene on behalf of the client and share with the court why you believe the records should not be released. In this way, you are advocating for the client because self-determination is being compromised in this particular situation. Often times like in this example, ethical issues do not always fit into a neat box but rather have many complicated components to them.

INFORMED CONSENT

> (a) Social workers should provide services to clients only in the context of a professional relationship based, when appropriate, on valid informed consent. Social workers should use clear and understandable language to inform clients of the purpose of the services, risks related to the services, limits to services because of the requirements of a third-party payer, relevant costs, reasonable alternatives, clients' right to refuse or withdraw consent, and the time frame covered by the consent. Social workers should provide clients with an opportunity to ask questions.

When discussing informed consent with the client, it is important to share that the client's records and services are completely confidential unless the client shares that he/she is a danger to him/herself, a danger to others, or gravely disabled. When the well-being of the client is compromised, the social worker can ethically break confidentiality to ensure the safety of the client. At that point the social worker must intervene and begin the process of implementing crisis evaluation services to assess if the client is a danger for suicide, and this will involve other entities getting involved such as a crisis evaluation team outside of your agency. The same scenario applies to the social worker regarding being a mandated reporter. The social worker can break confidentiality and report to a third party if there is any suspicion of child or elderly abuse. The client before beginning treatment needs to be aware of this as well as knowing that records can be released by the client's authorization. If the client were to sign a release of information for example, because the client is moving to a new city and wants their records transferred to the new treating therapist, this is legally being authorized by the client. At that point, the release of information is usually valid for 90 days and after that the contract can no longer be honored. Informed consent also extends to the services that will be provided to the client as well as discussing the limitations of what will be offered. Time should be used to allow the client to ask questions and to clarify any confusion the client may have regarding informed consent.

COMPETENCE

a. Social workers should provide services and represent themselves as competent only within the boundaries of their education, training, license, certification, consultation received, supervised experience, or other relevant professional experience.

b. Social workers should provide services in substantive areas or use intervention techniques or approaches that are new to them only after engaging in appropriate study, training, consultation, and supervision from people who are competent in those interventions or techniques.

Social workers should only practice within their scope of competence and nothing outside of that scope. Within the scope of practice of therapeutic services, the social worker can provide individual assessments, diagnose, create treatment plans, case manage, and implement therapeutic modalities such as cognitive behavioral therapy and family therapy services. Social workers on a macro level can help to create policies advocating for those that are underserved and do so much more within the scope to help better serve those that are most in need. The scope of a social worker is long and vast, but it is important to stay within the realm of the profession.

CULTURAL COMPETENCE AND SOCIAL DIVERSITY

a. Social workers should understand culture and its function in human behavior and society, recognizing the strengths that exist in all cultures.

b. Social workers should have a knowledge base of their clients' cultures and be able to demonstrate competence in the provision of services that are sensitive to clients' cultures and to differences among people and cultural groups.

c. Social workers should obtain education about and seek to understand the nature of social diversity and oppression with respect to race, ethnicity, national origin, color, sex, sexual orientation, gender identity or expression, age, marital status, political belief, religion, immigration status, and mental or physical disability.

Social workers should always show competence and respect for culture when seeing the client. When assessing the client, you may be using the medical model of treatment, but that should not be the only factor that you are assessing. Looking at the environment of the individual and culture is such an important and vital function regarding the client. Even if you do not agree with the cultural components of the client on a personal level, it is still showing respect and not allowing *egocentrism* to affect your ability to best serve the individual. In understanding the culture of an individual, the social worker better understands the whole person as treatment is being provided.

CONFLICTS OF INTEREST

a. Social workers should be alert to and avoid conflicts of interest that interfere with the exercise of professional discretion and impartial judgment. Social workers should inform clients when a real or potential conflict of interest arises and take reasonable steps to resolve the issue in a manner that makes the clients' interests primary and protects clients' interests to the greatest extent possible. In some cases, protecting clients' interests may require termination of the professional relationship with proper referral of the client.

b. Social workers should not take unfair advantage of any professional relationship or exploit others to further their personal, religious, political, or business interests.

Conflict of interest should not be taking place when treating a client. For example, if you are dating an individual and you are also providing therapy to this person, there is a conflict of interest that is taking place. When I was working for the county, one therapist was dating the clients that he was seeing and exchanging sexual favors for helping them get on permanent disability. This individual was eventually caught and had his license revoked but due to politics and the bureaucracy of a government agency, it took 8 years for him to finally lose his job and no longer have the ability to practice.

PRIVACY AND CONFIDENTIALITY

a. Social workers should respect clients' right to privacy. Social workers should not solicit private information from clients unless it is essential to providing services or conducting social work evaluation or research. Once private information is shared, standards of confidentiality apply.

b. Social workers may disclose confidential information when appropriate with valid consent from a client or a person legally authorized to consent on behalf of a client.

As stated earlier regarding commitment to clients, confidentiality should be protected at all costs unless criteria are met under these specific circumstances:

1. The client is a danger to self, others, or is gravely disabled.
2. There is a suspicion of child or elder abuse and you need to report your suspicion as a mandated reporter.
3. The client has signed a release of information and has requested records be sent elsewhere.

ACCESS TO RECORDS

a. Social workers should provide clients with reasonable access to records concerning the clients. Social workers who are concerned that clients' access to their records could cause serious misunderstanding or harm to the client should provide assistance in interpreting the records and consultation with the client regarding the records. Social workers should limit clients' access to their records, or portions of their records, only in exceptional circumstances when there is compelling evidence that such access would cause serious harm to the client. Both clients' requests and the rationale for withholding some or all of the record should be documented in clients' files.
b. When providing clients with access to their records, social workers should take steps to protect the confidentiality of other individuals identified or discussed in such records.

The client should have reasonable access to their records unless you as the social worker feel that it could compromise them. As mentioned earlier, if a client is to appear in court and you feel that the release of those records would compromise the client, then you have the right to intervene and limit access to those records. Even if the client is requesting it for him/herself, if you feel that the information may compromise that person, you can use your judgment in terms of how much information is going to be released.

SEXUAL RELATIONSHIPS

a. Social workers should under no circumstances engage in sexual activities or sexual contact with current clients, whether such contact is consensual or forced.

b. Social workers should not engage in sexual activities or sexual contact with clients' relatives or other individuals with whom clients maintain a close personal relationship when there is a risk of exploitation or potential harm to the client. Sexual activity or sexual contact with clients' relatives or other individuals with whom clients maintain a personal relationship has the potential to be harmful to the client and may make it difficult for the social worker and client to maintain appropriate professional boundaries. Social workers—not their clients, their clients' relatives, or other individuals with whom the client maintains a personal relationship—assume the full burden for setting clear, appropriate, and culturally sensitive boundaries.

This one is pretty simple: "Do not have sex with your clients!" This breaks all ethical principles in the sense of exploiting the client, potentially harming the well-being of the client, and just crossing clear and appropriate boundaries that should be established between the social worker and the individual being treated.

PHYSICAL CONTACT

Social workers should not engage in physical contact with clients when there is a possibility of psychological harm to the client as a result of the contact (such as cradling or caressing clients). Social workers who engage in appropriate physical contact with clients are responsible for setting clear, appropriate, and culturally sensitive boundaries that govern such physical contact.

Physical contact should be professional and not cross boundaries that are culturally insensitive and just overall cross appropriate and ethical boundaries. As a general rule, a handshake is a great way to greet your client and it is probably best to leave it at that.

SEXUAL HARASSMENT

> Social workers should not sexually harass clients. Sexual harassment includes sexual advances, sexual solicitation, requests for sexual favors, and other verbal or physical conduct of a sexual nature.

Sexual harassment should not be taking place in any form. When I worked for the county, one of my coworkers would only treat female clients even though our target population was the chronically and severely mentally ill. All of his individual sessions would be attractive females who did not meet the criteria of our clinic. Eventually, he crossed the line with one of his clients and began stalking this individual. The client's case had to be transferred to another therapist and the coworker was supposedly disciplined by the manager of the facility. Ideally, one would like to believe that the right action occurred, but just as described in looking at societal problems, there are so many factors on the micro, mezzo and macro levels that come into play. Four years later, this individual was eventually promoted and now manages a mental health facility. I have no idea if he learned from his past or is using his greater authority to continue what he did before.

DEROGATORY LANGUAGE

> Social workers should not use derogatory language in their written or verbal communications to or about clients. Social workers should use accurate and respectful language in all communications to and about clients.

Derogatory language should not be used when treating clients and when discussing cases among your peers. This also extends to supervision and just general case consultations. Regardless of how frustrated you may be with a case, it is still imperative to be respectful when addressing and discussing the individual that you are treating regardless of the setting or forum.

PAYMENT FOR SERVICES

> a. When setting fees, social workers should ensure that the fees are fair, reasonable, and commensurate with the services performed. Consideration should be given to clients' ability to pay.

b. Social workers should avoid accepting goods or services from clients as payment for professional services. Bartering arrangements, particularly involving services, create the potential for conflicts of interest, exploitation, and inappropriate boundaries in social workers' relationships with clients. Social workers should explore and may participate in bartering only in very limited circumstances when it can be demonstrated that such arrangements are an accepted practice among professionals in the local community, considered to be essential for the provision of services, negotiated without coercion, and entered into at the client's initiative and with the client's informed consent. Social workers who accept goods or services from clients as payment for professional services assume the full burden of demonstrating that this arrangement will not be detrimental to the client or the professional relationship.

Payment of services should be reasonable and setting a sliding scale fee to help an individual client is completely ethical. Bartering of services should never take place, for example exchanging therapeutic services for having your car washed by this person. It may seem like you are helping the client, but this type of action crosses boundaries and creates a conflict of interest that extends to multiple relationships. In this example you are a social worker as well as acting as a friend, and there is an overall unequal power distribution that is taking place between you and the client. Also as the therapeutic process goes on and more bartering of services continues to take place, this creates an unhealthy relationship dynamic where the client is in a position to be taken advantage of and is not in a healthy relationship dynamic to heal from their own wounds. Payment of services can be difficult to discuss and that is why it is very important to address that issue before the therapeutic process begins.

CLIENTS WHO LACK DECISION-MAKING CAPACITY

When social workers act on behalf of clients who lack the capacity to make informed decisions, social workers should take reasonable steps to safeguard the interests and rights of those clients.

As mentioned earlier regarding self-determination of your client, it is important to factor in the ability of the individual to make clear and sound decisions for themselves and for you the social worker to take appropriate steps to advocate on the client's behalf. The example provided earlier is if your client is to appear in court and has authorized the release of his/her records. In this instance if you believe that the client made this decision without having the right decision-making capacity, then it is your ethical duty to intercede and assist in any way that you can.

INTERRUPTION OF SERVICES

> Social workers should make reasonable efforts to ensure continuity of services in the event that services are interrupted by factors such as unavailability, relocation, illness, disability, or death.

If any interruption of services is going to take place, it is important to make sure that the issue is properly addressed with your client. Illness and unexpected events can take place and it is up to the social worker to figure out ways to best minimize the difficulty for the client. An example would be to have one of your colleagues provide short-term therapy during your absence, or at least have a discussion with your supervisor and find out the best way to minimize the disruption regarding the continuity of care.

TERMINATION OF SERVICES

a. Social workers should terminate services to clients and professional relationships with them when such services and relationships are no longer required or no longer serve the clients' needs or interests.

b. Social workers should take reasonable steps to avoid abandoning clients who are still in need of services. Social workers should withdraw services precipitously only under unusual circumstances, giving careful consideration to all factors in the situation and taking care to minimize possible adverse effects. Social workers should assist in making appropriate arrangements for continuation of services when necessary.

When terminating services with the client, it is important to review all of the goals that have been set forth during the therapeutic relationship and address if those goals have been met. If those goals have been met, then it is appropriate to terminate the case because the client has achieved their desired results. Other instances that may constitute termination may be the client moving, or the client finding a facility that is more appropriate for what he or she is trying to address. In those instances, it is important to make sure that the client has been properly linked with services and once you know that this is the case, you at that point can terminate the case. Before the client is transferred, it is up to you to make sure the client is continuing to receive services through you promoting a continuity of care, and making sure that the transition is being done as smoothly as possible.

VIGNETTE

Below is the same vignette from Chapter 2:

VIGNETTE

You are working at a mental health agency as a social worker and you have been there for four months. One day, your boss tells you that a client has been transferred to you, as the client was complaining about her previous social worker. Upon your initial session with the client, she shares that the previous social worker and herself had sexual relations, as she stated that "he promised me he would get me social security in exchange for going out with him." The client also shares that "I was terminated really quickly by him and there was no real explanation because I thought we were getting serious."

After completing the initial meeting with your new client, you take that information to your boss and he tells you, "That is why I transferred the case to you." You then ask the boss if any action is going to take place against the social worker and he tells you, "That is none of your business and I will take care of it." You then take the issue to your supervisor, and your supervisor tells you, "There is a boys' club here and you do not want to screw around with it. Just leave it alone because you do not want this going on your performance evaluation." As you spend time there, you realize that your boss, the accused social worker, and your supervisor are all friends.

QUESTIONS TO CONSIDER

1. What are the ethical issues regarding the treatment of clients that are being violated?
2. If you were to make a report to the NASW, how would you go about making that report?
3. How many individuals would you report regarding this whole situation?

REFERENCES

NASW (2017). Code of ethics of the National Association of Social Workers. Retrieved from: https://www.socialworkers.org/About/Ethics/Code-of-Ethics/Code-of-Ethics-English

NASW (2015). Code of ethics procedure manual of the National Association of Social Workers. Retrieved from: http://socialworkers.org/nasw/ethics/ProceduresManual.pdf

National Association of Social Workers, Code of Ethics. Copyright © 2017 by National Association of Social Workers, Inc. Reprinted with permission.

CHAPTER 4

Valuing Diversity and Advocating for Your Clients

WHAT IS CULTURE?

The NASW standards for cultural competence define culture as "a universal phenomenon reflecting diversity, norms of behavior, and awareness of global interdependence" (2015). Culture is the integrated pattern of human behavior that includes thoughts, behaviors, communications, actions, customs, beliefs, values, and institutions of a racial, ethnic, religious, or social group. Social groups may include lesbian, gay, bisexual, transgender people, people with a disability, older adults, military families, and immigrants and refugees. Culture engenders so many aspects of life which includes the healthy development of today's youth: closing the health gap, ending homelessness, addressing environmental issues, promoting social justice, and addressing income inequality. These are just a few cultural topics that as social workers we need to address moving forward. As a practitioner, it is important to look at all of the various components from a macro, mezzo, and micro perspective.

CULTURAL COMPETENCE IN SOCIAL WORK

Cultural competence can be understood in the context of behaviors, attitudes, and policies that enables a system to function effectively across various cultural dimensions. In this context, diversity includes:

- gender
- ethnicity
- religion
- sexual orientation
- religion
- socio-economic status

Establishing competence in social work requires constantly learning and expanding your ability to work with various cultures. Reynolds (1942) defines that there are five stages that are required for a social worker to develop cultural competency. These stages are:

- establishing self-awareness
- being culturally sensitive due to lack of understanding
- learning by trial and error
- establishment of knowledge
- establishment of competence

The framework that Reynolds sought to implement was to teach and educate others how to establish a form of cultural competence when working with a given culture. The model's strengths include the focus of taking self-responsibility for one's own biases and lack of knowledge, providing an evaluation standard of cultural competence, and an offering of stages that can be followed to achieve a form of competency. The biggest strength of the model is that it takes into account the importance of diversity, and how understanding and knowledge of any culture is a long-term process.

STAGE 1: ESTABLISHING SELF-AWARENESS

This stage can be defined by the statement "I do not want to say anything wrong and embarrass myself." As a social worker, you must confront situations that you may not understand or be able to relate to. When one feels uncomfortable due to lack of familiarity, this can lead to being overly self-conscious and wanting to retreat from the situation. As a social worker, it is important to be in tune with your own fears, but at the same time, embrace the opportunity to learn about a new culture. This is where humility and openness are required, and openly taking an active interest in what you are able to learn. It is also vital to be aware of any biases or ethnocentric beliefs that may hurt the process of helping the cultural group in need. Important social work tools to use include:

- rapport-building by starting where the client is at
- active listening
- being non-judgmental

STAGE 2: BEING CULTURALLY SENSITIVE DUE TO LACK OF UNDERSTANDING

This stage may involve the statement "I am going to jump in and learn." Reynolds describes that this is where an individual will draw from their own culture and begin to appreciate and identify the differences between the new culture and of one's own upbringing. This is what she defined as cultural sensitivity. She believed that this is where greater self-awareness and the capacity to really open and learn takes place. This is also the stage where genuineness and adaptation is required because the social worker will be facing situations outside of what they do not know. The metric for this stage is the beginning process of thinking outside of yourself because of greater self-awareness and cultural sensitivity.

STAGE 3: LEARNING BY TRIAL AND ERROR

This stage can be defined by the statement "I am still here and some things are working." Reynolds defines this stage as establishing more freedom when working with a given culture because of the expansive knowledge, self-awareness, and sensitivity that has been accumulated. This is where a greater understanding of the culture is comprehended by the social worker, and even though accidental mistakes are made, the social worker has the ability and confidence to address it and learn what is more culturally appropriate. This can take the form of communication gaps or other factors that may ensue. The social worker at this stage is able to differentiate between one's own beliefs and those of the culture being served.

STAGE 4: ESTABLISHMENT OF KNOWLEDGE

This stage can be defined by the statement "I have so much appreciation for their culture." This is where the social worker's abilities have expanded due to greater self-reflection and the capacity to be open to more diversity is established. The social worker can look at their experience and be objectively critical of what was done well and not done well in relation to the overall practice and cultural competency. The social worker at this stage not only thinks about traditional interventions to use, but can also acknowledge how cultural components need to come into play. In terms of competence, the social worker's knowledge, skills, and values are expansive from the macro, mezzo, and micro levels of practice.

STAGE 5: ESTABLISHMENT OF COMPETENCE

This stage can be defined by the statement "There is so much more to learn and I am just a student." The social worker here realizes the more one learns about a culture, the more there is to learn. An establishment of competence takes place during this stage, but at the same time, humility takes a strong hold knowing that no one person can truly be an expert on any culture outside of your own. Reynolds acknowledged that this level of competence is what creates great supervisors. Supervisors with this level of competence can effectively teach and guide those that are under his/her supervision. She believed that the supervision process when dealing with culture should be an egalitarian relationship. The reason being is that by the supervisor demonstrating humility to the supervised, the supervisor is actually modeling the attitude and behavior that the supervised should be demonstrating when away from supervision. This type of supervision also demonstrates and models how cultural competence is a lifelong journey and process.

SOCIAL WORK PRACTICE

The NASW amended a previous version regarding cultural competencies and the practice of social work (NASW, 2015). The ten standards below discuss the core practices that should be a guide for social workers to engage in when practicing out in the field*. The standards are below:

STANDARD 1: ETHICS AND VALUES

> Social Workers shall function in accordance with the codes, ethics, and standards of the NASW (2008) Code of Ethics. Cultural competence requires self-awareness, cultural humility, and the commitment to understanding and embracing culture as central to effective practice. (p. 4)

In relation to ethics and values, it is a matter as a social worker of addressing areas of conflict between your own personal values, and the values of those of other cultures. It is not having an ethnocentric approach, but being open-minded and respectful of all cultures. Also, it is understanding the interplay and disparity that exists between the values of the dominant culture, and the values of those who are marginalized or oppressed. As social workers, it is important to be a representative for those who need to be represented the most.

STANDARD 2: SELF-AWARENESS

> Social Workers shall demonstrate an appreciation of their own cultural identities and those of others. Social workers must also be aware of their own privilege and power and must acknowledge the impact of this privilege and power in their work with and on behalf of clients. Social workers will also demonstrate cultural humility and sensitivity to

---

* National Association of Social Workers, "Standards 1-10," Standards and Indicators for Cultural Competence, pp. 4-5. Copyright © 2015 by National Association of Social Workers, Inc. Reprinted with permission.

the dynamics of power and privilege in all areas of social work. (p. 4)

As a social worker, it is important to be self-aware and examine any possible biases, prejudices, and stereotypes that you may have. It is also important to look at your own perspective in relation to how you see power and privilege, as that can dictate how you will interact when working with the underserved population. It is also important to not only display cultural competence, but cultural humility which sees working with other cultures as a collaborative effort, versus trying to be viewed as an expert. Cultural humility takes on an egalitarian approach, and the community being served is the expert. It is up to the social worker to lean on their expertise and to help access the wealth of resources and knowledge that they have about their own community. This approach involves always being respectful and taking on the mentality of being a student each time you enter a cultural setting.

STANDARD 3: CROSS-CULTURAL KNOWLEDGE

Social workers shall possess and continue to develop specialized knowledge and understanding that is inclusive of, but not limited to, the history, traditions, values, family systems, and artistic expressions such as race and ethnicity; immigration and refugee status; tribal groups; religion and spirituality; sexual orientation; gender identity or expression; social class; and mental or physical abilities of various cultural groups. (p. 4)

As social workers, it is important to examine cultural values and world views pertaining to culture. Within that context, it is important to understand if the culture you are working with is more collectivist or individualistic in nature. Also, it would be important to identify relationally how they interact, meaning if they are low-contact or high-contact in nature. And it would be important to define how the culture views achievement, because this can help you in determining a culturally appropriate treatment plan. It would also be important to examine customs, traditions of family and the community. Is the structure of the family hierarchical, egalitarian, or patriarchal? Also intersectionality comes into play, looking at the interaction between other minority experiences, for example being a minority by culture as well as by sexual orientation.

STANDARD 4: CROSS-CULTURAL SKILLS

> Social workers will use a broad range of skills (micro, mezzo, and macro) and techniques that demonstrate an understanding of and respect for the importance of culture in practice, policy, and research. (p. 4)

In implementing cross-cultural skills, understand how cultural values and experiences of oppression dictate how a culture views the help of the social worker. This would affect the way in which a culture would seek out help for services. It would be important as the social worker to define what seeking help means to the culture you are working with. Gathering this information would be helpful in approaching the method you would use to assess and gather information, as well as structure your treatment plan.

STANDARD 5: SERVICE DELIVERY

> Social Workers shall be knowledgeable about and skillful in the use of services, resources, and institutions and be available to serve multicultural communities. They shall be able to make culturally appropriate referrals within both formal and informal networks and shall be cognizant of, and work to address, service gaps affecting specific cultural groups. (pp. 4–5)

In terms of service delivery, it would be the hope that the social worker is working for an agency that believes and practices the tenets that have been set forth. It would be ideal if the service agency would be inclusive and welcoming to all diverse consumers seeking their services. Along that line, it would be ideal if the agency's physical environment were also welcoming to all cultures, and that the policies and procedures of that agency would reflect an inclusive and culturally humble approach.

STANDARD 6: EMPOWERMENT AND ADVOCACY

> Social workers shall be aware of the impact of social systems, policies, practices, and programs on multicultural client populations, advocating for, with and on behalf of multicultural clients and client populations whenever appropriate. Social workers should also participate in the development and implementation of policies and practices that empower and advocate for marginalized and oppressed populations. (p. 5)

One of the best ways to empower and advocate as a social worker is to explore the socio-political history of the group being served and how that is impacting their experience. Are they being marginalized? Is there oppression taking place? These are avenues as social worker to explore. It would also be important to examine the social structures and see if there is any form of discrimination taking place. Empowering and advocating for a client is to look at the system as a whole and look at each facet from the macro, the mezzo, and the micro perspective.

STANDARD 7: DIVERSE WORKFORCE

> Social workers shall support and advocate for recruitment, admissions and hiring, and retention efforts in social work programs and organizations to ensure diversity within the profession. (p. 5)

A diverse workforce would promote cultural humility and an environment that would foster respect for differences. It would allow for appreciation of the diversity that does exist, because of the opportunity to continually learn and grow from one another. Also from a personnel perspective, a diverse workforce should be represented and the recruitment efforts should promote diversity when hiring employees. As a profession, social work seeks to promote all diverse cultures to enter the profession.

STANDARD 8: PROFESSIONAL EDUCATION

> Social workers shall advocate for, develop, and participate in professional education and training programs that advance cultural competence within the profession. Social workers should embrace cultural competence as a focus of lifelong learning. (p. 5)

Continuously engaging in professional education allows for one to always be a student, and to realize that there is always more to learn. From a cultural perspective, it is understanding that cultural competence can never be achieved, and so it is always being open to learning new information. It is identifying and challenging any assumptions that one may have, by being proactive to actually learn the truth.

STANDARD 9: LANGUAGE AND COMMUNICATION

> Social workers shall provide and advocate for effective communication with clients of all cultural groups, including

people of limited English proficiency or low literacy skills, people who are blind or have low vision, people who are deaf or hard of hearing, and people with disabilities. (p. 5)

It is important as the social worker to understand the role of language and communication patterns within and between cultures. This is vital in being able to most effectively communicate with the community that you are serving. Also, as a social worker, if you are treating anyone who is suffering from a disability that impairs their language capabilities, it is vital to ensure a timely professional response for translation or interpretive services.

STANDARD 10: LEADERSHIP TO ADVANCE CULTURAL COMPETENCE

Social workers shall be change agents who demonstrate the leadership skills to work effectively with multicultural groups in agencies, organizational settings and communities. Social workers should also demonstrate responsibility for advancing cultural competence within and beyond their organizations, helping to challenge structural and institutional oppression and build and sustain diverse and inclusive institutions and communities. (p. 5)

As a social worker, it is important to instill the professional value of promoting and modeling cultural humility. Cultural humility by the social worker needs to be practiced in the organizational setting, communities, and within the sociopolitical structures of society. It is imperative to maintain that standard in every facet of life as a social worker.

CULTURAL COMPETENCE VERSUS CULTURAL HUMILITY

Cultural competence is a conceptual framework to help providers understand, appreciate, and work with individuals from diverse cultures. Its components are:

- awareness and acceptance of cultural differences between and within cultures
- self-awareness of the differences between your own cultural beliefs and others
- knowledge of the client's culture, and adaptation of skills to better accommodate the client's culturally influenced needs

- cross-cultural skills in your treatment setting

Developing cultural competence results in an ability to understand, communicate with, and effectively interact with people across cultures (Donahue, 2018). It is the acknowledgment that there is a world outside of yourself and that other cultures may or may not reflect you own personal views. As a social worker, cultural competence requires you to:

- identify basic demographics
- identify your population's immediate environment and supports
- identify what helps and hinders tenancy

The goal of cultural competence is to build an understanding of minority cultures to better and more appropriately provide effective services. This requires the social work values of knowledge and training, and this practice allows for those you are serving to strive and obtain their goals through the promotion of skill building. What cultural competence is not is:

- tolerance
- assuming one is better than another
- belief that this is sufficient for a healthcare professional

The shortcomings of cultural competence are that it enforces the idea that competence in the understanding of another culture can exist. It also takes on the myth that cultures are monolithic and places too much focus on academic knowledge versus actual lived experience.

Cultural humility on the other hand reflects the complex attitude and sensitive skills required to meet the needs of clients and families in a way that empowers them to participate in a two-way therapeutic relationship, where both client and provider are understood to have something to contribute. There are three dimensions regarding cultural humility:

LIFELONG LEARNING AND CRITICAL SELF–REFLECTION

Practicing cultural humility is to understand that culture is an expression of self and that the process of learning about each individual's culture is a lifelong endeavor. It is understanding that no two individuals are the same and that each individual is complex with multidimensional roots.

RECOGNIZING AND CHALLENGING POWER IMBALANCES FOR RESPECTFUL PARTNERSHIPS

It is important to understand that while working to establish and maintain respect is essential in all healthy and productive relationships, the root of effective social work practice is acknowledging and challenging the power imbalances inherent in the client-provider relationship. This power imbalance needs to be recognized and the social worker must never abuse that power when serving their clientele.

INSTITUTIONAL ACCOUNTABILITY

There needs to be the acknowledgment of the intersection of individual, community, and macro forces that a client is experiencing in relation to racial injustice and oppression. The construct of solely pinning responsibility on the individual does not look at the person in the context of all life components.

The goal of cultural humility is to encourage personal growth and reflection around culture in order to increase awareness as services are being provided. The values required for cultural humility require introspection and co-learning with the clientele that you serve. The strengths of this model are that it encourages lifelong learning with no end goal, and it appreciates the journey of growth and understanding. It also puts professionals and clients in a mutually beneficial relationship and attempts to diminish the power imbalance in the working relationship. Practicing cultural humility allows a social worker to stop carrying the burden of feeling that one has to know everything about every culture that one encounters at work. Cultural humility also invites a social worker to check one's own assumptions and leave them behind, and instead approach each client relationship as a learner. This allows the power imbalance to become more equal and it empowers you to help understand the richness of the client's culture. In closing, in understanding the difference between cultural competence and cultural humility, cultural competence believes that:

- There is an end product to achieve.
- One can become an expert regarding another culture not your own.
- Objective best practices can be accomplished.

While on the other hand cultural humility believes:

- Learning about another culture is a lifelong process.
- The client is the expert of their own culture.
- Identifies subjective best practices knowing that culture cannot be put in a box

INTERSECTIONALITY

Intersectionality is a concept used in critical theories to describe the ways in which oppressive institutions (racism, sexism, homophobia, transphobia, ableism, xenophobia, classism, etc.) are interconnected and cannot be examined separately from one another. Many activists and thinkers helped to inform our current understanding of intersectional issues, particularly people who were part of the human rights movements (Crenshaw, 1994). Many grassroots women groups in the 1970s and 1980s sought to break down the hierarchies that create inequalities, such as patriarchy and capitalism. Women like Sojourner Truth have contributed to the development of intersectionality. Truth was a former slave in the United States who spoke both about her identity as an African American person, a woman, and an African American woman. During her speech in Akron, Ohio in 1851 (Collins, 2000), Sojourner Truth demonstrated that the concept of being a woman was culturally constructed through the discrepancies between her experience as an African American woman, and the qualities ascribed to women.

The actual term *intersectionality* first appeared in an article by Kimberlé Williams Crenshaw, published in 1991, which addressed the relationship between sex, gender, nation, race, and class. Crenshaw wanted to show how African American women had been excluded from women's equality struggles, particularly as it pertained to violence, and how all of the circles of an individual intersected to create oppression and discrimination. In attempting to provide a visual for intersectionality, it can be viewed through four circles, all within each other. The innermost circle represents a person's unique characteristics based off of:

- power
- privilege
- identity

The second circle from the inside represents aspects of identity. These include but are not limited to:

- gender
- age
- sexuality
- religion
- social status
- income
- education
- citizenship status
- disability

The third circle from the inside represents the different types of discrimination and attitudes that impact the individual's identity status. These include but are not limited to:

- ethnocentrism
- classism
- sexism
- heterosexism
- discrimination
- racism
- ableism
- homophobia
- ageism
- transphobia

The outermost circle represents the larger forces and structures that work together to reinforce exclusion. These include but are not limited to:

- immigration system
- educational system
- war
- capitalism
- globalization
- politics
- colonization
- the legal system
- the economy
- social forces
- historical forces

These are just a few examples of how discrimination, identity, and structure can interplay and affect the experience of an individual from a more holistic perspective.

FIGURE 4.1

Intersectionality takes a holistic approach because it involves looking at various aspects together. For example, instead of viewing race and gender separately, it would be looking at how they intersect together. A big part of intersectionality is about taking into account people's experiences and identities without placing them into fixed categories. Consider for a moment this quote from poet and activist Audre Lorde: "As a forty-nine-year-old Black lesbian feminist Socialist mother of two, including one boy, and a member of an interracial couple, I usually find myself a part of some group defined as other, deviant, inferior, or just plain wrong." In order to understand Lorde's experience, one can't just apply a strictly anti-racist, anti-homophobic, or gender equality perspective. Her identities cannot be seen as standing alone; it is the whole aspect of all the areas of her life that need to be looked at. Every person has their own unique history and experiences that determine their social location and, depending on who you are, one can experience a greater or lesser degree of privilege and exclusion. The rationale for an intersectional approach is not to show who is worse off in society, but as the Association for Women's Rights in Development notes, it is to reveal meaningful distinctions and similarities in order to overcome discriminations and to put the conditions in place for all people to fully enjoy their human rights (AWID, 2004). In this sense, intersectionality includes everybody and although the term intersectionality arose out of feminism, it can be applied to the experiences and circumstances of all individuals. Some examples where intersectionality comes into play today include:

- the Me Too movement
- DACA (Deferred Action for Childhood Arrivals)
- police violence against African Americans
- the alt-right movement and white privilege
- socioeconomic inequality

Lilia Watson stated regarding intersectionality, "If you have come to help me, you are wasting your time. If you have come because your liberation is bound up with mine, then let us work together." Intersectionality falls in line with the principles of social work because it looks at the evaluation of the various intersecting components of life, as well as providing the foundation and roadmap for activism and change. It does not pigeonhole social issues to one area, but rather looks at it from a mutual interaction perspective to effectively promote positive change.

REFERENCES

Association for Women's Rights in Development (AWID) (2004). Intersectionality: A tool for gender and economic justice. Toronto: AWID.

Collins, P. H. (2000). *Black Feminist Thought: Knowledge, Consciousness, and the Politics of Empowerment* (2nd ed.). New York: Routledge.

Council on Social Work Education (1969). Project to enhance the competence of social work personnel to understand and work with minority groups. Social welfare archives, (Box 3: Ethnic minority curriculum, 1969). University of Minnesota, Minneapolis, MN.

Crenshaw, K. W. (1994). Mapping the margins: intersectionality, identity politics and violence against women of colour. In M. A. Fineman, and R. Mykitiuk (Eds.), *The public nature of private violence*. New York: Routledge.

Donahue, L. (2018). Cultural Competence and Cultural Communication. Retrieved from: https://www.vanderbilt.edu/oacs/wp-content/uploads/sites/140/CulturalCompetence.pdf

Herzberg, L. (2013). Shared decision-making: a voice for the Lakota people. *Child & Family Social Work, 18*(4), 477–486.

Jani, J., Pierce, D., Ortiz, L., & Sowbel, L. (2013). Access to intersectionality, content to competence: deconstructing social work education diversity standards. *Journal of Social Work Education, 47*(2), 283–301.

Kohli, H., Huber, R., & Faul, A. (2010). Historical and theoretical development of culturally competent social work practice. *Journal of Teaching in Social Work, 30*(1), 252–271.

National Association of Social Workers. (2015). Standards and indicators for cultural competence in social work practice. Washington, DC: Author. Retrieved from https://www.socialworkers.org/LinkClick.aspx?fileticket=PonPTDEBrn4%3D&portalid=0

National Association of Social Workers. (2008). NASW standards for cultural competency in social work practice.

Reisch, M., (2007). Social justice and multiculturalism: persistent tensions in the history of U.S. social welfare and social work. *Studies in Social Justice, 1*(1), 67–92.

Reynolds, B. C. (1942). *Learning and teaching in the practice of social work*. New York: J. J. Little & Ives.

CHAPTER 5

Verbal Skills and Eliminating Counterproductive Communication

W hen meeting a client for the first time or continuously working with them throughout the therapeutic process, making sure that effective communication and healthy rapport is established is key. In this chapter, we will be going over ways to engage the client as well as focusing on ways of eliminating the barriers that can hinder communication. It is not only important to conceptualize and understand the material, but it is also important to practice in the classroom setting, and then to transition and actually implement what you are learning in your field placements. Rosen and Zlotnik (2001) explained that increased skills in student social workers are developed through actual practice in their field settings implementing the material. The experience is invaluable and even through the mistakes that will take place, great opportunities to learn and grow will arise, which will ultimately lead one to becoming a better social worker.

ENGAGING WITH THE CLIENT

When engaging with a client, it is important to be able to establish a healthy therapeutic relationship. Turney (2012) believes in the concept of recognition theory and that the therapeutic relationship is an ethical decision that needs to be made. This entails being able to build trust with the client as the practitioner but also being able to have the client feel like they are being understood. Rosen (1972) explained the importance of the social worker being congruent with the client when the individual is making their statements and evaluations regarding what is taking place in his/her life. There are two concepts that are related to congruence with the client:

1. stimulus response congruence—the social worker's response provides feedback to the client and the message is accurately received
2. content relevance—the extent to which the client views the feedback as relevant and substantial

An example of these would be the following:

Client	"I am ready to move out of my house but my parents are giving me so much grief and it makes me confused."
Social Worker	"It seems like being independent is important to you but with the pressure from your parents, you are having a hard time deciding what to do." (Stimulus response congruence)
Client	"That is exactly how I feel." (Content relevance)

In this example the social worker provided a response that was congruent to what the client was sharing. When the client felt that the message was received, content relevance was provided which lead to the client sharing, "That is exactly how I feel."

ESTABLISHING RAPPORT

Rapport is the ability of the client and social worker to establish a close and harmonious therapeutic relationship where the client's feelings are understood and easily communicated. Hersen and Thomas (2007) shared that individuals who see a counselor for the first time will often have a strange response when dealing with an authority figure. Seeing a counselor for the first time and sharing all of your personal feelings are difficult, and that needs to be understood by the social worker. Oftentimes this awkward dynamic can lead to ineffective ways of establishing healthy rapport. There are many generic statements about rapport such as "putting yourself in their shoes" and when the client is sharing difficult feelings to share affirmation statements like "the sun will come out tomorrow," but in the end, that is not establishing rapport. You are the clinician and your job is to do the hard work with the client and to explore whatever the client needs in order to get better. You are not their friend, spiritual advisor, or family member; you are the professional clinician that they have sought out for treatment.

One of my former colleagues who was a very nice person, when she would see a client, would quote the saying from the movie *Kung Fu Panda*, "Yesterday is history, tomorrow is a mystery, but today is a gift, that is why they call it the present." She would then make a weird grin to the client, and usually the client would just be silent. In her mind that was rapport, but in truth there was really no therapeutic alliance being established. All she was doing was taking away an opportunity to establish healthy rapport. It was her attempt to make the client feel better but in the end, it just changed the opportunity to establish a healthy therapeutic alliance. When establishing rapport, the focus should be on three aspects:

1. Stating the obvious—making a statement of truth about the actual situation to help establish a genuine bond with the client
2. Validating the story of the client—the client feeling you understand their point of view without any judgment about what is being said
3. Appropriate self-disclosure—using personal information about your life to help the client feel more comfortable about opening up

When it comes to "stating the obvious," instead of avoiding an uncomfortable feeling the client is having, it is better to just address it and be open about it. For example, let's say you have a client who is coming to see you for court ordered counseling and it is obvious that the client does not want to be there.

Social Worker	"So what brings you in today?"
Client	"I am here because it is court ordered."
Social Worker	"I am pretty sure that you would not be here unless you were forced by the courts, but since we will need to work together, let's try and make the most of it. How does that sound?" (Stating the obvious)
Client	"I guess, because there really is no choice."
Social Worker	"Who knows, you might even like it."
Client	"Maybe?"

In this example, the obvious was stated by acknowledging the client's desire to not be there, and a more genuine sense of rapport was established.

The second concept is "validating the story of the client." This means that even if you disagree with what the client is sharing, you still validate and contextualize the premise of what is being shared. I had a situation where I had a young man who was extremely talented but used all of his energy to sabotage his own life. His belief was that everyone around him was the cause of his failures and he refused to take any responsibility for his own problems. At the same time he was adamant that people recognize his talents and abilities. Below is an example of that dialogue:

Client	"Everyone in my life, including my friends and family, are the cause for me not getting into college and not being really successful. I know I am smart and talented."
Social Worker	"I can see that you are a very talented person and it must be really frustrating that those that you trust and love basically are the cause of your setbacks and failures in your life." (Validating the story)
Client	"I feel that way even if it may not be true."
Social Worker	"Are you saying that there may be some truth to what those around you are saying?"
Client	"I am saying that maybe it is not so black-and-white."

When I validated the client's story, he felt heard but it also opened the door for him to be open to the ways that he may be contributing to his own problems. This allowed for a healthier perspective of what he could do to make things better in conjunction with looking at his environment. When rapport was established with the client, it became much easier to begin the therapeutic relationship with him because his defense mechanisms began to break down. It opened the door for him to more safely explore how he has the power to contribute in creating the life that he wants.

The third concept is "appropriate self-disclosure." The general rule of thumb is that you can use appropriate self-disclosure if it is for the benefit of the client. An example would be disclosing a little about yourself because the client is having difficulty opening up. When sharing, it is important to not go overboard and to only share what is appropriate within the therapeutic relationship. The first example below is of appropriate self-disclosure:

Social Worker	"You shared that you suffer from anxiety. Can you share a little bit about your experience?"
Client	"It is hard to open up. I am sorry but I do not want to share right now."
Social Worker	"I totally understand how hard this must be for you. Would it be okay for you to share what you are comfortable sharing?"
Client	"I am not sure if I should even be here right now because I do not want to do this anymore."
Social Worker	"I know personally how debilitating anxiety can be as I suffered from it, too. It was so hard to seek help and share in a vulnerable fashion with a stranger, but it was one of the best things that I ever did. I do not blame you for leaving, but I do hope you know that you are not alone in terms of suffering from anxiety." (Appropriate self-disclosure)
Client	"Really? How did you overcome it?"
Social Worker	"It took a lot of work, starting exactly where you are today. Are you willing to give this a try?"
Client	"I am still hesitant and scared but yes, I am open to trying."

In this example, the social worker used some personal information to help the client feel like he/she was not alone and it helped the client to relax a little and be open to the therapeutic process. In this example, appropriate self-disclosure was utilized. On the flip side, an example of inappropriate self-disclosure would be treating the client like your friend and sharing in that manner. Below is an example of inappropriate self-disclosure:

Social Worker	"How are you doing today?"
Client	"I am doing okay but I am ready to discuss what happened to me this past week. How are you?"

| Social Worker | "Oh my god, I got totally wasted this past weekend and I did really stupid things. I think you are the one who should be counseling me this week because I lost control." (Inappropriate self-disclosure) |

When establishing rapport, it is important to state the obvious. Especially when you are meeting the client for the first time, validate their story by emotionally reflecting the belief system the client is holding, and use appropriate self-disclosure when it is for the benefit of the client.

VERBAL FOLLOWING SKILLS

It is important during the therapy session to have the client not only feel comfortable, but to expand and fully explain what is taking place in their life. Verbal prompts and following skills assist in this process. Furthering is the process of having the client continue to verbalize through the use of the social worker's prompts, using verbal and nonverbal methods. Examples of minimal prompts include:

- Nonverbal—nodding of head, using facial expressions, gestures
- Verbal—verbally saying "yes," "I see," "mm-hmm," etc.

You can also use accent responses that Hackney and Cormier (1979) describe as using a questioning tone while repeating a portion of the statement. An example of an accent response would be:

| Client | "I am so sick of my job and I have had it with my supervisor." |
| Social Worker | "Had it?" (Accent response) |

Paraphrasing can also be used, which is the process of using fresh words to restate the client's message concisely. An example of paraphrasing would be:

| Client | "I don't want to get into a living situation in which I will not be able to make choices on my own" |
| Social Worker | "So independence is a very important issue for you." |

When working with the client, it is also important to know when to properly use open-ended questions and closed-ended questions. Open-ended questions are directed at having the client expand expression to open the communication to go in a direction that the client would like to direct it. An example would be:

| Client | "I am so frustrated at my daughter right now and it is so hard to go there." |
| Social Worker | "What do you mean by that?" |

Client	"It is so hard to explain but I get so frustrated."
Social Worker	"You have mentioned your daughter. Tell me how she enters into this problem." (Open-ended question)

Closed-ended questions, on the other hand, are asked to elicit specific information. This is especially useful when you are doing your assessment because it helps in gathering the psychiatric and medical history of the client. Below is an example of using closed-ended questions:

Social Worker	"When did you begin seeing your primary psychiatrist?" (Closed-ended question)
Client	"I began seeing him one year ago."
Social Worker	"What medications are you currently taking?" (Closed-ended question)
Client	"I am taking Wellbutrin and I am doing well on it."

Also during the therapy process, there will be times when the client will make vague statements, and it will be the job of the social worker to gain more clarity regarding the statement. Seeking concreteness is the ability of the social worker to take a vague statement made by a client and have the individual personalize the information for greater clarity and understanding. The process of seeking concreteness involves:

1. clarifying the meaning of vague statements
2. assisting the client to personalize their statements
3. eliciting specific feelings from the client
4. eliciting details of the client's experience
5. focusing on the here and now

An example would be if your client made the statement "My last social worker did not answer my calls." That statement at face value would make it seem like the previous social worker never returned any calls, and it would be important to explore that. Also, given the fact that this was brought up by the client, this would be a great place to process and use this opportunity to build the therapeutic relationship. It is possible that the client does not trust you because of what took place in the past. Here is an example of the dialogue below:

Client	"My last social worker did not answer my calls." (Vague statement)
Social Worker	"Your last social worker never answered your calls?"
Client	"No, but when I really needed him he was not there to answer my call."
Social Worker	"When did this happen and what was the situation where you sought out his help?" (Clarifying the meaning of the vague statement)

Client	"Back in June I was in need of his assistance because I needed a letter from him for my court case showing compliance with my treatment."
Social Worker	"So what happened?"
Client	"I ended up having to get an extension from the judge and it delayed the chance for me to fulfill my probation."
Social Worker	"So you needed a letter of compliance from your social worker and he was unable to provide that to you when you had to show up to court." (Assisting the client to personalize their statement)
Client	"Yes, that is what happened and I was going to every session. I kept reminding him each week for one month and he promised to give it to me, and so when I called him the day before the court date, I was really in a crunch." (Eliciting details of the client's experience)
Social Worker	"How did that make you feel?"
Client	"I became really frustrated and felt really disappointed because I did everything that I was supposed to do, and because my social worker did not follow through, I suffered for it. It made me really mad." (Eliciting specific feelings from the client)
Social Worker	"I can see that given your previous experience, there is probably a lack of trust and I do not blame you. I cannot control what happened with you and your previous social worker, but I can say that I promise to follow through with whatever it is that you need going forward. Do you need a letter from me with your court case now?" (Focusing on the here and now)
Client	"Yes, and I really hope that I can trust you. I just want to fulfill my compliance with the court and move on with my life.

Verbal following skills are important tools that a social worker must use to be able to effectively gather the necessary information from the client that you are treating. Mastering the skills of furthering, paraphrasing, asking open-ended and closed-ended questions, and seeking concreteness takes practice, and are vital tools to the success of establishing healthy therapeutic relationships.

ELIMINATING VERBAL BARRIERS

Along with establishing and enhancing verbal skills when working with a client, it is also important to identify the barriers that can hinder the communication process. One verbal barrier is to use reassuring and sympathizing responses when a client shares something difficult. An example of this would be:

Client	"I am feeling so terrible after I lost my job. I am really worried about how I am going to pay my bills."

Social Worker	"It is all going to work out. Remember the sun will come out tomorrow." (Reassuring)
Client	"I don't know, because if I don't pay my rent, I have no place to live."
Social Worker	"It is all going to be okay, I promise." (Sympathizing)

A better way in handling this would be to own and establish the situation:

Client	"I am feeling so terrible after I lost my job. I am really worried about how I am going to pay my bills."
Social Worker	"That sounds terrible and what a difficult situation to be in. What is your plan right now?"
Client	"I don't know, because if I don't pay my rent, I have no place to live."
Social Worker	"Once again, this situation sucks and maybe we can use the time to figure out a way to get your rent and bills paid."

Another verbal barrier would be advising or giving suggestions. Your job as a therapist is not to provide answers in terms of how the client is going to fix their life, but rather it is giving the tools and direction to help the client figure out what he/she is going to do. An example of advising would be:

Client	"I am having so many problems at home right now and the situation continues to become more chaotic."
Social Worker	"I suggest that you move out to a new place because of all the difficulty you are going through." (Advising or giving a suggestion)

A better way to address that would be:

Client	"I am having so many problems at home right now and the situation continues to become more chaotic."
Social Worker	"It sounds like a really difficult situation to be in. Have you thought about the different options that are available to you in relation to your living situation?"

Other pitfalls to avoid is using sarcasm at the expense of the client and judging or criticizing the client.

Client	"I am having so many problems right now."
Social Worker	"You think you have problems?!" (Sarcasm)
Client	"I know I talk about the same issue but it is hard for me."
Social Worker	"We have been through this before and you are not doing what I am telling you to do!" (Judging, criticizing)

Trying to convince the client of your viewpoint is another verbal barrier that you want to avoid. If a therapist argues a point to a client, this can lead to the client shutting down and not allowing the individual to process and figure things out during the session time. This is also a countertransference issue, because the therapist's own perception of what is right and wrong is interfering with allowing the client to process freely without judgment. An example of trying to convince the client of your viewpoint is below.

Client	"I am seriously thinking about moving out of my parent's home and really starting to build my life."
Social Worker	"You don't want to do that and build up all that debt. Trust me, you want to stay there as long as you can and take advantage of living off of your parents." (Trying to convince the client of your viewpoints)
Client	"My whole point of leaving is to not depend on them anymore."
Social Worker	"Trust me, I did that when I was young and did not prepare, and my life was screwed. I know and you should learn from my mistakes." (Countertransference)

In this example, the social worker appears well-intentioned but the countertransference of the therapist is not allowing the client to effectively share and process his/her desires. Also, the social worker is assuming that the client is not prepared like the therapist wasn't in the past, and because of that, the social worker feels that he/she has the right to talk to the client in this manner. A more appropriate way of handling this would be:

Client	"I am seriously thinking about moving out of my parent's home and really starting to build my life."
Social Worker	"What has led you to make that decision?"
Client	"I am just at a point in my life where I feel like I need to be on my own."
Social Worker	"Have you prepared to move out in terms of figuring out finances, furniture, and things like that?"
Client	"I did not really think about that. I will definitely need to have a savings and I totally did not think about furnishings."
Social Worker	"It definitely helps, and I am really encouraged and excited for you as you take this next step."

Along the same lines, when a social worker is trying to convince the client of their viewpoint, this then will also direct the social worker to engage in asking leading questions. Asking leading questions is directing the client to do what you the social worker thinks the client should do. Using the same example of the client who wants to move out of his parent's home:

Client	"I am seriously thinking about moving out of my parent's home and really starting to build my life."
Social Worker	"What has led you to make that decision?"
Client	"I am just at a point in my life where I feel like I need to be on my own."
Social Worker	"Wouldn't that hurt your mom's feelings because you two are so close?" (Asking a leading question)

Client	"I know my mom will definitely need to adjust but it should be fine."
Social Worker	"Also wouldn't it put a financial strain on your family more if you sign an apartment contract and can't fulfill the contract?" (Asking a leading question)
Client	"Yeah, that would hurt my family for sure and I do not want to do that."

Another verbal barrier that involves convincing the client of your viewpoint is interrupting and dominating the interaction. If the social worker is not hearing what they want from the client, he/she will begin to interrupt the client and dominate the talk time in the therapy session.

An example of this would be:

Client	"I am seriously thinking about moving out of my parent's home and really starting to build my life."
Social Worker	"You don't want to do that; trust me, I know!"
Client	"I am just at a point in—"
Social Worker	"Point, nothing! You don't want to do that because it is the wrong choice and you should learn from me because I made the wrong choice at your age." (Interrupting and dominating the interaction).
Client	"It is—"
Social Worker	"'It is' nothing. You need to hear me because I have known you long enough to know what is best for you on this. I am the professional!" (Interrupting and dominating the interaction)

When it comes to the verbal barrier of trying to convince the client of your point of view, that will coincide with asking leading questions, issues of countertransference, and interrupting and dominating the interaction. It is important that you as a social worker have enough self-awareness to catch yourself if you are engaging in these barriers. It is also important to work with your supervisor if these issues come up.

Another verbal barrier that social workers will often engage in, especially when just beginning counseling services, is stacking questions. This is very common when you as the social worker are nervous because you have very little or no experience at all providing therapeutic services. An example of stacking questions would be:

Client	"I have had some serious difficulty in my life lately."
Social Worker	"What do you mean? How exactly? Is this something that has been recent?" (Stacking Questions)

In this scenario, the social worker is stacking questions one after the other, which in this case is most likely overwhelming the client.

Another verbal barrier that a new social worker might often engage in is fostering a safe social interaction. When a client begins to share very painful aspects of their life, it might be a natural instinct to not explore more and to change the topic of the conversation to a less emotionally charged issue. In doing so, you the social worker are denying the client the opportunity to gain further insight into their own life. An example of this would be:

Client	"I did not share this before, but I suffered from a lot of abuse when I was a kid growing up. It is even hard to bring it up now."
Social Worker	"What kind of abuse did you experience?"
Client	"I was physically and emotionally abused. There were nights when I often thought about hurting myself."
Social Worker	"You are not that kid anymore and I think it is best to discuss how well you are doing now. Look at how great your kids are doing now, right?" (Fostering a safe interaction)
Client	"No, you are right; my kids are doing great."

In this scenario, this was an opportunity for the client to discuss and share something really painful to the social worker, and the social worker did not allow that process to take place. Also the client had built enough trust in the social worker to not only bring it up, but to have the respect in the therapy process to go there. Instead, the social worker decided to foster a safe interaction by redirecting the topic to the client's own children. It is important as the social worker to honor when these moments come up because these are the moments where true growth can take place within the client. A better way to address it would have been:

Client	"I did not share this before, but I suffered from a lot of abuse when I was a kid growing up. It is even hard to bring it up now."
Social Worker	"What kind of abuse did you experience?"
Client	"I was physically and emotionally abused. There were nights when I often thought about hurting myself."
Social Worker	"That must have been really difficult. I thank you for having the courage to share this with me. Can you share more about what took place?"
Client	"My dad would often come home drunk and he would be violent with my mom, he would become violent and push me, and he would scream and threaten to hurt all of us."
Social Worker	"When did you start to feel suicidal?"
Client	"I started to feel like that nightly when I witnessed my dad hit my mother for the first time. I swore that I would never turn out that way."

| Social Worker | "And you didn't. In fact you deserve so much cred-it for how wonderfully you have raised your own kids." |

Here the client was able to explore the painful memories of the past, as well as connect with what the client has accomplished in his/her own life. This dynamic allowed for a full circle experience of past and present to merge, and allowed for the client to better emotionally come to terms with his/her life now.

The use of parroting is another verbal barrier that can often be done if you the social worker are nervous during the therapy session. Parroting refers to continuously repeating what the client is stating while phrasing it in question form. An example of parroting would be:

Client	"I have really had it up to here with my boss."
Social Worker	"Had it?"
Client	"Yeah, he was totally out of line, yelling at me in front of other staff."
Social Worker	"He was yelling?" (Parroting)
Client	"Yes, yelling. I felt completely embarrassed and devastated."
Social Worker	"Embarrassed and devastated?" (Parroting)

This is not only annoying to the client, but it is not allowing the therapy session to expand to allow for further exploration from the client. Using the same example, this is an opportunity to utilize the skills that we have covered during this chapter:

Client	"I have really had it up to here with my boss."
Social Worker	"Had it?"
Client	"Yeah, he was totally out of line, yelling at me in front of other staff."
Social Worker	"Why did he do that? Can you give more details?" (Furthering)
Client	"I had made a mistake in my last project, but that was because I was provided the wrong information from my supervisor. I actually took many steps to make sure that it did not go any further, and it didn't!"
Social Worker	"So you not only fixed a mistake made by your supervisor, but you went above and beyond to prevent the situation from getting worse. You should not have been criticized but commended for what you did." (Stimulus Response Congruence)
Client	"Exactly! However, I could not express that to everyone during the confrontation. I saved their ass!" (Content Relevance)

One of the biggest mistakes I made when I was providing counseling services at my first internship placement was going on fishing expeditions. This is when you are recklessly throwing out possible ideas for what may be the problem in the client's life without any real therapeutic work taking place. When I was doing this, it was a mixture of being inexperienced, as well my desire to have those breakthrough television moments. Back then, I loved watching talk shows and I loved when expert therapists would be the guests. There would be a person who was struggling with a life issue, and then the expert therapist would diagnose, create a plan, and wrap up all of their problems in 15 minutes. At that point the individual would have that breakthrough moment and the crowd would respond with "oohs and ahhs" over the insight that the therapist provided. The more and more I kept interning, I learned very quickly that TV was TV, and that in real life, therapy takes time and the process is not a 15-minute fix. An example of fishing would be:

Client	"I got into a fight with my boyfriend and it really messed me up."
Social Worker	"You did, what happened?"
Client	"We just began yelling at each other and there was no listening to each other."
Social Worker	"You had mentioned your dad in the past and how you two used to yell...that is why you are yelling with your boyfriend." (Fishing)
Client	"Excuse me? How does that relate and what does that have to do with my current argument with my boyfriend?"
Social Worker	"You see, your past is now coming to the present and that is the core of all of your arguments." (Fishing)
Client	"I am totally confused by what you are saying!"

What the social worker is saying might be true, but the way it is being approached in this example is totally irresponsible and wrong. The social worker had the right to explore issues of the past, but the progression needs to be natural and on the terms of what the client is actually saying. A better way to approach this would be:

Client	"I got into a fight with my boyfriend and it really messed me up."
Social Worker	"You did, what happened?"
Client	"We just began yelling at each other and there was no listening to each other."
Social Worker	"How did the argument happen?"
Client	"He was going on a trip and then I just became really overwhelmed because I was feeling abandoned. It was actually my fault because he did not even start the argument."
Social Worker	"Why do you think you responded this way?"
Client	"I don't know, but I remember my dad always having to go on trips and leave us when I was young."

Social Worker	"Do you think that there might be a connection between what happened with your dad when you were young and what happened with your boyfriend recently?" (Appropriate exploration)

In closing, it is important to work with your supervisor and give yourself permission to work through and figure things out. If any verbal barriers take place, it is an opportunity during supervision to discuss it and find out healthier ways to help your client. It is also normal for this to happen, especially if it is your first time providing any treatment. In reviewing verbal barriers, it is important to be aware of not stacking questions which can overwhelm the client. Also, you do not want to foster a safe interaction which would not allow for the client to explore their pain and deeper issues which is needed for effective therapy. Along the same lines, you want to avoid parroting by just repeating what the client is saying over and over in question form, because it will diminish the opportunity for the client to further the content of their interaction. Lastly, you want to avoid going on fishing expeditions because that will lead to reckless interpretations that can harm the client when seeking help. While focusing on ways of avoiding verbal barriers, it is also important to identify the healthy ways you are engaging that includes furthering, good non-verbal communication, and using open-ended questions.

REFERENCES

Hackney, H., & Cormier, L. (1979). *Counseling strategies and objectives*. Englewood Cliffs, NJ: Prentice-Hall.

Hersen, M., & Thomas, J. (2007). *Handbook of clinical interviewing with children*. Thousand Oaks, CA: Sage.

Rosen, A. (1972). The Treatment Relationship: A Conceptualization. *Journal of Clinical Psychology*, 38, 329–337.

Rosen, A. L., & Zlotnik, J. L. (2001). Demographics and reality: The "disconnect" in social work education (Study of gerontology neglected)(Abstract). *Journal of Gerontological Social Work*, 81.

Sowers-Hoag, K., & Thyer, B. (1985). Teaching social work practice: a review and analysis of empirical research, *Journal of Social Work Education, 21*(3), 5–15.

Turney, D. (2012). A relationship-based approach to engaging involuntary clients: the contribution of recognition theory. *Child & Family Social Work, 17*(2), 149–159.

CHAPTER 6

Treatment Planning and Assessing Motivation

SETTING GOALS AT THE BEGINNING STAGE OF TREATMENT

When you first see a client, there are specific areas that need to be covered in order for proper goals to be set. It is important to emphasize the importance of addressing deficit needs before transitioning into growth needs as a practitioner. If the order is not followed or it becomes intermixed, it leads to confusion and chaos for the client, and ultimately leads to a directionless focus in treatment. Addressing deficit needs first allows the client to form a more stable foundation to better achieve growth-need goals. In relation to goal setting at the beginning stage of treatment, it is important to cover the three main areas:

- emergency issues
- bio-psycho-social issues
- daily living skills

In relation to emergency issues, the following would need to be addressed:

- emergency medical issues where 911 would be needed
- suicide assessments
- mandated reporting that include child abuse and elder abuse
- Tarasoff, which is the duty to warn a potential victim that their life might be in danger

Let's look at the example below:

A client who is a 16-years-old male comes in to your clinic and states, "I am going to kill my brother and I am going to kill myself." The client adds, "My hand is bleeding and I have a really bad cut." You can see the blood streaming out of his hands and all over his arm. The client also shares,

"My mother is a drug addict and we are not being cared for at home."

At this point, what emergency issues would you need to address? The client is in a medical emergency, so someone should call 911 right away. Also, given the fact that the client has threatened suicide, a suicide assessment would be needed, as well as needing a consultation with DCFS because the child is a minor and his home appears to be unsafe. Given the fact that there was a direct threat to the brother which would invoke Tarasoff, the brother would need to be contacted, or at least the police would need to be notified of what took place. In emergency cases, it is important to remember that medical issues take precedence over mental health issues, and so the medical injuries of the client would be priority. In this scenario, the client would need to be taken to the hospital and have his physical injuries addressed first, before any suicide assessment takes place. In the ER, the admitting doctor will provide what is known as medical clearance, which is saying that the client's medical issues have been cared for, and that the client is physically able to be assessed for a psychological crisis. A treatment in addressing this client would be:

- 911 has been contacted and the client will be referred for treatment of his medical issues.
- The client at the hospital will then have a crisis evaluation performed in the emergency room upon medical clearance by the attending doctor.
- DCFS has been consulted since the client is a minor and an emergency worker is to follow up with the client tonight.
- The brother has been contacted by the therapist due to the threat made by the client, and the brother shared that he will contact police if the situation escalates when the client is released.

Bio-psycho-social issues refer to the biological, psychological, and the social issues that are involved with the client. Areas that need to be addressed include:

- medical issues (non-emergencies)
- mental health issues
- substance abuse
- social networks that include family and friends

Let's look at the example below using the same client:

> The client returns after being released from the hospital and shares, "I have not been in school for over three months and I have been loaded on bath salts and losing my mind." The client adds, "I am also hearing voices and I am having a changing mood throughout the day. My family and I barely talk and my mom and I are constantly fighting. I also was very psychotic when I threatened my brother."

In this case, the client has had his emergency medical issues addressed but would still probably need a general checkup on his overall health. The client is also using drugs as well as suffering from psychotic symptoms and mood swings. Also, within the client's home there is conflict between the mother and her children. Writing a treatment plan that would cover the needs of the client would include the following:

- Client will receive a referral for a medication evaluation with the staff psychiatrist.
- Client will follow up with his primary physician for a full medical evaluation.
- Client will begin individual counseling at the clinic site once a week with the assigned therapist.
- Client will be referred to a drug treatment program to address his addiction to bath salts.
- Client will be provided family counseling services if both the mother and brother agree to attend with the client.

Daily living skills refer to the areas of life that are necessary for the client's survival. Areas of daily living include:

- general relief if the client is in need of immediate financial assistance
- housing shelters
- food banks to help get free food
- social security to help someone with short-term, or if qualified, long-term disability
- employment services that include welfare-to-work services that provides basic needs support as well as educational and job training opportunities
- educational assistance

Once again using the same client, let's look at the vignette below:

The client has been compliant with treatment and has become more stable. The client is compliant with his psychiatric medications as well as attending both individual and substance abuse treatment during the week. The client also came with his mother and brother to begin family counseling services. The mother shares that the family is struggling daily to eat and that she is having a hard time finding a job. The mother also shares that she is afraid that the family will be evicted from their home and she does not want her children taken away from her. The client also shares that this has been affecting his ability to focus at school.

The family is struggling with basic necessities and is in need of immediate assistance. Services that could help the family would include:

- The family has been referred to General Relief so that the family can receive immediate cash aid.
- The family has been provided food bank resources where the family can pick up food weekly.
- The mother has been referred to welfare-to-work services that can assist her with job and educational training, while receiving temporary cash aid.
- The client is to meet with an educational specialist at his school along with his assigned social worker to help address the client's struggles at school.

It is important to remember that as a social worker, you encompass dual roles of being both:

- case manager (advocate)
- therapist (clinician)

Your job is to make sure that the client is linked to the appropriate resources that are available out in the community as well as properly diagnosing and providing proper therapeutic interventions. When you first see a client, it is important that before any intensive therapy is done, that at the beginning stage, you are making sure that the client's basic needs and resources are accounted for. Along with that, you also want to make sure that the client's primary mental health issues are addressed before engaging in insight-oriented therapy. Without doing that, you are then taking away from the client truly thriving and benefitting from the services that you provide. Let's take a look at the vignette from Chapter 1 below and practice developing an initial treatment plan using the three areas covered:

VIGNETTE

Mrs. H. has immigrated to the United States with her 10-year-old and her husband. She is living with her cousin in a house in Arcadia with her cousin's husband and their five children. Mrs. H. has been told by her cousin that she can stay there for three months, but no longer. Mrs. H. works odd jobs trying to support her family. She states that she has been having dizzy spells and has passed out a few times during the past two weeks. Her son is failing school and her husband is not working due to his own physical ailments. Mrs. H. comes to your mental health clinic and states that "I am feeling really depressed and unhappy right now. I am also beginning to hear voices telling me that someone is watching me and I have not slept for one week. Sometimes I feel like ending it all." She also is a recovering drug addict from her home country and states that "I have feelings of wanting to use cocaine again." Mrs. H. is crying in your office, asking you for help.

In addressing emergency issues with Mrs. H., what areas need to be addressed and incorporated in her treatment plan? In this case, the client is in crisis and a crisis evaluation would be needed. It is unclear if DFCS would need to be involved because the children may be in danger based on their current living situation. The mother seems to be well-intentioned but the environment may be harming her kids.

EMERGENCY ISSUES

- Client provided crisis intervention services and the emergency response team has been contacted
- DCFS was contacted for a consultation and follow-up services will take place with the family

In relation to the client's bio-psycho-social issues, the client is suffering from mental health symptoms of psychosis, the client is suffering from medical problems that need to be addressed, and client is suffering from an addiction to cocaine.

BIO-PSYCHO-SOCIAL ISSUES

- Client will be referred to a primary physician for a full medical evaluation.
- Client will be referred for a medication evaluation with a staff psychiatrist.
- Client will begin individual counseling services at the clinic site.
- Client will be referred for a substance abuse treatment program to address her addiction to cocaine.

Regarding daily living skills, the client and her family need to find a place to stay within the next several months, the client is in need of immigration services, and she needs access to help her find employment.

DAILY LIVING SKILLS

- Client will be referred to General Relief for temporary cash aid as well as housing assistance.
- The client will be referred to welfare-to-work services that can assist her with job and educational training, while receiving temporary cash aid.
- Client will be referred to immigration services to address her undocumented status at this time.

In putting this all together for Mrs. H. that includes all three areas that need to be addressed, her initial treatment plan would be:

- Client has been provided with crisis intervention services and the emergency response team has been contacted.
- DCFS was contacted for a consultation and follow-up services will take place with the family.
- Client will be referred to a primary physician for a full medical evaluation.
- Client will be referred for a medication evaluation with a staff psychiatrist.
- Client will begin individual counseling services at the clinic site.
- Client will be referred for a substance abuse treatment program to address her addiction to cocaine.
- Client to be referred to General Relief for temporary cash aid as well as housing assistance.
- The client has been referred to welfare-to-work services that can assist her with job and educational training, while receiving temporary cash aid.

- Client has been referred to immigration services to address her undocumented status at this time.

It is important to note that you would work with Mrs. H. at a pace that would be comfortable for her and not overwhelming. However, even though there are many goals, some of them can be achieved quickly and once completed, it would make the situation less overwhelming for Mrs. H. as a whole. Linking her to General Relief and welfare-to-work services would work hand in hand in assisting her, as well as working with you the social worker. At the beginning stage, it is very important to blend and to be diligent in your dual role as a social worker that includes being a case manager (advocate) and practitioner.

SETTING GOALS AT THE MIDDLE STAGE

It is important to note that when you are setting goals at the middle stage of treatment, you must first make sure that the initial goals at the beginning stage of treatment have been addressed and that you and the client are working as a team to try and meet those goals. By transitioning to this stage, deficit-need goals have been met and now growth-need goals can be properly addressed. Also in this stage, as the transition goes to growth needs, it is your job to prepare the client to begin the chosen therapeutic intervention that you the clinician will begin implementing. In this phase, some of the therapy models that might be used are:

- psychodynamic therapy
- (object relations) attachment theory
- behavioral therapy
- cognitive behavioral therapy
- intensive case management
- family therapy models (strategic and structural family therapy, Bowenian therapy)
- group therapy

It is important to note that as you are identifying and writing your outcome goals for the client, they must:

1. not be too abstract
2. not be too specific and limiting
3. be appropriate and specific

For example the statement "l will have a satisfying career" is too vague and it does not define the direction the client would like their career to go.

Another example statement "I will gain admission to UCLA Medical School" is too specific, because if that person does not get into that medical school, there is a neglect of the many other options that are available to that person. Finally, an appropriately specific goal will not be too vague and not too specific and will still have a clear direction of intent. Let's look below and put together these two statements so that an appropriate goal can be attained.

ABSTRACT GOAL

"I will have an outstanding career."

TOO-SPECIFIC GOAL

"I will gain admission to UCLA Medical School."

APPROPRIATE SPECIFIC GOAL

"I will have performed the behaviors to maximize my chances of getting into a top tier medical school while being prepared to accept alternate options that lead me to become a medical doctor."

It is also important to note that when you are writing your goals, the goals must:

- promote a direction towards positive change
- increase the motivation of the client

Promoting a direction towards positive change increases motivation and puts the focus on what is possible for the client. It also allows for both the client and therapist to have a directed focus with an agreed upon collaboration towards positive change.

Another effective way of making sure you are writing effective outcome goals is to use the acronym SMART. SMART stands for:

- Specific
- Measurable
- Attainable
- Realistic
- Timely

SMART goals come from George Doran (1981), who used this to more effectively guide management-based decisions. This is also effective when working with clients because it helps to create a healthy parameter in which effective and realistic goals can be attained for the client. In using SMART goals, it needs to be a collaborative effort where both the practitioner and client are able to see tangible and attainable outcomes to help improve the client's current situation. Hersh (2012) believes that using SMART allows for a summary of the work and exploration that has taken place during the session time. It also provides a positive direction that the client can seek to attain. Looking at each SMART acronym more in depth:

SPECIFIC

When setting a goal, it is important to be specific about what is to be accomplished. It is important for the client to have a clear direction for their goal similar to a mission statement that is done in business. This isn't a detailed list of how the client is going to meet their goals, but it should include answers to the popular "W" questions:

- Who—Consider who needs to be involved to achieve the goal besides the client. Will there need to be involvement from family members, or how is your role as the social worker going to come into play for the client? In the beginning stage of treatment, the "who" involves multiple members that include psychiatrists, medical doctors, substance abuse counselors, etc. It is vital when identifying the specifics to acknowledge who is going to be involved.
- What—Think about exactly what the client is trying to accomplish and if it is important for the client to become very detailed in discussing the "what."
- When—This will get more specific under the "Timely" section of defining SMART goals, but the client should at least set a timeframe for their goals.
- Where—This question may not always apply to the client, especially if the client is setting personal goals (i.e., reduce my depression), but if there is a location or relevant event, it is important for the client to identify it here.
- Which—This is where the client will identify any related obstacles or requirements that need to be met. This question can be beneficial in deciding if the client goal is realistic. For example, if the goal for the client is to never have conflict with people ever again, that clearly cannot be achieved and there will be an issue in achieving that goal. As a result, there would need to be a refinement of the specifics of the goal to "Have better conflict management skills through learning and practicing what I learn during sessions."
- Why—Here the client asks, "What is the reason for my goal?" When it comes to using this method for the client, the answer will be along the lines of personal growth or helping those that are close to that individual.

MEASURABLE

What metrics are going to be used to determine if the client meets their goals? This makes a goal more tangible because it provides a way to measure progress. If it is a goal that is going to take a significant amount of time to achieve, then setting milestones and subgoals will need to be addressed by the client.

ACHIEVABLE

This focuses on how important a goal is to the client and what the client can do to make it attainable. This may require developing new skills and changing attitudes. The goals that are being set are meant to inspire motivation and not promote any form of discouragement. The client here needs to think about how to accomplish the goal and if the client has the tools and skill set needed. If the client does not at the time possess the required tools, it would be important to consider what it would take to attain them.

RELEVANT

Relevance refers to focusing on something that makes sense with the broader desired goals for the client. For example, if the goal for the client is to eventually become a substance abuse counselor to help others who are suffering from addiction, the relevant goal for the client would then be for the client to overcome their own addiction first. There needs to be alignment and consistency with the broader scope and the current stage in relation to where the client is in his/her life.

TIMELY

Anyone can set goals, but if it lacks realistic timing, chances are the client is not going to succeed. Providing a target date for goals as well as asking specific questions about the goal allows for an effective deadline for the goal to be accomplished. If the goal will take three months to complete, it's useful to define the subgoals that should be achieved throughout the process. Providing time constraints also creates a sense of purpose and focus for the client.

When it comes to writing SMART goals, it is important to be prepared to ask the client a lot of questions. The answers will help fine-tune the subgoals and strategies, ensuring the goals are something that is actually attainable. While the goals should be as realistic as possible, it is important to approach writing SMART goals with a positive attitude. You as the social worker are working with the client to help this individual improve their life. This is something that requires work and effort from both the client and the clinician. Using the example of the individual who wants to get into a medical school and become a doctor:

INITIAL GOAL (THE APPROPRIATE SPECIFIC GOAL)

"I will have performed the behaviors to maximize my chances of getting into a top tier medical school while being prepared to accept alternate options that lead me to become a medical doctor."

1. Specific (What do you want to accomplish? Who needs to be included? When do you want to do this? Why is this a goal?)
   - Get into a top-tier medical school (2 years)
   - Do well in high school that includes a high GPA
   - Do well on my entry exams that include the SAT
   - Increase my extracurricular activities to enhance my portfolio
   - Family, Friends, Student Advisor at school
   - It has always been my dream to be a doctor
2. Measurable (How can you measure progress and know if you've successfully met your goal?):
   - high GPA
   - high scores on my SAT
   - multiple extracurricular activities
3. Achievable (Do you have the skills required to achieve the goal? If not, can you obtain them? What is the motivation for this goal? Is the amount of effort required on par with what the goal will achieve?):
   - I need to increase my GPA
   - My SAT scores meet the requirements
   - I need to engage in more extracurricular activities
   - I have two years before I apply for college and so I need to begin now
   - I will need to put in more effort with studying and after-school activities
4. Relevant (Why am I setting this goal now? Is it aligned with overall objectives?):
   - I am a sophomore in high school and I am two years from applying for college
   - I am much closer to my goals than ever before and I really need to get serious
   - I have the time and the resources to go for my goal and I am going to do it
   - I am going after my dream

5. Timely (What's the deadline and is it realistic?):
    ▸ I have two years until I apply for college and so this is my deadline

SMARTER IN CONCLUSION

In conclusion, SMART is an effective way of helping a client identify their goals and to make it more reasonable and effective for those goals to be achieved. If goals are not met, there is what is also known as SMARTER:

- Specific
- Measurable
- Achievable
- Relevant
- Timely
- Evaluate
- Redo

In two years, if the client was not able to achieve their goal of medical school, then it would be important to implement SMARTER (Doran,1981), where there is an evaluation of why the goal was not achieved, and what can be done to stick with the previous goal, or to redefine it. If the client wanted to continue to medical school, then the client would most likely need to go to junior college to increase their GPA as well as possibly contact graduate schools to see what it is they require, given the current situation of the client. Also, if the time frame did not match the client's circumstances, then it would be important to learn from why the goals were not achieved, and to take those lessons to the client's new goals.

EVALUATING CLIENT MOTIVATION

The transtheoretical model (Yang et al., 2015) is an integrative, bio-psychosocial model to conceptualize the process of intentional behavior change. Where other models of behavior change focus exclusively on certain dimensions of change, the transtheoretical model seeks to include and integrate key constructs from other theories into a comprehensive theory of change. The theory, instead of trying to figure out ways of motivating someone to do something, identifies the individual's current state of motivation and addresses what can be done based on their given motivational stage. The stages of change lie at the heart of the transtheoretical model. Studies of change have found that people move through a series of stages when modifying behavior. While the time a person can stay in each stage is variable, the tasks required to move to the next stage are not. Certain principles and processes of change work best at each stage to reduce resistance, facilitate progress, and to prevent relapse. These principles include decisional balance, self-efficacy, and processes of change.

The transtheoretical model recognizes change as a process that unfolds over time, involving progress through a series of stages. While progression through the stages of change can occur in a linear fashion, a nonlinear progression is common. Wu and Chu (2015) believe that the change process is a complicated and nonlinear process because both the strengths and weaknesses of the individual are addressed. Often, individuals recycle through the stages or regress to earlier stages from later ones because of that inner struggle. Below are the stages of change.

STAGES OF CHANGE

- Pre-Contemplation (Not Ready)—People are not intending to take action in the foreseeable future, and can be unaware that their behavior is problematic
- Contemplation (Getting Ready)—People are beginning to recognize that their behavior is problematic, and start to look at the pros and cons of their continued actions
- Preparation (Ready)—People are intending to take action in the immediate future, and may begin taking small steps toward behavior change
- Action—People have made specific overt modifications in modifying their problem behavior or in acquiring new healthy behaviors
- Maintenance—People have been able to sustain action for a while and are working to prevent relapse
- Termination—Individuals have zero temptation and they are sure they will not return to their old unhealthy habit as a way of coping

PRE-CONTEMPLATION (NOT READY)

People in the pre-contemplation stage do not intend to take action in the foreseeable future, usually measured as the next 6 months. Being uninformed or underinformed about the consequences of one's behavior may cause a person to be in the pre-contemplation stage. Multiple unsuccessful attempts at change can lead to demoralization about the ability to change. Pre-contemplators are often characterized in other theories as resistant, unmotivated, or unready for help. People in this stage are encouraged to learn more about engaging in healthy behaviors, thinking about the pros of changing their behavior as well as identifying the negative effects of their actions on those close to that person. Pre-contemplators typically:

- underestimate the pros of changing
- overestimate the cons
- often are not aware of making such mistakes

One of the most effective steps that can be done to help an individual at this stage is to encourage them to become more mindful of their decision making and more conscious of the multiple benefits of changing an unhealthy behavior (Prochaska et al., 1994).

CONTEMPLATION (GETTING READY)

Contemplation is the stage in which people intend to change in the next 6 months. They are more aware of the pros of changing, but are also aware of the cons. In a meta-analysis across 48 health risk behaviors, the pros and cons of changing were equal (Hall & Rossi, 2008). This weighting between the costs and benefits of changing can produce ambivalence that can cause people to remain in this stage for long periods of time. This is often characterized as constant and repetitive contemplation which leads to procrastination. Individuals in the contemplation stage are not ready for traditional action-oriented programs that expect participants to act immediately.

At this stage, participants are intending to start the healthy behavior within the next 6 months. It is best for the individual in this stage to learn about the kind of person they could be if they changed their behavior and learn more from people who behave in healthy ways. Others who have changed can positively influence and effectively help at this stage by encouraging the individual to work at reducing the cons of changing their behavior (Prochaska et al., 1994).

PREPARATION (READY)

Preparation is the stage in which people intend to take action in the immediate future, usually measured within 1 month. Typically, they have already taken significant action in the past year and the individual has a plan of action. This may be going to see a counselor, seeing a doctor, or quitting smoking. An individual at this stage should be recruited for action-oriented programs because the commitment is there to change. It is important for an individual at this stage to have taken small steps to prepare for the behavior change. People in this stage should be encouraged to seek support from friends they trust. During this stage contemplators should:

- Tell people about their plan to change.
- Think about how they would feel if they behaved in a healthier way.
- Identify their number one source of concern in terms of why they may fail.
- Learn that preparation is the key to sustaining the healthy behavior.

ACTION

Action is the stage in which people have made specific overt modifications in their lifestyles within the past six months. The action is observable and the overall process of behavior change is being sustained. An individual at this stage needs to work hard to keep moving forward by strengthening their commitments to change and fighting the urges to slip back. People in this stage maintain progress by:

- being taught techniques for keeping up their commitments
- substituting activities related to the unhealthy behavior with positive ones
- rewarding oneself for taking steps toward changing
- avoiding people and situations that tempt them to behave in unhealthy ways

MAINTENANCE

Maintenance is the stage in which people have made specific overt modifications in their lifestyles and are working to prevent relapse. While in the maintenance stage, people are less tempted to relapse and grow increasingly more confident that they can continue their changes.

People at this stage have changed their behavior for more than 6 months. It is important for an individual in this stage to be aware of situations that may tempt them to slip back into doing the unhealthy behavior (Prochaska et al., 1994). Relapse prevention techniques are important here because relapse can happen. It is important to note that relapse to an unwanted behavior is not failure, but part of the process of positive change. It is recommended that people in this stage:

- seek support from and talk with people whom they trust
- spend time with people who behave in healthy ways
- remember to engage in healthy activities to cope with stress instead of relying on unhealthy behaviors

TERMINATION

In this stage the individual has made the changes necessary and is able to function on his/her own. The individual takes full responsibility for the changes and is given the coping skills and tools to succeed.

DECISIONAL BALANCE

Decision-making was conceptualized by Janis and Mann (1977) as a decisional balance sheet of comparing potential benefits and consequences. Two components of decisional balance, the pros and the cons, have become core constructs in the transtheoretical model. As individuals progress through the stages of change, decisional balance shifts in critical ways. When an individual is in the pre-contemplation stage, the pros in favor of behavior change are outweighed by the relative cons for change and in favor of maintaining the existing behavior. In the contemplation stage, the pros and cons tend to be equal in weight, leaving the individual ambivalent toward change. If the decisional balance is tipped, however, such that the pros in favor of changing outweigh the cons for maintaining the unhealthy behavior, many individuals move to the preparation or even action stage. As individuals enter the maintenance stage, the pros in favor of maintaining the behavior change should outweigh the cons of maintaining the change in order to decrease the risk of relapse. Sound decision making requires the consideration of the potential benefits (pros) and costs (cons) associated with a behavior's consequences. Decisional balance is one of the best predictors of future change and identification of the stage is key (Khazaee-Pool et al., 2017). Once again, in looking at the concept of decisional balance through the stages of change:

- The cons of changing outweigh the pros in the Pre-contemplation Stage.
- The pros and cons are equal in the Contemplation Stage.
- The pros surpass the cons in the Preparation Stage.
- The pros far outweigh the cons in the Action Stage.

In review, the transtheoretical model is also based on critical assumptions about the nature of behavior change and population health interventions that can best facilitate such change. The following set of assumptions drives transtheoretical model theory, research, and practice (Prochaska, Redding, & Evers, 2002):

- Behavior change is a process that unfolds over time through a sequence of stages.

- Stages are both stable and open to change, just as chronic behavior risk factors are both stable and open to change.
- Population health initiatives can motivate change by enhancing the understanding of the pros and diminishing the value of the cons.
- The majority of at-risk populations are not prepared for action and will not be served by traditional action-oriented prevention programs.
- Helping people set realistic goals, like progressing to the next stage, will facilitate the change process.
- Specific principles and processes of change need to be emphasized at specific stages for progress through the stages to occur.

ASSESSING MOTIVATION WHEN WORKING WITH CLIENTS

One of the biggest energy-draining activities as a therapist is to spend your time trying to convince a client to change their negative behavior. I was taught in graduate school that it is the job of the social worker to motivate the client, but that is only partially true. As a social worker, you cannot force a client to want to do something even if it is positive, and so it is a matter of identifying their level of change and providing the best information that you can to the client based on that level of change. Using the transtheoretical model, it is best to equip the client with the tools that will most benefit them based on where the individual is at. The processes that are required are broken down into two categories:

- cognitive and affective experiential processes
- behavioral processes

Cognitive processes involve the processes that the client must acknowledge to promote change, which would include:

- consciousness raising
- dramatic relief
- environmental reevaluation
- self-reevaluation
- social liberation

Behavioral processes involve the actions that are required by the client and they are:

- self-liberation
- counter conditioning

- helping relationships
- reinforcement management
- stimulus control

Once the client stage has been identified, it is then the job of the social worker to help the client engage in the cognitive and behavioral processes to help the client move to the next stage. As a general rule, cognitive processing is more related to when a client is unwilling to change while behavioral processes take place when the client is ready to change.

FROM PRE-CONTEMPLATION TO CONTEMPLATION

At this stage the individual is about six months away from changing their behavior and the cons of their behavior far outweigh the benefits of changing. As the therapist, you can help the client by providing the following:

- consciousness-raising—providing facts about their actions and increasing awareness via information, education, and personal feedback about engaging in healthy behaviors
- environmental reevaluation—here you would help the client identify the effects their unhealthy behaviors have had on others and how the client could affect others more positively by changing their behaviors
- dramatic relief—here you would pay attention to the client's feelings and help them identify their feelings of fear and anxiety caused by the unhealthy behavior
- social liberation—this is helping the client identify that there is greater public support for their positive behaviors than for their unhealthy behaviors

FROM CONTEMPLATION TO ACTION

At this stage the individual is about six months away from changing their behavior and the pros and cons are about equal at this stage. The client is constantly contemplating change and often procrastinating to take action. At this stage, it is best to have the client engage in:

- self-reevaluation—here your job is to help the client identify a new self-image that is consistent with their desired healthy behaviors and who they want to be

FROM PREPARATION TO ACTION

Here the client is one month away from taking action and has taken the small steps to get to this point. The individual recognizes that the pros of changing the behavior outweigh the cons of not changing, and a declaration to friends and family has been made towards change. At this stage, it is important for the client to engage in:

- self-liberation—your job here is to have the client make the commitment to change and believe that change is possible
- helping relationships—you would work with the client to identify the people who would be supportive of their positive change efforts
- counter-conditioning—this involves helping the client find substitutes for the unhealthy behaviors—for example, exchanging eating carrot sticks for smoking cigarettes

FROM ACTION TO MAINTENANCE

The client at this stage has changed their behavior for 6 months or more and is working hard to continue to move forward. This is where a strengthening of commitment from the client is required, as well as a recognition that urges to slip back into the unhealthy behavior will occur. At this stage, it is important to work with the client to conduct:

- reinforcement management—it is important here for the client to increase the rewards that come from the positive behavior and reduce those that come from negative behavior
- stimulus control—having the client manage their environment by using reminders and cues that encourage healthy behavior and substituting them for those that encourage the unhealthy behavior

When working with a client, it is vital to do your best to reduce the resistance of the client and to do your best to maximize change for the client. In this chapter, we covered ways to clearly define goals for the client as well as assess the level of motivation by identifying the client's stage of change.

REFERENCES

Doran, G. T. (1981). There's a S.M.A.R.T. way to write management's goals and objectives. *Management Review, 70*, 35.

Hall, K. L., & Rossi, J. S. (2008). Meta-analytic examination of the strong and weak principles across 48 health behaviors, *Preventive Medicine, 46*, 266–274.

Hersh, D., Worrall, L., Howe, T., Sherratt, S., & Davidson, B. (2012). SMARTER goal setting in aphasia rehabilitation. *Aphasiology, 26*(2), 220–233.

Janis, I. L. & Mann, L. (1977). *Decision making: A psychological analysis of conflict, choice and commitment.* New York: Free Press.

Khazaee-Pool, M., Pashaei, T., Koen, P., Jafari, F., & Alizadeh, R. (2017). Decisional balance inventory (DBI) adolescent form for smoking: psychometric properties of the Persian version. *BMC Public Health, 17*(1), 1–7.

Prochaska, J. O., DiClemente, C. C., & Norcross, J. C. (1992). In search of how people change: applications to the addictive behaviors. *American Psychologist, 47*, 1102–1114. PMID: 1329589.

Prochaska, J. O., Norcross, J. C., & DiClemente, C. C. (1994). *Changing for good: the revolutionary program that explains the six stages of change and teaches you how to free yourself from bad habits.* New York: W. Morrow.

Prochaska, J. O., Redding, C. A., & Evers, K. (2002). The transtheoretical model and stages of change. In K. Glanz, B. K. Rimer & F. M. Lewis (Eds.), *Health behavior and health education: theory, research, and practice* (3rd ed.). San Francisco, CA: Jossey-Bass, Inc.

Wu, Y. K., & Chu, N. F. (2015). Introduction of the transtheoretical model and organisational development theory in weight management: A narrative review. *Obesity Research & Clinical Practice, 9*(3), 203–213.

Yang, H. J., Chen, K. M., Chen, M. D., Wu, H. C., Chang, W. J., Wang, Y. C., & Huang, H. T. (2015). Applying the transtheoretical model to promote functional fitness of community older adults participating in elastic band exercises. *Journal of Advanced Nursing, 71*(10), 2338–2349.

CHAPTER 7

The Beginning Stage of Treatment

CONFIDENTIALITY

When discussing issues of confidentiality with a client, it is important that the individual is aware of how their information will be protected, but also the limits of confidentiality and when it can be broken. Informed consent is the permission typically granted by a patient to a clinician, with the knowledge of the possible consequences. In relation to confidentiality the client should be aware that everything that is shared in the therapy session will remain confidential unless one or more of the following situations occur:

1. The client is a danger to him/herself, danger to others, or gravely disabled
2. There is a suspicion of child abuse
3. There is a suspicion of elder abuse
4. The Tarasoff rule applies

We will get into each one more specifically, but the client needs to be aware of where the limits of confidentiality lie. It is also important to be able to effectively communicate to the client so that they understand their rights, which informed consent is trying to accomplish. A typical way of addressing confidentiality with a client would go something like this:

"In relation to confidentiality, everything that you share with me will remain confidential. No family member, friends, or organizations will have access to information that you share during our sessions. The only time confidentiality can be broken is if you tell me you are going to hurt yourself, hurt others, or if you appear unable to care for yourself and are in grave danger. Also, as a mandated reporter, I am required to report any suspicion of child or elder abuse. If at any time you request your confidential information be sent elsewhere, say to your new therapist because you are moving to a new city, a release of information must be signed by you for any authorization of that information to be sent. Do you have any questions?"

At this point, you would address the following issues with the client and answer any questions that they may have regarding confidentiality before beginning any further. Also, it is typical that an informed consent form is signed by the client acknowledging that they understand what is being shared with them.

RAPPORT-BUILDING USING A PERSON-CENTERED APPROACH

As discussed previously in Chapter 5, establishing rapport is the ability of the client and social worker to establish a close and harmonious therapeutic relationship where the client's feelings are understood and easily communicated. Carl Rogers strongly believed that in order for a client's condition to improve, practitioners should be warm, genuine, and understanding. This approach is essential when you begin to first meet with a client. The starting point of the Rogerian approach to counseling and psychotherapy is best stated by Rogers (1986) himself:

> "It is that the individual has within himself or herself vast resources for self-understanding, for altering his or her self-concept, attitudes and self-directed behavior, and that these resources can be tapped if only a definable climate of facilitative psychological attitudes can be provided."

This is a vital perspective because when first meeting with the client, it is your job as the social worker to tap into the intrinsic and external resources that the client does have. It is also taking all of the information to help direct and guide the best course of action for the client. Rogers (1986) developed his theory based on his work with emotionally distraught individuals and claimed that everyone has a remarkable capacity for self-healing and personal growth leading towards self-actualization. He emphasized the person's current perception and focusing on the here and now. As you are discussing the issues of confidentiality, mandated reporting, and gathering personal information, it is important that a healthy relationship is established. Techniques that Rogers emphasized are listening, accepting, understanding, and sharing, which are more attitude-oriented than technique-driven. It basically comes down to treating the client like a competent and deserving human being. The Rogerian client-centered approach puts emphasis on the person coming to form an appropriate understanding of their world and themselves. In relation to the therapeutic process, Rogers emphasized the following six factors:

1. THERAPIST-CLIENT PSYCHOLOGICAL CONTACT

This first condition simply states that a relationship between therapist and client must exist in order for the client to achieve positive personal change. This is extremely important when you first meet with the client, because so much trust is being put in you as their social worker. Also when you are discussing the limits of confidentiality and issues of mandated reporting, it is vital that the social worker is conveying respect and autonomy to the client.

2. CLIENT INCONGRUENCE OR VULNERABILITY

A discrepancy between the client's self-image and actual experience leaves him or her vulnerable to fears and anxieties. The client is often unaware of the incongruence. When seeing a client, it is your job to help identify the strengths and resources that the client does have available to him/her. It is your job as the social worker to help align the individual to see their strengths and capabilities, and having the both of you work as a team to accomplish the goals set forth in treatment.

3. THERAPIST CONGRUENCE OR GENUINENESS

The therapist should be self-aware, genuine, and congruent. This does not imply that the therapist should be a picture of perfection, but that he or she should be true to him/herself within the therapeutic relationship. This also means being honest about addressing difficult issues, especially when discussing when confidentiality can be broken.

4. THERAPIST UNCONDITIONAL POSITIVE REGARD (UPR)

The client's experiences, positive or negative, should be accepted by the therapist without any conditions or judgment. In this way, the client can share experiences without fear of being judged. Oftentimes this can be difficult to do, but it is necessary as the social worker to convey this to the client.

5. THERAPIST EMPATHY

The therapist demonstrates empathic understanding of the client's experiences and recognizes emotional experiences without getting emotionally involved. This is vital, and it is important here to make sure that any countertransference issues be addressed if you are unable to provide empathic understanding to the client.

6. CLIENT PERCEPTION

To some degree, the client perceives the therapist's unconditional positive regard and empathic understanding. This is communicated through the words and behaviors of the therapist. It is important that your body language, voice tone, and overall energy as an individual convey an empathic and understanding tone to the client.

Rogers called his therapeutic approach client-centered or person-centered therapy because of the focus on the person's subjective view of the world (Kirschenbaum, 2012). Rogers regarded everyone as a "competent individual" who could benefit greatly from his form of therapy. When seeing a client for the first time, as you are performing your initial assessment, it is important that you are holding and implementing these humanistic values. The purpose of Roger's humanistic approach is to increase a person's feelings of self-worth, reduce the level of incongruence between the ideal and actual self, and help a person become more of a fully functioning person. It is important to treat every individual with this level of respect as you the social worker are providing treatment.

BEING A MANDATED REPORTER

Mandated reporters are individuals required by the law of a given state to report concerning suspicions. Most often the term "mandated reporter" refers to individuals required to report suspicions of child abuse or neglect, but in some states the law may require some people to report elder abuse, institutional corruption, or other behaviors. Most social workers in practice today have always been mandated reporters, but the role of mandated reporter is constantly evolving. For the first 75 years of child protective systems in the United States, private agencies like the New York Society for the Prevention of Cruelty to Children provided the means through which abused children were identified and protected from further harm. State and federal governments were largely removed from these processes until societal pressure required governmental response in the mid-twentieth century.

Since social workers work with children and families in a variety of settings and roles, the law in all 50 states requires social workers to report their suspicions of child abuse, elder abuse, and neglect. Social work setting such as schools, hospitals, mental health clinics, and nursing homes are the primary places where suspicions of maltreatment are reported by the social worker. As mandated reporters and ethical professionals, social workers have a professional obligation to seek out information to understand their legal requirement to report.

There were more than three million reports of suspected child abuse and neglect in 2011, but it is unclear exactly how many reports were based on the suspicions of social workers (US Department of Health and Human Services, Administration for Children and Families, 2011). However, more than one-half of all reports of suspected child abuse or neglect were made by professional reporters, including child care providers, educational personnel, law enforcement personnel, medical personnel, mental health professionals, and social services personnel (U.S. Department of Health and Human Services, Administration for Children and Families, 2011). Since social workers serve communities in a variety of roles and settings, reporting from social workers is vital regarding protecting those that are in danger.

CHILD ABUSE REPORTING

Mandatory reporters are required to report the facts and circumstances that led them to suspect that a child has been abused or neglected. They do not have the burden of providing proof that abuse or neglect has occurred. Permissive reporters follow the same standards when electing to make a report. The Department of Children and Family Services website (2017) states that the purpose and mission of the Child Protection Hotline (CPH) is:

- to act as the central point of entry for calls to DCFS regarding the possible abuse and/or neglect of children
- to receive calls of abuse and neglect involving children and assess the level of endangerment
- to obtain factual information regarding a specific incident and generate a referral for investigation, if appropriate
- to document and transmit all referrals of child endangerment to the appropriate office, timely
- to ensure child safety and protection

If there is any suspicion of child abuse, it is your job as the social worker to contact child protective services and to do a consultation with the worker you are speaking with. At this point, the worker on the other line will be taking specific information and your job is to report to the best of your abilities why you suspect there is possible child abuse. Once that information has been obtained, it is important that you obtain the case number that will be provided by the child protective worker, as well as the contact information of the person that you were speaking with. At that point, if the worker does not believe that there is enough evidence to investigate, he/she will let you know and you will document what took place in your client chart. However, if they do believe that there is enough evidence to investigate further, you will need to file the actual report.

In filling out the child abuse report, it is important that you fill out the information accurately and as detailed as possible. There are basically three sections that need to be filled out and we will be going over each section. The forms will vary from state to state but the core information will pretty much be the same. The process includes (California Department of Justice, 2005):

SECTION A. THE INVESTIGATING AGENCY

This is where you fill out the information that includes your place of work as well as the identifying information that you obtained when doing your consultation with the child protective worker.

1. Name and type of investigating agency

Here you fill in the name of your agency and identify which department of social service you work for. This could be police, sheriff, welfare, probation, mental health, etc.

2. Agency report number/case number

You would fill in your report number that was assigned by the child protective worker on the phone.

3. Agency address

You would enter the complete address of your agency.

4. Agency telephone and extension

You would provide the telephone number and extension of your workplace setting.

5. Name of investigating party and title

You would fill in your name and title.

6. Date report completed

Once completed you would put in the date that you completed the report.

7. Agency cross-reported to

This would be where you would put in the hotline information that will be given to you over the phone by the child protective worker.

8. Person cross-reported to

This would be the name and title of the child protective worker you notified about the suspected child abuse.

9. Action taken

This is where you would document what action is going to be taken as shared by the child protective worker. If there is the belief that there are substantiated findings (abuse more likely than not occurred), the worker will let you know when a worker will go out to investigate. If it is considered an emergency situation, the child protective worker will assign a worker to go out immediately after the completion of the call.

SECTION B. THE INCIDENT INFORMATION

1. Date of incident

Fill in the date the incident occurred if you have that knowledge. If you are suspicious but are not clear of dates, here you would report the meeting date with your client.

2. Time of incident

Fill in the time the incident occurred if you have that information. If you do not have a time, you would put in the time that the session took place.

3. Location of incident

You would fill in the address and description of premises where the incident occurred.

4. Type of abuse

This is where you would identify the type of abuse that you suspect or believe took place. The types of abuse include:

    a. physical
    b. mental
    c. sexual
    d. severe neglect

5. If abuse occurred outside of the home

Here, if the suspected abuse was not in the home, you can identify the outside location. The options include:

    a. family day care
    b. child care center

  c. foster family home

  d. small family home or group home or institution

  e. school

SECTION C. INVOLVED PARTIES

 1. Victims

Oftentimes the abuse victims will involve more than one person and it is your job to identify all potential victims. With that, you will need to identify:

  a. Name of victim: This includes nicknames or other names used, such as maiden names.

  b. Date of birth: Fill in the victim's date of birth.

  c. Sex: Here you would indicate whether the victim or victims are male or female.

  d. Race: This would be the nationality of origin of the victim(s). Did victim's injuries result in death? You never want it come to this, but if so, it is your job to report.

 2. Nature of injuries

Describe injuries: Here you would report to the best of your abilities what kind of injuries the victim has suffered which include broken bones, facial fracture, etc.

 3. Present location of victim

What is the victim's current location and is there more identifying information available, such as a phone number? Another identifiable source of information is to find out if the victim is developmentally disabled.

 4. Suspects

This is where the complete name of suspect(s), including any nicknames or other names used are listed. This would also include date of birth, gender, and race of the suspected perpetrators.

  a. name of suspects

  b. date of birth

  c. sex

  d. race

 5. Address location and physical features of suspect(s)

You would do your best to fill in the complete information requested of each suspect:

    a.   address
    b.   height
    c.   weight
    d.   eye color
    e.   hair color
    f.   social security number (if available)
    g.   driver's license number (if available)

6. Relationship to victim(s)

    a.   parent or stepparent of victim
    b.   brother or sister of victim
    c.   other relative of victim
    d.   friend or acquaintance of victim
    e.   stranger or unknown to victim
    f.   other

The process of filing a child abuse report can be extensive, but it is a vital part of the job and it is important to have a basic understanding of what you are supposed to do if you are ever in this situation. Basic rules to follow when there is suspicion is to:

1. Call the child protective hotline and get a consultation regarding what to do.
2. Remember that it is not your job to figure out if abuse occurred, but rather it is your job to report your suspicion.
3. Remember to gather the identifying information of the child protective worker including the case number.
4. If guided to do so, file the report.

ELDER ABUSE

Criminal elder abuse occurs when any person causes or permits an elder to suffer. This includes inflicting unjustifiable physical pain or mental suffering on the victim. It also covers situations where a person willfully causes or permits an elder to be placed in a situation in which the elder's health is endangered. By law the term elder means a person aged 65 or over, but abuse of a dependent individual from the age of 18–64 is also reportable if the individual appears disabled and in need of specific care (California

Legislation Institute, 2017). It also means the deprivation by a care custodian of goods or services that are necessary to avoid physical harm or mental suffering (Welfare & Institutions Code Section 15610). Based off of the same Welfare and Institutions code, elder abuse can be defined by the following:

- abandonment: the desertion of an elder by someone who is a caregiver
- abduction: the removal, without the consent of the conservator, of a conservatee to another state
- financial abuse: the illegal or unethical exploitation and/or use of an elder's funds, property, or other assets
- isolation: the intentional prevention of an elder from receiving mail, telephone calls, or visitors
- mental suffering: the infliction of fear, agitation, confusion through threats, harassment, or other forms of intimidating behavior
- neglect: the failure to fulfill a caretaking obligation such as assisting in personal hygiene, providing food, clothing or shelter, protecting an elder from health and safety hazards, or preventing malnutrition
- physical abuse: the infliction of physical pain or injury, sexual assault or molestation, or use of physical or chemical restraints for punishment

According to the National Institute on Aging (2017) website, signs that elder abuse is taking place are:

POSSIBLE PHYSICAL ABUSE AND NEGLECT INDICATORS:

- unexplained weight loss, malnutrition and/or dehydration, bedsores
- unseen physical injury—painful reaction when touched
- bruises, skin damage, or broken bones
- behavioral indicators
- agitation
- anger
- anxiety
- confusion or disorientation
- defensiveness
- depression
- fear
- helplessness
- hesitation to talk openly

- implausible stories
- non-responsiveness
- withdrawal

POSSIBLE RELATIVE OR CAREGIVER ABUSE INDICATORS

- the elder may not be given the opportunity to speak for him/herself
- obvious absence of assistance, attitudes of indifference, or anger toward the elder by family member or caregiver
- social isolation or restriction of activity of the elder
- conflicting accounts of incidents by the family or caregivers
- substance abuse by individual responsible for the care of the elder

Each state within their specified counties has an Adult Protective Services (APS) agency to help elder adults (65 years and older) and dependent adults (18–64 who are disabled), when these adults are unable to meet their own needs, or are victims of abuse, neglect, or exploitation. County APS agencies investigate reports of abuse of elders and dependent adults who live in private homes, apartments, hotels, or hospitals (CDSS, 2017). Under Penal Code 368 in California, elder abuse can be prosecuted as either a felony or a misdemeanor. It is the prosecutor's choice, depending on the defendant's criminal history and the facts of the case.

When elder abuse is prosecuted as a misdemeanor, potential penalties include up to one year in county jail and a fine of thousands of dollars. If it is prosecuted as a felony, the defendant may be sentenced to state prison for two to four years (CDSS, 2017).

TARASOFF

In 1976, the California Supreme Court ruled that psychotherapists have a duty to protect potential victims if their patients made threats or behaved as if they presented a serious danger of violence to another. In the case of Tarasoff v. the Regents of the University of California, the court determined that the need for therapists to protect the public was more important than protecting client-therapist confidentiality. Guided by the court decision, the state of California later passed a law stating that all therapists have a duty to protect intended victims by either warning victims directly, notifying law enforcement directly, or taking whatever other steps might be needed to prevent harm. The Tarasoff case is based on the 1969 murder of a university student named Tatiana Tarasoff. The perpetrator, Prosenjit

Poddar was an Indian graduate student at the University of California, Berkeley who had met Tarasoff at an event on campus. They ended up going out on several dates, and soon a disagreement on the seriousness of their relationship took place. Poddar eventually became obsessed with her, and when Tatiana rejected him, Poddar began stalking her and eventually psychological services at the university counseling center.

His therapist, Dr. Lawrence Moore, became concerned when his patient confessed his intention to kill Tarasoff. Dr. Moore eventually advised him that if the death threats continued, that he would have no choice but to have Poddar hospitalized. After the ultimatum was made, Poddar stopped attending treatment and eventually killed Tatiana Tarasoff. The case led to the "duty to warn" if any dangerous threat is made during a therapy session. If ever you are in a situation like this, by law it is your job to:

1. contact the individual that your client is making threats about and warn them
2. encourage the individual to contact the police and assist the individual if necessary
3. if you are unable to contact the individual, contact local law enforcement and file a report with the information that you do have
4. document in your chart your use of the Tarasoff rule, including documenting who you spoke with and the actions taken

CRISIS INTERVENTION SERVICES

A crisis is any situation in which a person's behaviors puts them at risk of hurting themselves or others and/or when they are not able to resolve the situation with the skills and resources available. Many things can lead to a mental health crisis. Increased stress, physical illness, problems at work or at school, changes in family situations, trauma/violence in the community, or substance use may trigger an increase in behaviors or symptoms that lead to a crisis. These issues are difficult for everyone, but they can be especially hard for someone living with a mental illness. Miller (2011) cites three areas of crisis:

- developmental crisis
- situational crisis
- existential crisis

DEVELOPMENTAL CRISIS

A developmental crisis is the result of a normal life event like a pregnancy or graduation that causes stress and strain on an individual (James, 2008). While developmental crises are normal, they may need close monitoring to ensure that a client returns to normal functioning. A way of conceptualizing a developmental crisis is to consider the different life stages and mourning of what your life used to be compared to what it is going to be now. An example would be getting married and transitioning from living on your own to now living with someone. Even though it is a joyous occasion, the transition can lead to a crisis given the changes that will be taking place.

SITUATIONAL CRISIS

A situational crisis is the most common kind of event when we consider crisis intervention. This is an event that is so overwhelming and sudden that it overwhelms normal coping (Schottke, 2001). Examples of situational crises include sexual assault, a motor vehicle accident, or sudden loss of a loved one. This is the most common form of crisis that emergency responders and other crisis intervention workers (hotline workers, social workers) are likely to encounter.

EXISTENTIAL CRISIS

Existential crises are based on larger concepts of a person's purpose and attainment of actualization, a deep sense of personal fulfillment (Olson, 2013). Often existential crises are related to situations of regret or belief that life has passed them by or realization that one will not reach goals they had set for themselves at a certain age (Price, 2011). Existential crises are particularly common at life transition points like 30, 40, and 50 when people "take stock" of their life. A significant existential crisis can predispose suicide and may be linked to the markedly high suicide rate among men and women between 45 and 54 (MacDonald, 2015).

WARNING SIGNS

It is important to be able to identify warning signs of a crisis. Sometimes family, friends, or co-workers observe changes in a person's behavior that may indicate an impending crisis. Other times the crisis comes suddenly and without warning. Warning signs include:

- inability to deal with daily tasks like bathing or eating
- excessive mood swings going from anger to becoming depressed
- becoming more threatening and violent

- abusing drugs
- experiencing of psychotic symptoms like delusions or hallucinations
- isolating from family or friends

SITUATIONAL STRESSORS

Situational stressors identify external events that may induce a crisis. Examples include:

- a family stressor
- a break-up in a relationship
- trauma
- work or school stress
- financial issues
- an unsafe living environment
- experience of discrimination

If as the social worker you are in a crisis situation, it is important to do the following:

1. Assess the crisis and implement crisis intervention services
2. Implement de-escalation techniques
3. Ensure safety of the client either by staying with the client or having someone watch them
4. Contact the local mental health crisis team to come out for an evaluation
5. Wait and ensure safety of the client

SHORT ASSESSMENT

Most people know CPR to stand for cardiopulmonary resuscitation, which is a lifesaving technique useful in many emergencies, including heart attack or near drowning, in which someone's breathing or heartbeat has stopped (Mayo Clinic, 2018). Similarly, if you have a client who is in a mental health crisis, it is important to act quickly and to implement a short crisis assessment using CPR. CPR from a mental health standpoint is an acronym for:

- Current plan
- Previous attempts
- Resources to execute the plan

This information, along with other information you gather, will be enough for you to quickly assess the severity of the client's threat of self harm, to contact the crisis evaluation team, and to pass along pertinent information that the crisis team will need when they arrive. Unless you are actually designated to write a hold and have an individual who is suicidal taken to the hospital, your job is keep the client safe and to make sure that the crisis team is as prepared as possible. Below is the information you would need when performing a short assessment:

CPR MODEL

- current plan
- previous attempts
- resources to execute the plan
- mental health diagnosis
- mental health history
- substance abuse history
- medical history
- compliance with medications
- recent trauma or circumstance that triggered the symptoms

Just gathering this information is enough to figure out the severity of the crisis quickly and to have enough information to pass along to the crisis evaluation unit if you need to make the call. Using CPR is vital because if a person has a plan, has attempted before, and has access to execute that plan, it automatically becomes a high-risk situation. Below is an example using the CPR model:

- Current Plan: "I want to kill myself by jumping in front of a train."
- Previous Attempts: "I have never attempted before."
- Resources: "There are no trains nearby where I live."
- Mental health Dx: No diagnosis
- Mental health Hx: No history
- Substance Abuse: Occasionally smokes marijuana
- Medications: Is not taking any psychiatric medications
- Trigger: I am sixteen years old and my mom took away my Xbox and I cannot go out with my friends.

Given this example, what would the risk factor for this client be?

- high
- medium
- low

In this example the risk of harm is low. The client is not a threat to harm himself; he is acting out because he is unable to play video games and go out with his friends. The client also has no extensive history of mental illness, is not on any medications, and is making a threat of jumping in front of a train even though there is no access to trains. Given the information from the short assessment, it would be useful to take the session time and process the client's frustration because no crisis team would be needed.

Below is another example:

- Current Plan: "I want to kill myself by jumping off of my 12th floor balcony."
- Previous Attempts: "I was hospitalized last month for 2 weeks because I tried to stab myself in the throat."
- Resources: "I am right in front of the balcony right now."
- Mental health Dx: Schizophrenia Paranoid Type
- Mental health Hx: 10 years of mental health treatment and hospitalizations
- Substance abuse: Client has a long history of abusing crystal meth and cocaine
- Medications: Abilify, Haldol
- Trigger: Client stopped taking his meds and began believing that aliens are trying to steal his thoughts. Client believes that the world will end soon.

Given this example, what would the risk factor for this client be?

- high
- medium
- low

In this example the risk factor would be very high and immediate action would be required, including contacting 911. The client has a plan, has attempted before, and has the resource to execute the plan. The client also has an extensive mental health history that includes multiple hospitalizations, has a diagnosis of schizophrenia which is a chronic and severe mental illness, has not taken any medications, and is on the verge of jumping out of his balcony. At this point, you would take the information that you have obtained from the short assessment, contact the crisis evaluation team, and report the information.

DE-ESCALATION TECHNIQUES

Along with the short assessment, it is important to also utilize de-escalation techniques to help the client from acting out in a harmful manner. It is important to remain calm and to implement the following techniques:

- not arguing
- listening
- acting supportive
- moving slowly
- showing spacing
- honoring body space

WHEN THE CALL GOES INTO THE CRISIS HOTLINE

Everyone is aware of 911, where any individual who is in a medical emergency can call at any time, 24 hours a day, and receive immediate assistance. Similarly this applies to an individual who is in a mental health crisis. When a person out in the community is in a mental health crisis and is in a non-medical emergency, they can call 911 and the call will then get routed to the 24-hour crisis line that is available throughout any particular county. From there, a phone agent will gather information from either the individual in crisis or the family member or friend who is making the call. Basic information is taken (address, telephone number, contact person, etc.) to the psychiatric information (mental health diagnosis, mental health history, substance abuse history, level of coping, etc.) of the client. This is known as a mini-assessment and it is up to the phone agent to gather as much important information as possible so that the level of crisis can be properly assessed.

From there, there are supervisors who will take all of the crisis call information from the agents and begin to prioritize crisis calls based on the severity of the case. This stage is very important because if a situation is potentially violent, law enforcement needs to go out and assess the situation to make sure it is safe, so that a proper crisis evaluation can take place. Also, the most important calls that require immediate action are the calls that need to be addressed first. Once the calls have been prioritized, the supervisors on scene will dispatch crisis teams out into the community to do crisis evaluations. Crisis evaluations are done with a partner, and it is important that the two individuals who go out on the calls have great teamwork, and are able to think quickly on their feet. As the crisis team goes to the specified location of the call, usually the home of the individual, one member will interview the individual in crisis, and the other worker will gather information from the family member or friends who are on scene. From there, the two members will discuss the information that they have received and then the two workers will then go back and interview the individual in crisis together. It is at this point where the crisis team will decide if the client meets criteria for hospitalization.

THE CRISIS EVALUATION

A crisis evaluation is not a therapy session but rather a quick and time-limited approach where the goal is to have the client back to his/her previous level of functioning before the crisis occurred. This is important to understand because long-term therapy requires a person to improve upon their life situation and how they cope, and is done over several months exploring every area of the individual's life. Crisis intervention on the other hand is a one-time intervention that is all about just getting the individual back to how they were previous to wanting to commit suicide. The information that is sought out during this time is for nothing more than assessing for writing a hold which is an application that sends the client to the hospital. Once the client is restored to his/her level of functioning, whether through the crisis assessment or through hospitalization, the client can then be referred for long-term therapy.

WRITING A HOLD

Writing a Hold is the legal term for the right to hospitalize an individual out into the community based on the criteria for "danger to self, danger to others, or gravely disabled." *Danger to self* means that you have a very high risk of killing yourself; *danger to others* refers to the very high risk of a person hurting someone else due to their mental state, and *grave disability* means that if the crisis team left the scene, that an individual may die due to the inability to take care of him/herself. This is something that should be taken very seriously by the crisis workers and if the team decides to hospitalize an individual, they are taking away his/her freedom and that individual is being taken to the hospital even if it is against their will. Once the crisis team fills out the paperwork to write the hold, it becomes a legal document, the ambulance is called and the individual is put in a gurney with restraints on their ankles and wrists, and taken away to the nearest psychiatric hospital. In the United States, people often assume that if a person is mentally ill, that this is automatic grounds for hospitalization, but that is not the case. Regardless of a mental illness, it is up to the crisis team to evaluate if this person meets criteria for hospitalization. Oftentimes, family members will get upset and want their family member hospitalized because he/she is hard to live with, but a crisis evaluation team will not decide hospitalization based on the inconvenience of the living situation on the family and solely upon whether criteria for hospitalization is met.

From there, once the individual is at the psychiatric hospital, the individual will be reevaluated again and if there is agreement among the staff at the hospital that this person meets criteria, the individual is held at this hospital until the client is stabilized. Stabilization of treatment includes 24-hour monitoring and medication stabilization. A client is held for a minimum of 72 hours (3 days) to up to one month depending upon how functional the client is. While the client is in the hospital, he/she will also receive short term individual counseling as well as group counseling services. Once stabilized, the client will meet with the staff social worker and nurse to establish a follow-up treatment plan once the individual is released.

FOLLOW-UP CARE

After the client is released, follow-up care is very important. Continuity of care needs to be established so that the risk factors for an individual to go back into crisis mode become reduced. An individual upon release is given an appointment at the nearest mental health facility within four to five days of release, is provided a one month supply of psychiatric medications and assigned a case manager who will help establish the services that the individual needs. The case manager at the mental health facility, after performing a full psychiatric evaluation, will link the individual to the necessary services that he/she needs. For example, the case manager can make a referral for individual therapy, group therapy, a medication appointment with a staff psychiatrist, referral for a substance abuse treatment program, referral for a medical checkup, employment services, supportive services for the family so that they can address the stress of caring for a family with a mental illness, their general relief, etc. Follow-up care is vital to the success of a person overcoming their crisis because without continuity of care, the likelihood of the client going back into crisis and being suicidal again becomes extremely high.

PUTTING IT ALL TOGETHER

When beginning your initial assessment with the client, it is important to establish rapport with your client as well as address all legal mandates that include informed consent, being a mandated reporter, and addressing issues of danger to self, danger to others, and grave disability. A good exercise to practice in class is to pair up with another student and to go over all of the information that was covered during this chapter. Also with more practice, you will become more fluid and confident when addressing all of this when working with a client at the initial assessment.

REFERENCES

California Department of Justice (2005). A guide to reporting child abuse to the California Department of Justice. Retrieved from: http://ag.ca.gov/childabuse/pdf/8583guide.pdf

California Department of Social Services California (2017). Adult Protective Services. Retrieved from: http://www.cdss.ca.gov/Adult-Protective-Services

California Legislative Information (2017). Chapter 11 Elder Abuse. Retrieved from: https://leginfo.legislature.ca.gov/faces/codes_displaySection.xhtml?lawCode=WIC&sectionNum=15610.07.

James, R. K. (2008). Crisis intervention strategies. Belmont, CA: Brooks/Cole.

Kirschenbaum, H. (2012). What is "person-centered"? A posthumous conversation with Carl Rogers on the development of the person-centered approach. *Person-Centered & Experiential Psychotherapies, 11*(1), 14–30.

Los Angeles County Department of Children and Family Services (2017). Report child abuse. Retrieved from: http://dcfs.lacounty.gov/contactus/childabuse.html

MacDonald, D. K. (2015) Understanding and preventing male suicide. Retrieved from http://dustinkmacdonald.com/understanding-and-preventing-male-suicide/

Mayo Clinic (2018). Cardiopulmonary resuscitation CPR: first aid. Retrieved from: https://www.mayoclinic.org/first-aid/first-aid-cpr/basics/ART-20056600

Miller, G. (2011). Fundamentals of crisis counseling. Hoboken, NJ: John Wiley & Sons.National Institute on Aging (2017). What are signs of abuse? Retrieved from: https://www.nia.nih.gov/health/elder-abuse#signs

Olson, A. (2013). The theory of self-actualization: mental illness, creativity and art. *Psychology Today*. Retrieved from https://www.psychologytoday.com/blog/theory-and-psychopathology/201308/the-theory-self-actualization

Price M. (2011) Searching for meaning. *Monitor on Psychology. 42*(10), 58.

Rogers, C. (1959). A theory of therapy, personality and interpersonal relationships as developed in the client-centered framework. In S. Koch (Ed.), *Psychology: A study of a science. Vol. 3: Formulations of the person and the social context.* New York: McGraw-Hill.

Rogers, C. (1986). Carl Rogers on the development of the person-centered approach. *Person-Centered Review, 1*(3), 257–259.

Schottke, D., & Pollak, A. N. (Eds.) (2001) Emergency medical responder: Your first response in emergency care. American Association of Orthopaedic Surgeons. Suffolk, MA: Jones & Bartlett.

Tarasoff v. Regents of the University of California, 551 P.2d 334 (Cal. 1976).

U.S. Department of Health and Human Services, Administration for Children and Families (2011). Retrieved from: https://www.acf.hhs.gov/sites/default/files/cb/cm11.pdf

CHAPTER 8

The Initial Assessment

INITIAL ASSESSMENT

One of the main roles of the social worker in the initial assessment is to determine whether a client is suffering from a psychological or behavioral disorder and what environmental factors and stressors are contributing. During the clinical interview, the social worker will gather information regarding a client's family history, social life, employment, financial situation, previous experience in mental health treatment, and other factors that can impact mental health and well-being. The assessment provides the social worker with a comprehensive picture of the client's life, which helps in determining the diagnosis and course of treatment. The goal of this chapter is to break down the basic components that are necessary for a thorough and complete assessment, so that you the social worker will have a strong clinical foundation.

BASIC INFORMATION

The basic information regarding an initial assessment can often be over-looked but often provides valuable information. Even before the client begins sharing more personal and in-depth thoughts and feelings, the basic information that a social worker gathers can provide the direction regarding what is going on with your client. A good rule of thumb when doing an initial assessment is to gather the basic information at the beginning of the assessment before the client gets too personal, because oftentimes when the client begins to share more painful experiences and feelings, the ability to gather that information becomes harder and harder. Similar to when a person sees a physician for a routine check-up, a set of basic questions are asked of the client at the beginning of the meeting because the physician wants to rule out any immediate potential red flags. And if there are red flags, the physician will then know what direction to take the examination. This is the same approach the social worker is displaying to the client in being thorough in ruling out any immediate dangers. The following is included regarding a client's basic information:

- name
- age
- relationship status
- current living situation
- employment
- education
- religious affiliation
- medical history
- mental health history
- substance abuse history
- family history
- family dynamics
- social environment
- any recent stressor or circumstance that has taken place
- level of coping
- why the client has come in to treatment

Here is a sample of a client with just the basic information that is gathered.

- Name: John Smith
- Age: 20
- Relationship status: Single
- Current living situation: Lives at home with his parents
- Employment: Unemployed
- Education: High School
- Religious affiliation: Christian
- Medical history: Severe back pain
- Mental health history: None
- Substance abuse history: Oxycodone addiction for 2 years
- Family history mental illness: None
- Family dynamics: Positive and supportive
- Social environment: Client states he has no social support
- Any recent stressor or circumstance that has taken place: Client states that he is feeling "really down" and it just hit him hard a few days ago.
- Level of coping: Staying home and having thoughts of suicide
- Why the client has come in to treatment: The client shares, "My faith in God is what brought me here."

Just with the information that we have without even going into figuring out what John's possible diagnosis is, what do we know about this client already? For one, we know that the client is deeply religious in his faith and that this is a primary motivator for him seeking treatment. We also know that he has severe back pain and that may be the reason why the client is having a substance abuse problem with Oxycodone. Also, given the potential severity of his back pain, this may also be the reason why the client is unemployed and has no social support outside of his home. The client is sharing that he just recently began feeling down, but just from the basic information that has been gathered, it is possible that his symptoms have been an issue for several years.

Let's try one more as this client example will be used throughout the rest of the chapter.

- Name: Tony Johnson
- Age: 34
- Relationship status: Recently broke up with girlfriend
- Current living situation: Lives alone in Pasadena
- Employment: Unemployed as he just recently was fired from his job
- Education: College
- Religious affiliation: None
- Medical history: None
- Mental health history: None
- Substance abuse history: Drinking 3–4 times a week for the past few weeks
- Family history mental illness: None
- Family dynamics: Distant
- Social environment: Client states he has a few close friends
- Any recent stressor or circumstance that has taken place: Client states that he began feeling suicidal after he lost his job and girlfriend within the same week.
- Level of coping: Staying home having suicidal ideations
- Why the client has come in to treatment: The client shares, "My friend dragged me here but I do not want to be here."

From the example provided above with just the basic information, what do we know about our client Tony? The client has had two big stressors in his life, which were losing his job and losing his girlfriend all within the same week. The client has no significant mental health or medical history, and the client has begun drinking heavily after his stressors began. It seems that the client did not have a drinking problem before these events, and if this is the case, his overall level of coping has deteriorated significantly. The client also appears to not have strong social support within his own family but appears to have a strong support with his friend who brought him to treatment. In relation to his motivation, the client appears to not be very motivated as it was his friend who brought him to treatment. Given just this information, it would be important to assess for suicide when continuing on with the assessment. This would fall in line with the next portion of the assessment process.

MENTAL STATUS EXAM

The mental status exam is the observation portion of the assessment where you the practitioner are looking at various aspects of the client. This portion of the assessment is present-oriented and only takes into account what is currently happening. It is a systematic way of collecting data on the client that can provide insight into possible mental health disorders the client is displaying. The various domains that are assessed are:

- appearance
- attitude
- behavior
- mood and affect
- speech
- thought process
- thought content
- perception
- cognition
- insight and judgment

APPEARANCE

As a practitioner, you would take a look at the presentation of the client in terms of height, weight, grooming, and attire. If the client is unkempt in his appearance, this might indicate possible drug use or schizophrenia, and if the client is displaying over the top attire, this may be signs of bipolar disorder. Other areas to look for is if the client looks pale due to possibly being malnourished, or if there are needle marks or bruises anywhere, because they may be indicators of abuse or neglect. All presentation that the client displays needs to be taken into account.

ATTITUDE

This aspect takes into account the client's intention when coming to treatment. Questions that you may want to consider when assessing this portion are:

Is the client being cooperative?

Cooperation shows motivation for treatment while being uncooperative may be a sign of not being motivated.

Does the client appear angry or hostile?

Angry or hostile behavior may be a sign of bipolar disorder.

Does the client appear to be acting cautious or suspicious?

Being cautious or suspicious might indicate symptoms of anxiety or schizophrenia.

Is the client not acting age appropriate during the session?

If the client is showing regressive behaviors, this may be an indication of a developmental disability.

BEHAVIOR

In assessing behavior, you as the practitioner are looking for any possible abnormalities. Some behaviors to look for include:

akathisia—the physical side effects of taking an antipsychotic medication
catatonia—the inability to move properly and freely
dystonia—tremors that usually come from a neurological condition

In working with older adults, you want to be able to differentiate from behavioral symptoms of depression versus medical conditions of Parkinson's disease or possible Dementia.

MOOD AND AFFECT

Mood describes how the client feels from their own observations and some questions to ask regarding mood are:

- Do you feel happy? (euthymic)
- Do you feel unhappy? (dysphoric)
- Do you not take pleasure in things you usually enjoyed before? (anhedonia)
- Do you feel angry?
- Do you feel anxious?

Affect refers to the nonverbal cues the client is displaying while expressing their emotions. Questions to consider are:

- Is the affect congruent or incongruent with what the client is sharing?
- Is their affect appropriate or inappropriate?

- Is the affect blunted or flat? (Possible depression or Schizophrenia)
- Is the affect overly exaggerated? (Possible Bipolar Disorder or Borderline Personality Disorder)
- Is the overall affect constricted? (Possible neurological injury)

It is important to take into account both the mood and affect of the client during the MSE.

SPEECH

When assessing for speech, it is important to look out for the following:

- aphasia—the inability to speak (Possible neurological condition)
- echolalia—repetition of another person's words (Signs of Schizophrenia, Autism, and in older adults Alzheimer's)
- neologisms—client's use of their own made up words (Signs of Schizophrenia)

Also in general, if the speech of the client is slow, this may be due to depression or other medical conditions that would need to be explored. Pressured and rapid speech could be signs of anxiety or bipolar disorder.

THOUGHT PROCESS

Looking at the client's thought process would be by listening to the client in their own words. It is important to look for any symptoms of any possible mental health disorder which would include:

- flight of ideas—rapid thoughts that come out through rapid speech (Schizophrenia or Bipolar Disorder)
- poverty of thought—the overall decompensation of thinking (Schizophrenia, Depression, or Dementia)
- delusions—a false belief that cannot be proven but is believed with complete faithfulness (Schizophrenia)

There are specific types of delusions to look out for that are consistent with symptoms of schizophrenia:

- paranoid delusion—being extremely fearful without reason
- delusions of reference—taking daily ascents of life and tying it into a delusion that is not true
- grandiose delusions—an over exaggeration that is not based on reality

Another aspect to look out for is *phobias*, which are irrational fears that do not pose any actual threat that are consistent with anxiety disorders like obsessive-compulsive disorder.

PERCEPTIONS

Perceptions look into the sensory experience of the client. *Hallucinations* are false sensory experiences that are not actually taking place in reality. This is consistent with schizophrenia, and the various types of hallucinations are:

- auditory—hearing something that is not there
- visual—seeing something that is not there
- tactile—feeling something that is not there
- olfactory—smelling something that is not there
- gustatory—tasting something that is not there

The various types of hallucinations as stated before are congruent with schizophrenia, but also can be a sign of a substance induced disorder.

COGNITION

In looking at cognition, the practitioner is assessing for the understanding, memory, and overall thinking of the client. Some questions to ask are:

- What is today's date? (orientation)
- Count backwards from 100 by 3s? (concentration)
- Please repeat these numbers back to me: 10, 12, 29, 37. (short-term memory)
- Can you share a significant event that took place 10 years ago? (long-term memory)

INSIGHT

Insight looks into the client's ability to understand their own symptoms. The greater the understanding by the client, the greater the opportunity to gain compliance from the client in terms of treatment. It also allows the client to be more self-aware and to be more actively engaged in their own treatment. Especially in treating clients with schizophrenia, the earlier the client can be treated after having their first psychotic episode, the greater the chance of overcoming and living a higher quality of life.

JUDGMENT

Judgment looks into the client's ability to make reasonable decisions in their own life. Questions to consider when assessing judgment of the client include:

- Does the client display good self-awareness?
- Is the client able to manage their symptoms when around other people?

- Is the client prepared to address both their symptoms and persona goals?
- Does the client display good impulse control?

Severe impairments in judgment may take place due to the mental illness, and so it is important to work with the client to best prepare them as they move further along in treatment.

DIAGNOSING THE CLIENT

When diagnosing a client, there are many different disorders to consider but we are going to focus on what is in the DSM-IV and the Axis I diagnostic criteria*. In the DSM-5, there are no axis codes, but in terms of establishing a strong foundational knowledge base, this will be the focus for diagnosis in this section. The purpose and goal of doing this is to have you the social worker establish a strong clinical foundation, which will allow you to explore and understand the complexities of the DSM in an easier fashion. When considering a diagnosis for a client, it is important to remember seven categories. The categories are:

- major depression
- bipolar disorder
- schizophrenia
- schizoaffective disorder
- anxiety disorders
- medical issues
- substance abuse

When giving a diagnosis, you are doing three things in relation to the seven categories:

- You are picking the diagnosis that justifies the criteria for your client.
- You are trying to rule out the other categories to get a clear diagnosis.
- If you combine categories, the combinations must match the criteria in the DSM.

In relation to the third premise, each specific disorder will either stand alone in relation to its criteria, or the diagnostic criteria will involve multiple categories. Please use the following criteria below:

---

* American Psychiatric Association, Diagnostic and Statistical Manual of Mental Disorders. Copyright © 2013 by American Psychiatric Association Publishing.

- Major Depression—Category 1 only
- Bipolar Disorder—Category 1 and 2
- Schizophrenia—Category 3 alone
- Schizoaffective Disorder—Category 1, 2, 3, and 4
- Anxiety Disorders—Category 5 only
- Medical Issues—Category 6 with Category (1–5)
- Substance Abuse—Category 7 with Category (1–5)

As long as you understand these three aspects moving forward, you will be fine. Let's take a look at each category.

CATEGORY 1

The first category is major depression. The symptoms for MDD include:

- having symptoms for at least two weeks
- feeling depressed most of the day almost everyday
- loss of interest in activities that one used to enjoy
- significant weight loss or weight gain
- excessive guilt
- thoughts of suicide

The criteria for MDD is pretty straightforward with the client experiencing depressive symptoms for at least two weeks experiencing fatigue, loss of energy, feelings of worthlessness, and in severe cases recurrent thoughts of death. To provide a diagnosis of major depressive disorder, the client would simply need to meet the symptom criteria for this disorder. Using the seven categories, this is what MDD would look like:

- Major Depression **Yes**
- Bipolar Disorder **No**
- Schizophrenia **No**
- Schizoaffective Disorder **No**
- Anxiety Disorders **No**
- Medical Issues **No**
- Substance Abuse **No**

CATEGORY 2

The second category is bipolar disorder. The essential feature of Bipolar 1 Disorder is a clinical course that is characterized by:

- having a manic episode
- having symptoms of major depression

- is not because of substance use or a medical condition

This portion of the DSM when describing bipolar disorder appears to be like it is coming from another language, but simply put, it is saying that if you give a diagnosis of bipolar disorder to a client, you are ruling out the other categories mentioned except for major depression. Bipolar includes depressive symptoms along with an elevated mood known as a manic episode. Using our seven criteria pattern, this is an example of what bipolar disorder criteria would look like.

- Major Depression **Yes, meets criteria**
- Bipolar Disorder **Yes, because there is a manic episode**
- Schizophrenia **No**
- Schizoaffective Disorder **No**
- Anxiety Disorders **No**
- Medical Issues **No**
- Substance Abuse **No**

Let's take a look at the symptoms for mania below.
Manic Episode:

- experiencing an elevated mood for at least 7 days or more
- increased self-esteem or grandiosity
- the need for less sleep
- more talkative and more active than usual
- having racing thoughts and rapid speech
- seeking excess pleasurable activities that are possibly dangerous

For a client to be diagnosed with bipolar disorder, they have to meet the criteria for major depressive disorder, along with experiencing a manic episode, which occurs at least for one week at a time, along with at least three other manic symptoms. In putting a manic episode into simpler context, four things can happen during a manic episode:

- intense elation or happiness
- intense irritability and anger
- intense anxiety
- psychotic features such as delusions, a/h, v/h

When a client is in a manic episode, one of these four symptoms can occur, but when the mania is over, the client will then go down to more normal levels or go into major depression. Going back to the beginning of the criteria for bipolar disorder, let's go over it using the seven criteria again:

- Major Depression—In bipolar disorder, there is the presence of major depression
- Bipolar Disorder—This disorder means there is the presence of a manic episode along with meeting criteria for major depression (Category 1 and 2).
- Schizophrenia—**No.** There can be psychotic symptoms in bipolar disorder but it is caused by the manic episode which can have residual effects, whereas here psychosis is taking place throughout for an individual. It is important here to acknowledge if psychosis does exist in the client, to figure if it is based off of criteria of schizophrenia or due to a manic episode. This would need to be ruled out to justify bipolar disorder.
- Schizoaffective Disorder—**No.** There is no sign of both the symptoms of schizophrenia and bipolar disorder in relation to this client.
- Anxiety Disorders—**No.** Once again intense anxiety can take place with bipolar disorder but it would only be occurring primarily in the manic episode. Anxiety disorders are usually taking place due to feared events and avoidance, not because of an elevated mood.
- Medical Issues—**No.** Medical issues can often be the cause of mental health symptoms or may often mimic symptoms that are not due to a mental illness. For example dementia has similar characteristics to major depression, but they are completely separate in terms of criteria. Here bipolar disorder is not due to any medical condition.
- Substance Abuse—**No.** Drug use can lead to mental health symptoms. For example, cocaine use can lead to experiencing bipolar symptoms. If it is a drug that is contributing to the client experiencing bipolar symptoms, then the diagnosis of bipolar disorder would not be justified. In this case the client would be diagnosed with a **mood disorder unspecified.**

Looking at the criteria that are in the DSM at the beginning describing bipolar disorder, there are also the stated categories we went over in bold: presence of one or more manic or mixed episodes (bipolar disorder). Category 2 is met.

Having one or more major depressive episodes. (Major Depression) Category 1 is met.

Episodes of moods not due to a substance-induced mood disorder (Substance Abuse). Category 7 is not met.

The mood disorder is not due to a general medical condition (Medical). Category 6 is not met.

The episodes are not due to either schizophrenia, or schizoaffective disorder (Schizophrenia and Schizoaffective Disorder). Category 3 and 4 are not met.

Remember that bipolar disorder is met with the presence of a manic episode along with criteria for major depression.

CATEGORY 3

The third category is schizophrenia. Schizophrenia is a chronic illness that is debilitating, involving delusions or false beliefs, along with hallucinations and overall negative symptoms that make it difficult to engage socially and perform daily activities. The criteria for schizophrenia include the following:

- disorganized and flat behavior
- experiencing delusions that do not hold in reality
- having hallucinations where actual sensory experiences are not happening
- incoherent speech and communication
- low energy
- lack of emotions
- socially isolated

It is important to note here that both bipolar disorder and schizophrenia can display similar symptoms of psychosis, but the differential component is the manic episode. The mania is the cause of the psychosis in bipolar disorder whereas in schizophrenia, there is an absence of a manic episode. Also regarding positive and negative symptoms of schizophrenia, the positive symptoms represent the delusions and hallucinations whereas the negative symptoms describe the physical and social difficulties experienced by a client. Below, using the seven categories, are the criteria for schizophrenia:

- Major Depression **No**
- Bipolar Disorder **No,** the psychosis is not due to a manic episode occurring
- Schizophrenia **Yes**
- Schizoaffective **No**
- Anxiety Disorders **No**
- Medical Issues **No**
- Substance Abuse **No,** there is no drug use that appears to be the cause of the symptoms

CATEGORY 4

The fourth category is schizoaffective disorder. Schizoaffective disorder often confuses clinicians but simply put, it is meeting criteria for bipolar disorder as well as for schizophrenia. In bipolar disorder, the mania is the cause of psychosis in the client whereas in schizophrenia, there is no mania taking place. Let's take a look below at the criteria for schizoaffective disorder:

Experiencing the following:

- a depressive episode
- a manic episode
- symptoms of schizophrenia which include delusions, hallucinations, affect
- not due to substance use or a medical condition

Using our seven-category analysis, let's take a look at what schizoaffective disorder looks like:

- Major Depression **Yes**
- Bipolar Disorder **Yes**
- Schizophrenia **Yes**
- Schizoaffective **Yes**
- Anxiety Disorders **No**
- Medical Issues **No**
- Substance Abuse **No**

Here you can see that categories 1, 2, 3, and 4 are met, which would be the criteria for schizoaffective disorder. This can be confusing because so many categories are met, but it is an important diagnosis and it becomes more clear with greater exposure to the various mental illnesses. Schizoaffective involves the first four categories, meaning that the client has suffered from a depressive episode, a manic episode, as well as psychotic features that are attributed to schizophrenia. Simply stated again, a schizoaffective disorder is someone who has both bipolar disorder and schizophrenia all together. The client with this disorder meets criteria for multiple symptoms that are not due to any substance or medical issues. At this point, hopefully there is some clarity regarding the distinctions between bipolar disorder, schizophrenia, and schizoaffective disorder.

CATEGORY 5

The fifth category is anxiety disorders. There are many types of anxiety disorders that include social phobia, panic disorder, obsessive compulsive disorder, and post-traumatic stress disorder. For this category, these are all included but we will be primarily focusing on GAD or Generalized Anxiety Disorder. The criteria for GAD are:

- experiencing excessive anxiety and worry
- feeling restless or keyed up
- irritable
- muscle tension
- racing thoughts
- experience of fatigue
- difficulty sleeping

An anxiety disorder is experiencing excessive worry, feeling restless and keyed up, and anticipating fatalistic outcomes before an outcome has occurred. This leads to avoidance of the feared situation and experiencing of anxiety attacks. Below using the seven categories, this is what GAD would look like:

- Major Depression **No** (Possible secondary symptoms due to fatigue)
- Bipolar Disorder **No**
- Schizophrenia **No**
- Schizoaffective **No**
- Anxiety Disorders **Yes**
- Medical Issues **No**
- Substance Abuse **No**

With anxiety disorders, it is very important to rule out bipolar disorder because mania can lead to excessive anxiety as well. However if there is intense anxiety due to a manic or mood elevation, once that episode is over, the primary symptoms of anxiety should dissipate as well. This is different from the fear of experiencing another anxiety or panic attack in the future associated with an anxiety disorder, and constantly feeling on edge because of it. That is an important distinction between the two disorders to note. It is also important to be mindful of the fact that oftentimes a secondary diagnosis of major depression will accompany an anxiety disorder, because the energy that is used constantly being in an anxious and overwhelmed state, can lead to secondary depressive symptoms such as fatigue and lack of motivation.

CATEGORY 6

The sixth category is regarding medical issues of the client. In relation to mental health symptoms, you are stating that there is a medical issue that is contributing to the mental health symptoms of the client. For example, an individual who is suffering from an overactive thyroid will secondarily experience symptoms that meet criteria for depression. In this example, if the client would just be put on anti-depression medication without addressing the medical problem of the thyroid, the mental health issue of depression would continue to exist. It is important to note here that it is the medical problem that is the primary cause of the depressive symptoms. Also using this example, the client does not meet full criteria for major depression because of the medical issue. Using the seven categories, the criteria of a client who had an overactive thyroid with depressive symptoms would look like this:

- Major Depression **Yes**
- Bipolar Disorder **No**
- Schizophrenia **No**
- Schizoaffective **No**
- Anxiety Disorders **Yes**
- Medical Issues **Yes**
- Substance Abuse **No**

The medical category is the combination of one of the first five mental health disorder categories in conjunction with a medical issue that is contributing. Depression can be caused by a wide range of factors, and it is inherent in several medical illnesses. A principle diagnostic characteristic of a disorder in this category is that it is not the result of some mental disorder, but instead a consequence of medical conditions that are not always linked to a mental health diagnosis. An example of this is when a mother gives birth and experiences postpartum depression or even worse, postpartum psychosis; it is the medical issue of the pregnancy that is a direct cause of the mental health symptoms being experienced. An example diagnosis in this category for the male with the overactive thyroid would be *depression due to a general medical condition.*

CATEGORY 7

The seventh category is substance abuse. Similar to the medical component, you are combining the use of a substance, and saying that there appears to be a direct correlation between the drug use and the mental health symptoms the client is displaying. For example, crystal meth can often lead an individual to experience bipolar symptoms that include a fluctuating mood and psychosis. If the client never had any of these symptoms prior to the drug use with no family history of mental illness, and the client only began experiencing the fluctuating mood after the drug use began, the client meets the criteria for Category 1, 2, and 7. Using this example and the seven criteria format, the following example would look like this:

- Major Depression **No** (Covered in Category 2 already)
- Bipolar Disorder **Yes**
- Schizophrenia No
- Schizoaffective No
- Anxiety Disorders No
- Medical Issues No
- Substance Abuse **Yes**

When there is substance use involved, a common diagnosis will include the term unspecified. Using this example above, a preliminary diagnosis for this client would be Mood Disorder Unspecified. This means that the client meets two categories in this case, the **Substance Use** along with **Bipolar Disorder.** *Unspecified* also means that the client did not fully meet the criteria for bipolar disorder on its own merits. It is important to note that in any criteria that we have covered in the DSM, it will always state that it cannot be due to a general medical condition or substance use. That is important to recognize, because that will change the diagnostic criteria for the individual you are treating.

In closing, we have completed going over the seven categories in relation to differential diagnosing. The purpose of this section was to provide as simple an explanation possible regarding this very difficult material. Please do not beat yourself up too much if it is still confusing, and know that with time and practice, it will become easier to understand. By going through this, we have laid the foundation of assessing through the lens of a medical model. The following sections will begin the process of taking everything you have learned and putting it all together.

VIGNETTE

As we go into writing the presenting problem, the diagnostic summary, and treatment plan, let's take a look at our client Tony again. Below is his basic information as well as statements provided by the client during your initial session.

VIGNETTE

Name: Tony Johnson
Age: 34
Relationship Status: Recently broke up with girlfriend
Current Living Situation: Lives alone in Pasadena
Employment: Unemployed as he was just recently fired from his job
Education: College

Religious Affiliation: None

Medical History: None

Mental Health History: None

Substance Abuse History: Drinking 3–4 times a week for the past few weeks

Family History Mental Illness: None

Family Dynamics: Distant

Social Environment: Client states he has a few close friends

Any Recent Stressor or circumstance that has taken place: Client states that he began feeling suicidal after he lost his job and girlfriend within the same week.

Level of Coping: Staying home having suicidal ideations

Why the client has come in to treatment: The client shares, "My friend dragged me here but I do not want to be here."

The client also shares "I have not gone out of my house for the past two weeks and all I do is sleep." He also added, "I just think about what happened over and over and I just stay in bed." The client Tony says he just feels tired all of the time and can barely get enough energy to get food for himself. He also added that he can't focus on anything and he cannot concentrate at all. Tony did not acknowledge having thoughts of suicide without any specific plan.

WRITING THE PRESENTING PROBLEM

When writing the presenting problem for an initial assessment, it is important that the content provided is consistent and in line with the diagnosis that you are providing. Oftentimes an inexperienced clinician will put in information that is not pertinent to the initial assessment and is more relevant for case notes when therapy is being provided. Writing a presenting problem for an initial assessment needs to be directly related to the self-reports of the client and focused on the client's most immediate needs. When writing a presenting problem, it is necessary to have four components:

- direct quotes from the client related to the DSM diagnosis
- trigger, or recent event that took place
- the client's level of coping
- the client's risk factor for suicide

Next is an example of a Presenting Problem:

The Ct shared, "I have not gone out of my house for the past two weeks and all I do is sleep." The Ct added, "I just think about what happened over and over and I just stay in bed." The Ct stated that he began feeling this way after he lost his job and after his girlfriend broke up with him. The Ct shared that he has been drinking three to four times a week and that he has never drank like this in the past. The Ct stated that he has thoughts of suicide without a plan and it feels to him that "My whole world is ending."

The presenting problem is broken down into its four components below: Direct quotes from the client related to the DSM diagnosis

> *The Ct shared that, "I have not gone out of my house for the past two weeks and all I do is sleep." The Ct added, "I just think about what happened over and over and I just stay in bed."*

Trigger, or recent event that took place

> *The Ct stated that he began feeling this way after he lost his job and after his girlfriend broke up with him.*

Level of coping

> *The Ct shared that he has been drinking three to four times a week and that he has never drank like this in the past.*

Level of suicide

> *The Ct states that he has thoughts of suicide without a plan and it feels to him that "My whole world is ending."*

Given just the information provided from the presenting problem, what diagnosis would you give this client? From the given information, it appears that the client has a diagnosis of Major Depression. The quotes provided by the client are in line with major depression as the client just recently had the trigger of losing his job and his girlfriend. The client's level of coping is poor as he is drinking three to four times a week which he reported that he has never done, and he is having thoughts of suicide without a plan which is also consistent with the criteria. It is important to note that the information that is in the presenting problem needs to be directly tied in with the diagnostic summary. The presenting problem reflects the self-reports of the client, and the diagnostic summary is taking that information and using it to justify a diagnosis. If there is no consistency within these two components, the assessment is then lacking the proper justification of the diagnosis being presented.

DIAGNOSTIC SUMMARY

As previously stated, the diagnostic summary is where the clinician is taking all of the information that they have gathered from the client and putting it all together for a diagnostic formulation. This is the portion of the assessment where the use of the medical model and the ecological perspective are combined to provide a picture of what is taking place with the client. From the medical standpoint, the clinician is looking at the mental, emotional, and physical symptoms of the client, while at the same time looking at the environment (job, relationship, family) and how it is contributing to his/her symptoms. This should all be reflected in your summary. In writing your diagnostic summary, it is important to have the following four components:

- Identify the client from an ecological perspective
- The DSM-V criteria for your chosen diagnosis for the client
- Differential diagnosing (ruling out the six categories to justify your diagnosis)
- The mental status exam

Given the presenting problem of the client, we will need to take a look at the criteria for Major Depression:

- having symptoms for at least two weeks
- feeling depressed most of the day almost everyday
- loss of interest in activities that one used to enjoy
- significant weight loss or weight gain
- excessive guilt
- thoughts of suicide

The client here does meet the criteria for major depression based upon the self-reports of the client. Once it is clear that the criteria for major depression are met, we can begin the process of differentially diagnosing and justify that major depression is the most accurate diagnosis for the client. Below is the rule out using the DSM and the seven categories:

- Major Depression—the client meets criteria **(Yes)**
- Bipolar Disorder—there is an absence or presence of a manic or hypomanic episode **(No)**

- Schizophrenia—there appears to be no symptoms of hallucinations or delusions **(No)**
- Schizoaffective Disorder—the client does not meet criteria **(No)**
- Anxiety Disorders—the client has anticipatory anxiety but it is not his primary symptoms **(No)**
- Medical Issues—the client did not report any medical issues that may be contributing to his depressive symptoms **(No)**
- Substance Abuse—the client began consuming excess alcohol once he lost his job and girlfriend **(No)**

If we take this same information and take a look at the DSM V and the justification portion for a major depression diagnosis, you will be able to see that what we did above is the exact same thing that the DSM V is trying to explain. After explanation of criteria in the DSM for any diagnosis, there is also a justification portion that tells you exactly what is required. In looking at this portion in the DSM for major depression, all that is being asked is to do what we have been doing which is go over the seven categories. Below are the written criteria justifying how to give a major depression diagnosis as well as the category in **bold** describing what it is saying:

Bipolar Disorder—no manic episode/**Category 2 (No)**

Schizoaffective disorder—the depression is not due to suffering from other mental health disorders **Schizophrenia, Bipolar Disorder, and Schizoaffective/Category 2, 3, 4 (No)**

Secondary depression—not a secondary symptom because of a medical issue **Medical/Category 6 (No)**

Active alcoholism or alcohol withdrawal, and any other drug **Substance Abuse/Category 7 (No)**

Not due to anorexia nervosa and the significant weight loss **Medical/Category 7 (No)**

In the elderly, depression not due to dementia or Alzheimer's **Medical/Category 7 (No)**

Not because of secondary symptoms of an anxiety disorder **Anxiety Disorders/Category 5 (No)**

The language of the DSM can be confusing, but the justification section of the DSM is only explaining what was mentioned before—rule out the other categories to justify your diagnosis:

- Major Depression **Yes**
- Bipolar Disorder **No**
- Schizophrenia **No**
- Schizoaffective **No**

- Anxiety Disorders **No** Anxiety symptoms appear to be a secondary symptom of his depression
- Medical Issues **No**
- Substance Abuse **No** Alcohol appears to not be the cause of the depression

Using the seven categories that have been mentioned, we have successfully justified our preliminary diagnosis. At this point, the presenting problem, criteria for major depression, and the ruling out of the other six categories have been completed. From here, we now need to officially write the diagnostic summary which also includes the diagnosis and treatment plan for the client. Let's take a look at the Diagnostic Summary for this client below:

VIGNETTE

The Ct is a 34-year-old Caucasian male who was self-referred and lives alone in the city of Pasadena. The Ct displays symptoms of fatigue, lack of energy, lack of interest in activities that he used to enjoy, feelings of worthlessness, and feeling depressed nearly every day for the past two months. The Ct denies any mood symptoms, denies any psychotic symptoms, denies any medical symptoms, and states that he has begun consuming a 12-pack a night three to four times a week. The Ct does acknowledge symptoms of anxiety, stating features of anticipatory anxiety when he knows that he has to prepare for something the next day. At present time the Ct denies any S/I or H/I. The Ct's affect appears depressed and flat. The Ct is sleeping more than eight hours a day and is eating at least two meals a day.

The summary is broken down into its four components:

ECOLOGICAL MODEL

The Ct is a 34-year-old Caucasian male who was self-referred and lives alone in the city of Pasadena.

DSM CRITERIA FOR MAJOR DEPRESSION

The Ct displays symptoms of fatigue, lack of energy, lack of interest in activities that he used to enjoy, feelings of worthlessness, and feeling depressed nearly every day for the past two months.

DIFFERENTIAL DIAGNOSIS: RULING OUT
THE OTHER SIX CATEGORIES

The Ct denies any mood symptoms, denies any psychotic symptoms, denies any medical symptoms, and states that he has begun consuming a 12-pack a night, three to four times a week. The Ct does acknowledge symptoms of anxiety, stating features of anticipatory anxiety when he knows that he has to prepare for something the next day.

MENTAL STATUS EXAM

At present time the Ct denies any S/I or H/I. The Ct's affect appears depressed and flat. The Ct is sleeping more than eight hours a day and is eating at least two meals a day.

As we can see from the summary, the client is a 34-year-old Caucasian male who lives by himself in the city of Pasadena. The client meets criteria for Major Depression as the symptoms from the DSM V have been listed and which is consistent with the self-report that was provided in the presenting problem section. The presenting problem and the diagnostic summary here is consistent with the diagnosis of Major Depression and in relation to differential diagnosing, the other six categories have been ruled out. Also, the mental status exam that has been performed is also incorporated. The only part left is to write the official diagnosis and treatment plan of the client.

DIAGNOSIS:

F33.1 Major Depressive D/O, Recurrent, Moderate (Primary)
F10.20 Alcohol Use Severe (Secondary)

PROBLEMS WITH THE SOCIAL ENVIRONMENT:

Substance Use, Relationship Issues, Employment related issues, Social Support

TREATMENT PLAN:

Ct provided a crisis evaluation at the time of the assessment (Date).

Ct is to be referred for a medication evaluation with the staff psychiatrist on (Date).

Ct to be referred for a medical evaluation (Date).

Ct to be referred to an alcohol treatment center to address his drinking issues (Date).

Ct is to attend individual counseling once a week for the next ten weeks beginning on (Date).

Ct to be referred for employment services on (Date).

Ct's progress to be monitored and reevaluated in 2 months (Date).

LCSW VIGNETTE FROM CHAPTER 1

In closing out this chapter, let's take a look at the vignette that was provided in the first chapter of this book. Below is the vignette:

VIGNETTE

A client John, aged 30, comes in to see you at your clinic. The client states that he hears voices and that he believes that his neighbor is out to get him. He shares that his neighbor puts flowers in a way that John does not like, "and there are billboards that prove that my mind is being read." John adds, "I have not slept for one week just thinking about it and I have stopped using cocaine for the past several months." John adds that he has had thoughts of suicide and "I get really sad about my future." John's mother is crying as she shares, "We have had so much mental illness in my family and he gets the ups and downs just like me."

What are the diagnostic considerations for this client?

A. schizophrenia
   bipolar disorder
   schizoaffective disorder
   major depression

B. substance induced psychotic disorder
   major depression
   bipolar disorder
   schizophrenia
C. bipolar disorder
   psychotic disorder unspecified
   major depression
   r/o schizoaffective disorder
D. substance abuse
   bipolar disorder
   major depression
   schizophrenia

As stated before in Chapter 1, the answer is C. It is important to understand that when you are given these questions, your job is to pick the best group of categories that would best define the client's possible diagnosis. You can only go off of the information that you have and do your best to come up with the best grouping. Using the seven categories that we covered in this section, let's take a look at what the client meets:

Major Depression Category 1 only

John does have depressive episodes, but given the fact that there is also mood elevation with him, the answer would be (No).

Bipolar Disorder Category 1 and 2

John is having ups and downs and does meet criteria here (Yes).

Schizophrenia Category 3 alone

John is hearing voices and has bizarre behaviors but there are also mood fluctuations and drug use that is involved, so the answer would be (No).

Schizoaffective Disorder Category 1, 2, 3, and 4

John meets the criteria of a depressive episode, a manic episode, and psychotic symptoms, but there is a possibility that his drug use may be the cause, so this could be a tentative (Yes).

Anxiety Disorders Category 5 only

John here does not meet criteria based off the information that we have (No).

Medical Issues Category 6 with Category (1–5)

Given the information, there is no indication of any medical symptoms of the client (No).

Substance Abuse Category 7 with Category (1–5)

John has been using cocaine and that may be the cause of both his fluctuating mood symptoms as well as his psychotic symptoms. We could give a tentative (Yes).

Looking at what we do know, there is a family illness of bipolar disorder in the family as the mom stated, and the client has multiple symptoms that could be either:

- Bipolar Disorder (family history) Category 2
- Mood Disorder Unspecified (Cocaine may be causing the bipolar symptoms) Category 2 and 7
- Psychotic Disorder Unspecified (Cocaine may be causing the schizophrenia symptoms) Category 3 and 7
- r/o Schizoaffective Disorder (r/o stands for rule out, which here means that this diagnosis is a strong possibility and so it is important to explore this more. If he did not take cocaine, he would meet criteria for sure, but it is unknown how much the cocaine use is contributing given the information that we have.)

This would be the ideal grouping given the vignette, but with answer choices provided, choice C has three of the four possible choices to consider. Choice D would be chosen, if a person taking the exam is just looking at symptoms and not differentially diagnosing at all. As stated before, this is considered a very difficult question in the LCSW exam, and if you can get a grasp of what is trying to be accomplished, you are already ahead of the game. It is my hope that you have a better foundation regarding the diagnosing process and that this will set a foundation for you to be well prepared for your clinical licensing exam in the future.

REFERENCES

American Psychiatric Association (2013). Diagnostic and Statistical Manual of Mental Disorders DSM-5. (5th ed.). American Psychiatric Publishing.

CHAPTER 9

Middle-Stage Therapy Models

BRIEF THERAPY MODELS

Brief therapy models focus on utilizing evidence-based practices in a time limited fashion, that addresses and aids in resolving a client's presenting problem. The models are task oriented, focusing on developing solutions and have become an essential part of practice utilized by social workers and other psychotherapists. Brief therapy models began when seeking to address substance abuse problems and have extended to address intrapsychic issues within an individual. Brief models focus on behavior changes and actions that are needed to create the change that is required. The ultimate goal is to reduce the undesired goal by eliminating the unhealthy behaviors that lead to the negative outcome, and promoting the desired goal by changing and engaging in positive healthy behaviors to create positive change. In using a brief therapy model, it is important to address the following assumptions that are involved for effective outcomes.

COLLABORATION

The therapist-client relationship is a collaborative effort and it is through this dynamic that change can possibly occur for the client who is seeking treatment.

CHANGE CAN TAKE PLACE RATHER QUICKLY

Since this is a brief and time-oriented approach, it is the goal to make immediate change and to produce quick results.

THE FOCUS IS PRESENT-ORIENTED

In using these models, one will not be able to address severe traumas or unresolved past issues, but problems that are in the present and tangible can be addressed with action.

IT IS ABOUT BEING PRACTICAL

The best approach will be practical and the practitioner recognizes that what happens outside of the office with the client in terms of results is more important than what takes place in the office.

UTILIZE THE STRENGTHS AND RESOURCES OF THE CLIENT

By identifying and utilizing the strengths and resources available to the client, this will allow for a greater opportunity for the desired change to occur. Also, this will allow for the client to maintain and sustain the change once it is achieved.

SMALL CHANGES CAN LEAD TO BIG RESULTS

The small changes made by the client can lead to significant outcomes, because it is the small changes that open the door for greater outcomes in the immediate future.

GOALS SHOULD BE CONCRETE AND ACHIEVABLE

The goals that are set forth should not be abstract and difficult to achieve, but rather, they must be easily understood. Goals should be tangible and focused when being set with the client.

Because it is the goal for change to occur quickly, the client needs to be aware that it will take hard work, commitment, and a direct focus on achieving the desired goals. There will most likely be homework assignments and tasks that will need to be completed in a timely manner. Also with using a brief therapy model, it is important to be parsimonious in the sense that if there are two equally effective treatments to address the client's problem, the one requiring less energy and time would be preferable to use. In closing, brief therapy models are a task centered with numerous applications, that extend both in micro and macro fields of social work.

REALITY THERAPY

Reality therapy is a model introduced by William Glasser, with the focus on addressing a client's choice and their own personal ability to solve whatever is going wrong in his/her life. The focus of the model is present-oriented and the goal is to help create a better future by focusing on the here and now. William Glasser, the creator of reality therapy in the early 1960s, began to use control theory in the late 1970s to better explain his work, and then renamed it choice theory in the 1990s. Choice theory is at the core of what reality therapy is attempting to do. Glasser developed reality therapy based on the belief that a particular mental diagnosis does not matter and that ultimately, it comes down to how a person thinks and perceives their own personal situation. Glasser believes that the underlying problem of all individuals is the same. He believes that at the core of all problems is unhappiness, and that it mainly stems from unsatisfying relationships or lack of relationships at all. Glasser believes that unsatisfying relationships lead to psychological problems and also psychological problems conversely lead to unsatisfying relationships. Therefore, for therapy to be successful, therapists must help their clients to develop a satisfying relationship and teach them to choose more effective ways to behave.

The focus of reality therapy is to break things down into step-by-step methods that can make the solutions simpler. The process involves being able to analyze the situation and figure out from the situation what can be changed. From there, it is a matter of having a plan and making sure that the plan is properly executed. It is a very systematic approach that promotes personal accountability and empowers the individual to see that they alone are the solution. The process is broken down into four parts that include:

- What are your thoughts about the situation?
- How do you feel about what is taking place?
- What are the actions that got you into this situation in the first place?
- How did you physically react to the situation?

The focus is on the client's thoughts, their feelings, the actions that they took, and how they physically responded. From there, the choice can be made to address the four components in a more positive and solution-oriented way:

- How must I think when I address this issue?
- By changing my thought processes about the situation, how do I feel?
- What are the actions that will need to be done in order for success to occur?
- How does this physically make me feel about what is happening?

Reality therapy acknowledges, accepts, and takes responsibility for the positive and negative consequences of one's own actions. Because of the ability to always make a choice, an individual must also accept the outcomes of their own lives. In understanding this construct, Reality therapy focuses on these tenets:

- Control—establishing and acceptance of what you can and cannot control
- An individual only has control over how they see their own life situation.
- An individual does not have control over what other people think, or how they behave.
- Discord happens when an individual tries to control others, or believes that he/she can be controlled by others.

Some consequences are natural like overeating, while others are imposed, such as incurring a fine for driving over the speed limit. With our choices, we are all born with five genetically encoded needs: survival, love and belonging, power, freedom, and fun (Corey, 2001, p. 231). More specifically:

- **survival**—you must be able to provide and care for yourself
- **love**—building relationships is the most important part of life next to survival, and the therapeutic process needs to be cooperative
- **power**—an individual needs to feel that they have control over how he/she lives and has the power to create the life that he/she wants
- **freedom**—an individual needs to feel that there is freedom to choose at any time and that this can be exercised continuously
- **fun**—an individual must enjoy the process of change and take pleasure, even through the struggles

Choice theory makes the assumption that everyone has an inner- and outer-quality world. In the inner realm is the storage of all your positive and negative experiences in relation to all of your experiences, and so it is extracting from the knowledge that has been accumulated by exploring it in therapy. From there it is clearly defining how both worlds can be of a quality that will make the individual happy.

CHOICE THEORY AND DEPRESSION

Glasser believed that at the core of depression was unfulfilled and unhappy relationships. It is in looking at the relationship dynamics of an individual where the client's quality world becomes exposed, and that includes the unhealthy behaviors that have led to the lack of fulfilling relationships. He believed that a cycle would take place where the client would express anger and frustration due to the unfulfilling relationships and complain about it. From there helplessness becomes the primary emotion, which then leads to depression. Glasser believes that once an individual is in a depressed state, it allows a person the excuse to gain sympathy from others and allows a safer space for the client to express how helpless he/she feels. It provides a paradoxical outcome in the sense that the individual gets to exert control over others where direct attention and care is provided to him/her, and a sense of control over the symptoms takes place. Understanding this dynamic helps to understand the reality therapy paradigm of ACHE below:

A = Anger
C = Control
H = Help
E = Excuse

Depression is a coping mechanism that does four things:

- It helps people deal with **anger**, an emotion that is more dangerous than the passivity associated with depression.
- It gives people a measure of **control** over circumstances that may seem out of our control (e.g., illness or death).
- It helps to secure **help** from friends, doctor, and/or institutions.
- It provides an **excuse** for not doing what we should.

THE WDEP SYSTEM

The WDEP was developed by Robert Wubbolding (1988) and sums up much of Glasser's philosophy in a summary form:

W = WANTS (WANTS, NEEDS, AND PERCEPTIONS)

The question of "What do you want out of your life?" is explored here. In the therapy session, it is important to identify the successes as well as the failures. In identifying the failures, it is important to identify what was not achieved that the client was trying to get. That provides valuable insight into what it is the client really wants. In fact, it often becomes the most important information that is gathered because it provides direct knowledge into what kind of quality world the client is seeking. It is important as the therapist to remain nonjudgmental and to be supportive throughout this exploration process.

D = DIRECTION

In addressing direction, it is important to identify where the client wants to go as addressed in the previous section, and to identify the direction that the client is currently going in. Usually, it is in the opposite direction of their wants and so it must be defined. For the client and therapist to gain insight, it is important to ask questions to help define where the client is currently at. Some examples include:

- What has been your contribution in relation to the situation you are currently in?
- Describe your past week and how your actions directed what is happening now.
- If you could go back and change things, what would you do differently?
- In making those changes, what is the outcome you would have liked to have achieved?

It is here that the therapist aims to change the behavior instead of trying to change attitudes and feelings. The questions are action-based and solution-focused. Listening to a client talk about feelings is only productive if it leads to change in what the individual is doing.

E = EVALUATION

After exploring the "what" the client wants and identifying the undesired direction the client is going in, it is important to take that information and evaluate what is actually taking place. Some questions to ask the client include:

- Looking back on all that we have discussed thus far, how would you describe where you are at?
- What have been the positive outcomes of your behaviors?
- What have been the negatives?
- In comparing the positives and negatives of your situation, is the current situation more positive or negative for you?
- How are your current actions affecting your relationships with others?

It is important to be respectful to the client at all times, but the use of confrontation would be beneficial here. It is vital when using this therapy model to keep the client accountable for their actions and the consequences for what has occurred. In using confrontation here, the practitioner is also identifying and modeling the behaviors and actions that are required to achieve the desired results. Evaluation is performed from the perspective of self-empowerment and the ability of the individual to make effective change.

P = PLANNING AND COMMITMENT

Once the client has identified what he/she wants to change in their life, there needs to be an action plan. If a plan doesn't work, then another can be created, as outcomes are key for this therapy model. Any form of rigidity is addressed by the therapist as flexibility is a necessary virtue of this therapy model. All plans that are made need to be:

- simple
- attainable
- measurable
- immediate

IMPLEMENTING REALITY THERAPY

In implementing reality therapy, let's look at the following vignette and then use this to put together a plan for the client:

VIGNETTE

Tammy is struggling with alcoholism and was recently fired from her job. She was given an ultimatum by her family to get help or to leave the home. Tammy has been drinking a quarter bottle of vodka every night for the past year; this began after she and her husband divorced after 10 years of marriage. Tammy is currently living with her parents and her two children. She has not only lost her job, but she was recently jailed for her second DUI in the past year. When she appeared in court, the judge told her to get help, which includes intensive treatment. The judge warned that if her behavior continues, the court will be forced to involve the department of children and family services, because she does not appear to be able to take care of her two kids. Tammy is in your office as she has a court order for treatment. She shares, "I want my life back, which includes sobriety and creating a normal life for my kids." She adds that "When life overwhelms me, I lose it and just go straight for the bottle." Tammy adds that "When my life was in order, I would not go to the bottle but would work out, and really lean on my friends and family for support. This time around, I just withdrew and gave my life to alcohol."

IDENTIFYING TAMMY'S UNSATISFYING RELATIONSHIPS AND THE MAIN BEHAVIOR CAUSING IT

As mentioned earlier, the core of reality therapy is the unsatisfying relationships that are taking place in a person's life. For Tammy, the unsatisfying relationships are:

- with her two children
- with her ex-husband
- with her parents
- with her employer
- with the law
- with herself (addiction)

And the client's main behavior that is causing all of this discord is:

- Behavior—drinking vodka every night

In identifying her unsatisfying relationships, it is important to note how her alcohol abuse has affected all of her close relationships in her life. The main component and behavior that has contributed to these unsatisfying relationships is her alcoholism.

GO OVER THE FIVE BASIC NEEDS

In addressing her five basic needs as listed with reality therapy:

- survival—you must be able to provide and care for yourself.

Tammy is unable to care for herself and her children because she is killing herself by drinking away her life.

- love—building relationships is the most important part of life next to survival, and the therapeutic process needs to be cooperative.

Tammy is hurting the ones that she loves the most, which are her children and her parents. She is neglecting and sabotaging her love relationships.

- power—an individual needs to feel that they have control over how he/she lives and has the power to create the life that he/she wants.

Tammy is displaying no power in her life as her addiction to alcohol is taking it away. She is choosing to act powerless by continuing to drink.

- freedom—an individual needs to feel that there is freedom to choose at any time and that this can be exercised continuously.

Tammy is exercising her freedom to drink and the consequences include the loss of her marriage, strained relationships, loss of job, and two DUIs.

- fun—an individual must enjoy the process of change and take pleasure, even through the struggles.

Tammy has the opportunity to turn her life around and really focus on building a quality life for herself. This process will be hard but can be fun at the same time.

IDENTIFY THE DEPRESSION CYCLE ACHE

- A = Anger

Tammy, when she feels her life becoming difficult and out of control, will get angry and then start drinking.

- C = Control

Tammy tries to gain control over external things she has no control of by drinking, which is her choice to do.

- H = Help

Tammy, instead of seeking and asking for help when needed, uses drinking and depression as a way to avoid and not address the problems in her life

- E = Excuse

Tammy is hiding behind her depression and alcohol abuse to avoid changing her life, even though the choice to change is always available to her.

USE THE WDEP SYSTEM

In using the WDEP system, you would want to go over the questions in each section with Tammy to help establish a realistic plan.

W = WANTS (WANTS, NEEDS, AND PERCEPTIONS)

"What do you want?"

> *Tammy wants to get sober and rebuild her relationships with her children and her parents. She also wants to get a full-time job again and take care of herself again.*

"What kind of person would you be if you were the person that you wish you were?"

> *Tammy sees herself living a healthy lifestyle that includes taking yoga classes as well as possibly going back to school to get her graduate*

degree in marketing. It has been her dream to work in advertising but she hasn't pursued it.

D = DIRECTION AND DOING

"What are you doing now?"

> *Tammy is drinking every day and her life is falling apart.*

"What did you do during the past week?"

> *Tammy lost her job, drinks every day, and had to appear in court for her second DUI.*

"What would you want to do differently this last week?"

> *Tammy would want to be sober and live a normal life which would include working and spending time with her children.*

"What stopped you from doing what you say you wanted to do?"

> *Tammy, instead of focusing on her responsibilities, decided to focus all of her attention on drinking.*

"What do you see for yourself now and in the future?"

> *Tammy sees herself getting sober and reconnecting her life back with her family.*

E = EVALUATION

"Is what you are doing helping or hurting you?"

> *Tammy has identified how drinking is hurting her life.*

"Is what you are doing what you want to be doing?"

> *Tammy states that she has no choice but to seek help and treatment or go to jail.*

"Does you behavior match up with what you believe?"

Tammy believes that there is a really healthy person inside of her but she is scared.

"Is your behavior against the rules?"

Tammy believes and knows that alcohol will always be a problem for her and she will always need to be sober.

"Is what you want in your best interests and in those of others?"

Tammy acknowledges that getting sober is in the best interest of herself and those that she cares about the most.

P = PLANNING AND COMMITMENT

As stated before, once the client has identified what she wants to change in her life, there needs to be an action plan. All plans that are made need to be:

- simple
- attainable
- measurable
- immediate

Tammy's treatment plan would include:

- Go into an inpatient program for the next three months to get sober and completely detox from her alcohol addiction.
- After completion of the inpatient program, attend AA meetings and get a sponsor to support her sobriety.
- Attend individual counseling once a week to address her addiction and depressive symptoms.
- Remain compliant with all court ordered mandates to remain out of jail.
- Attend family counseling services so that her children and her parents can also be helped during this process.
- Supportive services referrals to Tammy's children and parents that include counseling and group services.

In closing, reality therapy is very behavior-specific and it involves detailing an action plan that is easy to comprehend.

SOLUTION-FOCUSED THERAPY

Solution-focused therapy, which was developed by Shazer and Bergand, believes in the premise that the solutions to one's problem lies in the history of the individual when the person was not suffering from the problem. The therapy model is a logical approach that looks at when the problem was not a problem for the individual, and identifying what that person did during those times versus the times when it actually became an issue. An example would be a person who has difficulty with driving because of a recent accident. It would then be important to identify the traits and qualities the individual possessed before the accident happened. From there, the practitioner would create a set of solutions based upon the healthy behaviors that the individual previously engaged in. This requires a collaborative effort from both the client and therapist, and also requires that the client is self-motivated in their endeavor to change. The key is to help the client describe the details of when their life was better, and to take those skills to progress towards a better solution for the future.

It is required that the practitioner take a positive and solution-focused stance. The overall attitude of the practitioner should be positive, respectful, and hopeful. SFT assumes that all people are strongly resilient and continuously utilize this skill to deal with the ever-changing world. Further, there is a strong belief that most people have the strength, wisdom, and experience to effect change. SFT approaches client resistance in a more client-focused view stating that it is:

- a client's natural protective mechanisms or realistic desire to be cautious and go slowly
- it is the therapist's error providing an intervention that does not fit

It is up to the practitioner to lead from behind, to allow the client to feel a sense of control over the process, and to coordinate with the client during the direction of positive change.

KEY CONCEPTS AND TOOLS FOR SFT

The main construct of the solution-focused model is that focusing on the problem is not an effective way of solving the problem. When solely focusing on the problem, it diverts away from healthy coping because a negative viewpoint becomes the foundation. In implementing this model, it is important to note the following assumptions:

- that change is actually possible
- the focus and energy of the time-limited model will be on addressing solutions

- that the client is the expert in their own life and that they already have the solutions
- finding the solutions is about identifying the existing resources that are available to the client to make the changes

It is in working through these assumptions, that a detailed action plan can be developed during the therapy process.

IDENTIFYING PAST SOLUTIONS

Identifying how the client successfully handled similar problems in the past allows the client to develop a sense of confidence, and diverts the client from viewing the situation through a negative filter. Even though this is a current problem for the client, there were times in their life that it was not an issue, and in that exploration lies the solutions. Some questions to ask are:

- "When was this not a problem for you?"
- "During that time, what were the behaviors and actions that you were engaged in?"

In identifying past successes for the client, this will open the door to develop a plan for present and future success.

IDENTIFYING EXCEPTIONS

When exploring for possible past solutions with the client, it is also important to explore when exceptions occurred. An *exception* is when the client looks at similar problems in the past that are currently happening now, and identifies the times when bad outcomes did not occur. This could have taken place by accident, but it is identifying those times because solutions lie in those exceptions. Questions to ask may include:

- "When was this a problem, but a good outcome took place?"
- "What specifically did you do during that time that may have helped you get a good outcome?"

More specifically, it is thought of as a time when a problem could have occurred, but did not.

PRESENT- AND FUTURE-FOCUSED QUESTIONS
VS. PAST-ORIENTED-FOCUSED QUESTIONS

Questions are an important communication element of all models of therapy. Therapists use questions often with all approaches while taking a history, when checking in at the beginning of a session, and when finding out how a homework assignment went. However, [SFT] therapists make questions the primary communication and intervention tool. These therapists tend to make no interpretations, and they very rarely directly challenge or confront a client…. The questions that are asked by [SFT] therapists are almost always focused on the present or the future…. This reflects the basic belief that problems are best solved by focusing on what is already working and how clients would like their lives to be, rather than focusing on the past and the origin of problems…. The questions that are asked by [SFT] therapists are almost always focused on the present or on the future, and the emphasis is almost exclusively on what the client wants to have happen in his or her life (Trepper et al., 2012, p. 24).

It is important to clarify that past-oriented questions are only used to identify possible solutions to use for the future. The goal is present- and future-oriented, and even past questions are used to address the present situation.

USING COMPLIMENTS

Compliments are an important tool in solution-focused therapy, as they validate what the client is already doing well in achieving the desired goal. It is providing positive feedback as well as validating how the client is taking initiative in solving their current dilemma. Validating what the client is already doing well and acknowledging how difficult their problems are encourages the client to change while giving the message that the therapist has been listening and cares (Berg & Dolan, 2001). In SFT therapy, compliments are often conveyed in the form of appreciatively toned questions of:

- "How did you do that?"
- inviting the client to do more of what is working

Once an SFT practitioner has created a positive framework via compliments and through discovering some previous solutions and exceptions to the problem, the client can then be gently invited to do more of what has previously worked, or to try making positive changes, also known as experiments, to help improve the situation. You as the therapist are giving a gentle nudge to do more of what is working for the client, as well as combining other aspects that could work. It is rare for a SFT practitioner to make a suggestion or assign homework that is not based on the client's previous solutions or exceptions. It is always best if the changing of ideas and assignments come from the client, rather than coming from the therapist because:

- the previous assigned behaviors are familiar to the client
- the new experiments are truly coming from the client's own motivation

USING THE MIRACLE QUESTION

The *miracle question* tool is a powerful way of taking the first small steps towards a solution by helping the client describe small, realistic, and doable steps that can be done as soon as the next day. The miracle question was developed by taking what is perceived to be desperate situations and trying to find a way for an individual to get out of that helpless and depressed state. Using Tammy as an example from the previous vignette, here is an example of using the miracle question:

Social Worker:	I am going to ask you a rather strange question that requires some imagination on your part; do you think you can use your imagination?
Tammy:	I think so; I will try my best.
Social Worker:	Great. I want you to imagine that after we talk and you go back home and finish the rest of your day, it is time to go to bed and everybody in your household is sound asleep and the house is very quiet. In the middle of the night there is a miracle that occurs and your problems are all solved. But because this happens when you are sleeping, you have no idea that there was a miracle and that the problem was solved. So when you are slowly coming out of your sound sleep the next morning, what would be the first small sign that will make you wonder that there must've been a miracle and your problems are all gone? How would you discover this?
Tammy:	I suppose I would feel like getting up and facing the day without having a headache from drinking all night, and instead of wanting to cover my head under the blanket and just hide there, I would get up and exercise because I am sober and physically and mentally fit.
Social Worker:	Suppose you do get up and face the day, what would be the small thing you would do that you didn't do this morning?
Tammy:	I suppose I would say good morning to my kids in a cheerful voice instead of barely acknowledging them or not seeing them like this morning.
Social Worker:	What would your children do in response to your happy greeting?
Tammy:	They would probably be surprised at first to hear me talk to them in a cheerful voice, and then they would calm down and ask me, "What is going on with you, mom?"
Social Worker:	So, what would you do then that you did not do this morning?
Tammy:	I would probably crack a smile, start crying, and hug them both, letting them know that I will always put them first in my life from now on.

These small steps would then become the building blocks of implementing an immediate behavioral change that was just envisioned during the use of the session. This is often the longest question asked because this allows the client to freely and without restriction explore how they want their life to be. In the case of Tammy, it would be a great start to rebuild the relationship with her kids and to start the process of her recovery. Being able to wake up sober and greet her kids and make a proclamation of change is not only possible, but could be enacted the next day.

SCALING QUESTIONS

Scaling questions can be used to help tangibly identify where the client is at and how they see their current situation. They can be used to address multiple areas, including a client's level of motivation, happiness, and progress. Usually scaling questions go from a scale of 0 to 10, where 0 reflects the lowest level of satisfaction and 10 represents ultimate satisfaction.

Once again using Tammy as an example using the scaling question:

Social Worker:	Given what you described about your difficulty being able to make it to session today, on a scale of 1–10 with 1 being not well and 10 being very well, how would you score your overall mental and physical health at this moment?
Tammy:	Given how crappy I feel because I am shaking from not drinking last night, and with my children so disappointed in me, I would give it a 1.
Social Worker:	What are other factors that are making your scale score so low?
Tammy:	My kids not only hate me, but my parents are disappointed with me and we all had to move in together because of what I have done. And I lost my job and my husband and I divorced due to my failure to get a grip on my drinking.
Social Worker:	You have been through quite a lot already and it makes sense that you are scoring your well-being so low.
Tammy:	That is why I am here, because I need to start somewhere to begin turning my life around.

COPING QUESTIONS

These types of questions are a powerful reminder that all individuals engage in positive actions even when facing overwhelming difficulty, and when life is not going the way the individual wants. If in the midst of despair, an individual is able to get out of bed, get dressed, feed their children, and do many other things that require major effort, that is a form of positive coping. The individual should be acknowledged for that. Below are examples of coping questions that can be directed to the client:

- "How have you managed to carry on given all of this difficulty?"
- "How have you managed to prevent things from becoming worse?"

Coping questions allow the client to temporarily escape their negative viewpoint and see a different way of looking at their coping. Oftentimes, an individual will not see how much resilience and determination is being expressed, and objectivity becomes lost. It is important for the practitioner to validate what the client is doing well.

CONSULTATION

It is important to consult with your colleagues and/or supervisor to see how effectively you are implementing the model. If your other colleagues are able to observe your sessions, they would be able to provide valuable feedback in terms of what is going well and what can be improved upon. An important question to ask your colleague or supervisor is:

- "Do you feel like there is anything that I did not cover that I needed to during session?

Even if there is no observation from your peers, you can still go over the case during consultation and ask the question after your review of what took place.

PUTTING SOLUTION-FOCUSED THERAPY TOGETHER

It can be difficult to cohesively put together all of the different components, and so we are going to use the vignette of the client Tammy again below:

VIGNETTE

Tammy is struggling with alcoholism and recently was fired from her job and was given an ultimatum by her family to get help or to leave the home. Tammy has been drinking a quarter bottle of vodka every night for the past year. This began after she and her husband divorced after 10 years of marriage. Tammy is currently living with her parents and her two children. She has not only lost her job, but she recently was jailed for her second DUI in the past year. When she appeared in court, the judge told her to get help, which includes intensive treatment. The judge warned that if her behavior continues, the court will be forced to involve the department of children and family services because she does not appear to be able to take care of her two kids. Tammy is in your office as she has been court ordered for treatment. She shares, "I want my life back which includes sobriety and creating a normal life for my kids." She adds that "When life overwhelms me, I lose it and just go straight for the bottle." Tammy adds that "When my life was in order, I would not go to the bottle but would work out, and really lean on my friends and family for support. This time around, I just withdrew and gave my life to alcohol."

Below is an example of using the different components of solution-focused therapy with Tammy:

Social Worker:	Hi Tammy, it is nice to meet you, what brings you in today?
Tammy:	I have a lot going on, and truthfully I really am not sure if I want to be here or not.
Social Worker:	I appreciate your honesty. If it is okay to ask, what is the reason you are here today?
Tammy:	I have been court ordered for treatment because I received my second DUI, and I am at risk of losing custody of my children as well. In this past year, my husband divorced me and I had to move in with my parents because I cannot afford to care for myself and my kids.
Social Worker:	That is a lot to go through. "How have you managed to carry on given all of this difficulty?" **(Coping question)**
Tammy:	Honestly, I am just taking it day by day, and this is the first day that I have been sober because I chose not to drink last night. My body is going through withdrawal which I hate though.
Social Worker:	That is great that you are taking that first step. That is huge. (Compliment) Were there situations in the past where you were able to not drink for extended periods of time? **(Looking for previous solutions)**
Tammy:	Yes.
Social Worker:	How did you do it?
Tammy:	I honestly prioritized my life, putting my family first, and instead of going to happy hour, I would go the gym. Instead of alcohol, my life was more focused on family and friends, and I was planning to go back to graduate school. **(Previous solutions shared)**
Social Worker:	That is wonderful that you were able to do that. You substituted exercise and the people close to you to be the priority of your life over alcohol and you had even bigger goals to get your graduate degree. **(Restating the solutions that the client accomplished in the past)**
Tammy:	I was able to do that but it feels so long ago now.
Social Worker:	If you were able to be in that space before, you should be able to do it again. Just from this I can see your strength and desire to live a great life. **(Compliment)** Were there times as well when you could have had a DUI but it did not happen? **(Looking for an exception)**
Tammy:	Yes, it did. One time me and my close friends were all hanging out a bar for my friend's birthday. I was really sick and so I could not drink, but I still had a really good time. I just really enjoyed the food and it was the first time in a long time, that I was not scared to drive home. I was not scared to see police cars on the street.

Social Worker:	That could have gone badly but instead you were able to make the most of the situation and be sober. Also as you stated before, that situation allowed you to honor how you did live your life before, when alcohol was not the priority in your life. **(Redirecting back to solutions)**
Tammy:	Yes, that is true and I wish I could be like that going out all of the time. **(Client in a solution-focused mindset)**
Social Worker:	Given what you described about your difficulty being able to make it to session today, on a scale of 1–10 with 1 being not well and 10 being very well, how would you score your overall mental and physical health at this moment? **(Scaling question)**
Tammy:	Given how crappy I feel because I am shaking from not drinking last night, and with my children so disappointed in me, I would give it a 1.
Social Worker:	What are other factors that are making your scale score so low?
Tammy:	My kids not only hate me, but my parents are disappointed with me and we all had to move in together because of what I have done. I lost my job and my husband and I divorced due to my failure to get a grip on my drinking.
Social Worker:	You have been through quite a lot already and it makes sense that you are scoring your well-being so low.
Tammy:	That is why I am here, because I need to start somewhere to begin turning my life around.
Social Worker:	I am going to ask you a rather strange question that requires some imagination on your part; do you think you can use your imagination?
Tammy:	I think so, I will try my best.
Social Worker:	Great. I want you to imagine that after we talk and you go back home and finish the rest of your day, it is time to go to bed. Everybody in your household is sound asleep and the house is very quiet. In the middle of the night, there is a miracle that occurs and your problems are all solved. But because this happens when you are sleeping, you have no idea that there was a miracle and that the problem was solved. So when you are slowly coming out of your sound sleep the next morning, what would be the first small sign that will make you wonder that there must've been a miracle and your problems are all gone? How would you discover this? **(Miracle question)**
Tammy:	I suppose I would feel like getting up and facing the day without having a headache from drinking all night, and instead of wanting to cover my head under the blanket and just hide there, I would get up and exercise because I am sober and physically and mentally fit.
Social Worker:	Suppose you do get up and face the day, what would be the small thing you would do that you didn't do this morning?
Tammy:	I suppose I would say good morning to my kids in a cheerful voice instead of barely acknowledging them or not seeing them like this morning.

Social Worker:	What would your children do in response to your happy greeting?
Tammy:	They would probably be surprised at first to hear me talk to them in a cheerful voice, and then they would calm down and ask me, "What is going on with you, mom?"
Social Worker:	So, what would you do then that you did not do this morning?
Tammy:	I would probably crack a smile, start crying and hug them both, letting them know that I will never not put them first in my life ever again.
Social Worker:	That is something that you can do tomorrow. What will you be doing in the next week that would indicate to you that you are continuing to make progress? **(Present- and future-oriented question)**
Tammy:	Besides rebuilding my relationship with my kids, I can start looking at an inpatient alcohol treatment center so that I can really get clean. **(Solution-focused goals)**
Social Worker:	That is great. For this week let's focus on rebuilding communication with your children and finding an inpatient setting for you to go to. **(Restating the agreed-upon goals)** I can help you with that. Is there anything that I did not ask that you think it would be important for me to know? **(Invitation to add further information)**

MOTIVATIONAL INTERVIEWING

Motivational interviewing is a brief therapy model that uses the practitioner as a helper in the change process for the client, while the client finds the desire and ultimately makes the decision towards positive change. The process of this model is a democratic process, and the goal is to work collaboratively together. Usually in the beginning process of therapy, the client overestimates the benefits of their current lifestyle and choices, and devalues the benefits of actually changing. It is during this time that the practitioner must help prepare the client for change through psycho-education, and to help the client at least see more of the benefits of actually changing. It is important during this process to be empathic, non-confrontational, and open-minded towards the individual. It is important to promote a safe environment for the client and to understand the unique perspective that the client is providing. In this dynamic, establishing trust with the client is essential because that is the element that is central to the collaborative effort required for positive change. As the practitioner, it is important to respect and understand the client's perspective even if you disagree. It is up to you to use the resistance that the client will have regarding change and convert that into genuine motivation. Here are motivational interview techniques that can be used during a session:

ASKING FOR PERMISSION

Asking for permission is basically asking respectfully if the discussion regarding the client's harmful behaviors can be addressed. This shows respect for the client and takes away the authoritarian view that client can have with the therapist. Some questions to ask include:

- "Is it okay if we discuss some of the behaviors that you are engaging in?"
- "I know that you are having some heart issues, can we talk about how your daily living may be contributing?"

PROMOTING CHANGE QUESTIONS

The construct of using change questions is to help guide the client in the direction towards positive change. Change questions can include:

- "If your situation does not change, what quality would you need to develop to deal with this on a daily basis?"
- "If you did decide to change, what is one possible positive that could come out of it?"

EXTREME CHANGE QUESTIONS

These types of questions can be used when the client is in the pre-contemplation stage of motivation and shows little desire to change. Questions that can be asked include:

- "If you do not change, what is the worst that could happen to you?"
- "What is the best-case scenario for you if you stay where you currently are? And what could be the alternative for you?"

PROMOTING CHANGE THROUGH FUTURE-ORIENTED QUESTIONS

This concept is similar to the miracle question used in solution-focused therapy and it helps to identify what the client actually wants out of their life.

- "Let's say that you turned everything around for yourself, what would your life look like in the next year?"
- "If you did make the changes, what would your relationship with your daughter look like?"

USING SCALING QUESTIONS

As mentioned before with SFT, scaling questions allow for the practitioner and client to assess tangibly where the client is at. The following example is below:

- "On a scale of 1–10, how motivated are you to change?"
- "You currently stated a 2, what would it take to move you up to a 5?"
- "On a scale of 0–10, what is your current level of resistance?"
- "Can you describe where the resistance to change is coming from?"

USING OPEN-ENDED QUESTIONS

As a practitioner, it is important to use this tool so that you and the client can delve deeper into what is going on with the client. Open-ended questions allow for the client to expand their point of view about what is taking place in their life.

- "Tell me what has happened since our last session?"
- "What are the aspects of your life that are working for you right now?"
- "Describe your relationship with your partner right now?"

USING REFLECTIVE LISTENING

Reflective listening is used to show the client that you understand what the client is sharing, and it also demonstrates respect for the client. Examples include:

- "What I am hearing from you is..."
- "To rephrase what I heard, I heard you say..."
- "Is it true that you are sharing...?"

NORMALIZING THE EXPERIENCE

Normalizing is used to help the client understand that what they are going through is difficult, and that anyone would struggle with what is taking place in their life. It is also being able to convey that others are have gone similar experiences, and that they are not alone. Normalizing statements include:

- "A lot of people struggle with making changes in life because it is often easier to keep things the same."
- "I'm sure that many people feel that way and there is no reason to feel any shame about it."
- "There are always positive and negative consequences when engaging in a change effort."

WEIGHING THE PROS AND CONS

Weighing the pros and cons is known as a decisional balance. This is where the client will look at the positive and negative of their actions, and ultimately see how they weigh their current situation. Early on, most people will see more benefits in not changing, often seeing the change process as too difficult. However, as greater preparation occurs, the pros and cons will become more even, and eventually, the benefits of change will far outweigh the consequences. Example questions to ask include:

- "What are the benefits of changing?"
- "What are the consequences of not changing?"
- "It looks like the benefits of changing outweigh the decision to stay the same. What can we start with first to move towards change?"

BEING COLUMBO

Being Columbo is basically acting as a detective and identifying the inconsistencies in the statements made by the client during session. The goal is to identify the discrepancies in relation to the client's own value system, and to help piece together what can be done moving forward. Examples include:

- "You mentioned that drinking alcohol makes you more sociable with others, but at the same time, you are losing your support system in terms of friends and family. That is confusing."
- "You shared that it is your goal to be healthy, but you are smoking a pack a day. Does this make sense to you?"
- "You mentioned how you want to save money to buy a house, yet you are maxing your credit card. That seems contradictory to me."

PROVIDING FEEDBACK

Providing feedback in the form of questions allows the client to safely receive information, as well as allowing for self-evaluation. Feedback questions include:

- "Your drug of choice has had some serious consequences, including the loss of your job. How has that affected you?"
- "Your family during this time has been concerned about what has been going on with you. How do you see the situation?"
- "You shared last session that you are afraid that you won't follow through with treatment. Why did you share that?"

In closing, motivational interviewing techniques are effective on their own, but are also useful in conjunction with other therapy models. The techniques are powerful and allow for a healthy therapeutic alliance to be established. It also allows you as the practitioner to help guide the client to assess their level of motivation, find ways to improve their inner desire for change, and to go in the direction towards positive change.

COGNITIVE BEHAVIORAL THERAPY

Cognitive behavioral therapy is an effective form of therapy that is used to treat depression, anxiety disorders, substance abuse issues, and eating disorders. It is an evidence-based practice that has been proven to be effective in alleviating symptoms that an individual is suffering from. CBT is based off of research and clinical practice, and has been proven effective in promoting positive change. CBT is a short-term therapy and during the course of treatment, the client is able to identify irrational thoughts and belief systems, and is able to reframe and address the perspective from a more rational point of view. The ultimate outcome of the therapy model is to teach the client that though they cannot control their outside environment, they are able to control their thoughts, their feelings, and their behaviors in relation to their environment.

In relation to the thought process of CBT, there is a concept known as *automatic negative thoughts*. These thoughts are the immediate thoughts that emerge when confronted with an external situation. Automatic thoughts can either help or hurt the overall well-being of an individual based upon whether they are positive or negative. Negative automatic thoughts come through by perceived bad experiences in the past and the negative interpretation of it. Often, the viewpoint is illogical and non-objective. However, once these automatic negative thoughts become the actual belief of the person, this will lead to avoidant behaviors, and often be accompanied by symptoms of anxiety and depression. This can affect the many areas of one's life including family, friends, and employment. As the practitioner, it is important to conduct a *functional analysis*, which is identifying the beliefs and behavioral patterns of the individual, and how it is contributing to their current pathology. This allows for greater conceptualization of the client's specific belief patterns and behaviors. Ultimately this information would be used to educate the client, identify and disprove irrational and distorted beliefs, and ultimately reframe the client's thoughts and behaviors towards healthier means.

In addressing the behavioral components, it is important for the client to learn new skills and utilize healthier coping skills than those used in the past. This will require the client to slowly expose themselves to the situations that were previously being avoided because of the automatic negative thoughts, to slowly ingratiate oneself to disproving the irrational beliefs through engaging in positive behaviors while facing the avoided situation, and after the fact developing an overall healthier belief system because of the reframed experience. This is known as exposure therapy, and it is common when treating clients with phobias and anxiety disorders. Ultimately, the individual is able to not only become more rational in their thoughts, but more rational and purposeful in their own actions.

THE TENETS OF CBT

The tenets of cognitive behavioral therapy are a guide to help promote and maximize the outcomes for the clients that are being served. The best way to promote that is to follow some guidelines associated with CBT (Beck, 2011). Cognitive behavioral therapy is based off several core principles:

- Psychological issues are based off of irrational and faulty thinking that are not based on rationale and facts.
- Someone suffering from psychological issues can learn better ways of coping to help alleviate the unwanted symptoms that are occurring.
- By slowly engaging and seeking evidenced-based solutions, greater confidence and belief in oneself will naturally emerge.
- What is learned and practiced in the therapy session by the client will translate when it is used outside of the therapy session.

HOMEWORK IS AN IMPORTANT FEATURE IN THE USE OF CBT

Practitioners using this model will emphasize what is going on in the person's present life, versus fixating on what led them to the situation that comes from the past. Though information about the past is gathered, it is only used to address how their thought processes are currently being used. The focus is present- and future-oriented in its application and all interventions reflect that focus.

IMPLEMENTING COGNITIVE BEHAVIORAL THERAPY (USING THE ABCD MODEL)

In implementing CBT, it is important to understand the dynamic that is taking place with the client. In any situation that the client is involved in, the following occurs:

- A = the stimulus or environment
- B = thoughts
- C = feelings, physical reactions
- D = action

In any circumstance, any event which is A, can then trigger a thought which is B, which then will evoke a feeling which is C, and then will then lead to an action D. For example, take a random occurrence as a stranger passing by without acknowledging you while walking on the sidewalk. This incident is completely out of your control in terms of whether or not that stranger acknowledges you, and has nothing to do with what you did or did not do. However, that incident (A), based on how it is interpreted, will trigger automatic thoughts (B), and will then cycle to a physical sensation and feelings (C), and will produce an action (D). Looking at it using the model:

- A = The stimulus or environment: A stranger passes by without acknowledging you
- B = Thoughts: "I am no good and such a loser that no one wants to talk to me."
- C = Feelings, Physical Reactions: Anxiety, Dejection, and Feeling Physically Tense
- D = Action: Make the decision to not greet anyone on the street

If the client were to interpret the situation as shown above, it would be educating the client that it was not the circumstance that was the cause of how he felt and acted, but that the event was the trigger or stimulus for the already existing automatic negative thoughts that are constantly going off within the client's own head. The client in this situation does not know what the other individual was thinking, and so the decision to no longer greet anyone comes from an irrational point of view.

USE SEQUENTIAL QUESTIONING

When implementing CBT, it is important that when your client is describing situations about what is taking place in their life, that you are organizing the framework by asking sequential questions. Sequential questioning involves addressing:

- A = Event "What was the situation that took place?"
- B = Thought "What were you thinking when this happened?"
- C = Feeling, Physical Sensation "What were you feeling when all of this was taking place?"
- D = Action "How did you respond after that?"

For example, using the stranger who passes by without acknowledging the client, there would need to be follow-up questions that address the thought process of the client (B), the feelings and physical sensations of the client (C), and the action that was taken by the client (D). Below is an example:

Social Worker:	You seem very discouraged right now.
Client:	Yes, I had something just happen on the way here.
Social Worker:	**(A = Event)** What was the situation that took place?
Client:	**(A)** A stranger passed by without acknowledging me when I looked at him.
Social Worker:	**(B = Thought)** What were you thinking when this happened?
Client:	**(B)** I am no good and such a loser that no one wants to talk to me.
Social Worker:	**(C = Feelings)** What were you feeling when all of this was taking place?
Client:	**(C)** I had a lot of anxiety and my body began tensing up.
Social Worker:	**(D = Action)** How did you respond after that?
Client:	**(D)** I made the decision not to greet or acknowledge anyone after that.

By going through sequential questioning, you are able to see the cycle of how the event (A), triggered the automatic thought (B), which then produced the feelings and physical sensations (C), which lead to the action (D).

IDENTIFY COGNITIVE DISTORTIONS

Cognitive distortions are simply ways that our mind convinces us of something that isn't really true. These inaccurate thoughts are usually used to reinforce negative thinking and are part of the automatic negative thoughts that occur from a negative cognitive schema. Cognitive distortions without being challenged and looked at can seem internally rational and accurate, but really only serve to keep a person from continuing to feel bad about oneself. For instance, a person might tell themselves, "I always fail when I try to do something new and so there is no point in trying." This is an example of all-or-nothing thinking or black-and-white thinking, and puts belief systems in absolutes. If this individual were challenged rationally, there would at least be one situation that the individual did succeed in and thus would dispute the irrational and distorted claim.

Cognitive distortions are at the core of what many cognitive behavioral therapists try to address and help a person to change in psychotherapy. By learning to correctly identify a cognitive distortion, an individual can then answer the negative thinking back, and refute it. By challenging the negative thinking over and over again using reason and facts, the negative cycle will diminish overtime and be automatically replaced by more rational and balanced thinking. Here are the most common cognitive distortions:

- **all-or-nothing thinking**—thinking that something is all good or all bad. Thinking in absolutes, black-and-white thinking
- **overgeneralization**—viewing a negative event as a never ending pattern of defeat
- **mental filtering**—dwelling only on the negatives and foregoing the positives
- **magnification or minimization**—blowing things out of proportion or shrinking the importance of an event
- **emotional reasoning**—basing decisions solely on how you feel even though feelings are not a good predictor of outcomes
- **personalization and blame**—blaming oneself for something that you were not entirely responsible for. Excessive guilt that is irrational
- **labeling**—instead of "I made a mistake" it becomes "I am a jerk and I am a loser."
- **should statements**—"I should do or should have done this," "I must do this" versus focusing on what can be done
- **catastrophizing**—expecting a disaster before doing something "What if I totally just lose it and break down?"
- **fallacy of fairness**—the belief that you know what is fair and that others who do not agree with you are just wrong
- **control fallacy**—the belief that you are at the mercy of your environment and have no control of your life
- **being right**—the belief that others have to prove that you are wrong versus being open-minded and listening to all possible perspectives
- **being a martyr**—seeing all of your self-sacrifice and self-denial as a righteous act, and being angry that others are not wanting to help you in return
- **jumping to conclusions** in the form of:
    - ▸ **mind reading**—assuming that people are acting negatively to you when there is no definitive evidence. You are assuming that you can read other people's minds.
    - ▸ **fortune-telling**—predicting that things will turn out badly without any factual evidence
    - ▸ **"what if" statements**—a hypothetical statement that is neither true nor false that either will make you feel hopeful or feel anxiety about the future

Identifying cognitive distortions is vital in helping the client to identify and challenge their unhealthy thought processes. Looking back at the previous example with the stranger passing the client by:

Social Worker:	You seem very discouraged right now.
Client:	Yes, I had something just happen on the way here.
Social Worker:	**(A = Event)** What was the situation that took place?
Client:	**(A)** A stranger passed by without acknowledging me when I looked at him.
Social Worker:	**(B = Thought)** What were you thinking when this happened?
Client:	**(B)** I am no good and such a loser that no one wants to talk to me.
Social Worker:	**(C = Feelings)** What were you feeling when all of this was taking place?
Client:	**(C)** I had a lot of anxiety and my body began tensing up.
Social Worker:	**(D = Action)** How did you respond after that?
Client:	**(D)** I made the decision not to greet or acknowledge anyone after that.
Social Worker:	Did you ever meet that stranger before?
Client:	No, I never saw that person before.
Social Worker:	So the stranger not acknowledging you probably had nothing to do with you and was probably more about that person just being that way or having a bad day.
Client:	I did not think about it that way. I assumed that I was the cause of his unhappiness. **(Personalization and blame)**
Social Worker:	Also, when you decided to not greet or acknowledge anyone after that, weren't you assuming that all people would then be unhappy and not want to acknowledge you?
Client:	Yes, after that I assumed that all people who I was around would not want to acknowledge me at all. **(All-or-nothing thinking)**

It is important to use sequential questioning to identify the internal cycle that is taking place within the client, as well as being able to identify the cognitive distortions which are causing and discord based on the client's misperception.

IDENTIFY THE COGNITIVE SCHEMA OF THE CLIENT

A *cognitive schema* is an organizing framework of the mind. Schemas represent patterns of internal experiences that include memories, beliefs, emotions, and thoughts. The patterns of thoughts if it comes from a maladaptive framework, will then produce automatic negative thoughts. Maladaptive schemas can come from bad experiences that have been interpreted in an irrational manner. As CBT is being performed, automatic negative thoughts will be challenged going from the irrational to the rational, but it is also important to identify the organizing framework from where these thoughts stem from. For example, let's take a look at Jason who is an 18-year-old student with some automatic negative thoughts:

- "I do all of this because my parents want me to instead of me wanting to."
- "I have to fulfill what my friends want or else I will not fit and I'll disappoint them."
- "The more I do, the more is required of me."
- "Accomplishments just mean more pressure and stress."

The core or cognitive schema for Jason would be something to the effect of "I must live for others and not for myself." It appears that Jason is doing well in school but his interpretation of his circumstances, even positive ones, are creating a negative cycle, and appear to be stemming from his negative cognitive schema. Here is another example:

> *Three people get into the exact same accident at the intersection and all three individuals were uninjured. Damages to the cars are equal as the front bumper has a slight dent and the severity of damage is exactly the same for all of them.*

Now let's take a look at the automatic thoughts of each person involved in the accident:

> *Person 1- "This is another example of how my life always sucks."*

> *Person 2- "I need to be more careful and be even more cautious about driving as well as every area of my life."*

> *Person 3- "I am so thankful that no one was hurt and it could have been much worse. I am so blessed and will need to be more careful when going through an intersection."*

In this example, the first person with their automatic thought of "This is another example of how my life always sucks" has a cognitive schema that is something to the effect of:

> *"My life sucks no matter what."*

The second person with the automatic thought of "I need to be more careful and be even more cautious about driving as well as every area of my life" probably has a cognitive schema of:

"Life is about being careful and cautious no matter what."

And finally the third person with the automatic thought of "I am so thankful that no one was hurt and it could have been much worse. I am so blessed and will need to be more careful when going through an intersection" has a cognitive schema of:

"I have a really great life and I am so blessed."

In this example, the exact same thing happened to each of the three individuals, and yet the incident was interpreted in three different ways based on the automatic thought that emerged, and the cognitive schema of each individual. It is vital to educate and teach the client how the external environment is the trigger for the internal cycle of thoughts, feelings, and emotions that emerge from it.

GOING FROM THE IRRATIONAL TO THE RATIONAL USING THE ABCDEF MODEL

When the client comes into therapy and begins a working relationship with you using cognitive behavioral therapy, it is important to understand the structured dynamic that is taking place within the therapeutic relationship. As discussed earlier, the ABCD model for the client is:

- A = the stimulus or environment
- B = thoughts
- C = feelings, physical reactions
- D = action

When going over this with the client, you are helping the client to identify their cognitive distortions and make more sense of it from a rational point of view. *Irrational thinking* is thinking without reason or inadequate use of information. Conversely, *rational thinking* is using logic and reasoning that is based on facts. Having the client understand this dynamic is your role to help the client go from:

- the irrational to the rational
- eliminating negative behaviors to engaging in positive behaviors that will benefit the client

To do this, the following model must take place:

- A is the external (activating) event to which the individual is exposed
- B is the belief that the individual has about A
- C is the emotion or behavior that results from B
- D is the action that resulted from C
- E is the social worker's attempt to dispute and alter the individual's irrational belief
- F is the alternate thought (rational) or belief that results from D

Your job as the therapist in the therapy session is to take ABCD from the client and to use E and F to create an alternate solution:

- Dispute and alter the individual's irrational belief (**E**)
- Provide an alternate thought or rational belief (**F**)

This then will help to create a positive action for the client. Looking at the previous interaction with the client identifying the stranger not acknowledging him:

Social Worker:	You seem very discouraged right now.
Client:	Yes, I had something just happen on the way here.
Social Worker:	**(A = Event)** What was the situation that took place?
Client:	**(A)** A stranger passed by without acknowledging me when I looked at him.
Social Worker:	**(B = Thought)** What were you thinking when this happened?
Client:	**(B)** I am no good and such a loser that no one wants to talk to me.
Social Worker:	**(C = Feelings)** What were you feeling when all of this was taking place?
Client:	**(C)** I had a lot of anxiety and my body began tensing up.
Social Worker:	**(D = Action)** How did you respond after that?
Client:	**(D)** I made the decision not to greet or acknowledge anyone after that.
Social Worker:	Did you ever meet that stranger before?
Client:	No I never saw that person before.
Social Worker:	So the stranger not acknowledging you probably had nothing to do with you and was probably more about that person just being that way or having a bad day. **(E = Disputing the irrational belief)**
Client:	I did not think about it that way. I assumed that I was the cause of his unhappiness. **(Personalization and blame)**

Social Worker:	So it is a fair and logical assumption that since the stranger does not know you, his not acknowledging you had nothing to do with you. **(F = Alternate rational belief)**
Client:	Yes, that makes complete sense.
Social Worker:	Also when you decided to not greet or acknowledge anyone after that. Weren't you assuming that all people would then be unhappy and not want to acknowledge you? **(E = Disputing the irrational belief)**
Client:	Yes, after that I assumed that all people who I was around would not want to.
Social Worker:	Is it fair to say that the stranger's behavior had nothing to do with you, and it would be silly to not be friendly to others assuming that all people are unfriendly? **(F = Alternate rational belief)**
Client:	Totally! It kind of seems silly now, and I can recognize that the circumstance was not the cause of my thoughts, but more about me.

PUTTING IT ALL TOGETHER

Let's take a look at the vignette below and begin to put everything we learned about CBT together:

VIGNETTE

Paul, age 40, comes in and shares that "I suffer from a lot of anxiety and I always feel on edge." The Ct states that he has come in because "recently I interviewed for a job that I really wanted and I was not offered the job." He adds that "I always fail and things never really work out for me." The Ct adds that "other people do not really understand me and because I am so different, I cannot really relate to people." The Ct currently lives in an apartment by himself, but he shares that "I need to find a job fast because my savings is dwindling down." He adds that "I am good for about four more months, and after that I will be on the street." Paul states that he has two good friends and that "I have a pretty good relationship with my family" but "like I said, I am so different from others that I cannot really be understood. I can tell that people do not really like me. I am very intuitive and I can feel things a lot of times." Paul adds that "Wherever I go, I always feel like I am at the mercy of others." He adds that he drinks about three times a week having about 4–6 beers when he goes out.

From here, let's perform the following:

- Establish an initial treatment plan for the client
- Identify the cognitive distortion of the client's statements
- Use sequential questioning (**ABCD**)
- Create transition questions to challenge irrational belief (**E**) and to create an alternate thought (**F**)

INITIAL TREATMENT PLAN FOR THE CLIENT:

- Refer for crisis intervention services if needed
- Provide a referral for medical check-up
- Provide a referral to a psychiatrist for a medication evaluation
- Referral for alcohol treatment centers as well as AA
- Provide individual counseling to the client on a weekly basis
- Provide a referral for employment services as well as to the employment benefit services

USING CBT WITH EACH OF THE CLIENT'S STATEMENTS

Client statement

> *"I suffer from a lot of anxiety and I always feel on edge."*

Cognitive distortion

- All-or-nothing thinking

Sequential questioning

- What do you feel anxious about? (**B**)
- How does that make you feel? (**C**)
- When did this happen? (**A**)
- How did you respond? (**D**)

Transition questions (**E** and **F**)

- Do you always feel anxious?
- When do you not feel anxious?

Client statement

> *"I always fail and things never really work out for me."*

Cognitive distortions

- all-or-nothing thinking
- catastrophizing
- overgeneralizing

Sequential questioning

- Was there a time when a situation did not work out for you? (**A**)
- How did you feel when that happened? (**C**)
- What were you thinking at that time? (**B**)
- How did you react to that? (**D**)

Transition question (**E** and **F**)

- Is there a time when something did work out for you?
- So that means that sometimes you do have success?

Client statement

> *"Other people do not really understand me and because I am so different, I cannot really relate to people."*

Cognitive distortions

- blaming
- labeling
- mental filtering

Sequential questioning

- How do you feel when you think this?
- When you are around others, how do you respond?
- In what ways are you the same as others?
- When you identify these traits, how do you feel?

Transition question (**E** and **F**)

- If you were to focus on these similarities, how could you use this to better engage with others?

Client statement

> *"Like I said, I am so different from others that I cannot really be understood."*

Cognitive distortions

- labeling
- personalization

Sequential questioning

- Was there a circumstance that made you feel misunderstood? (**A**)
- What were you thinking during that time? (**B**)
- How do you feel when you think this way? (**C**)
- How did you react when that happened? (**D**)

Transition question (**E** and **F**)

- What do you want to be understood about?

Client statement

"I can tell that people do not really like me."

Cognitive distortions

- mind reading
- personalization

Sequential questioning

- How do you feel when you think this way? (**C**)
- Was there a time when people did not like you? (**A**)
- What were you thinking during this time? (**B**)
- How did you react when this happened around others? (**D**)

Transition question (**E** and **F**)

- Are you able to read people's minds?
- Can you try to read mine right now?

Client statement

"I am very intuitive and I can feel things a lot of times."

Cognitive distortions:

- emotional reasoning

Sequential questioning

- Was there a time where you can explain when you used your intuition? (**A**)
- How did you respond? (**D**)
- How did you feel when that happened? (**C**)
- What were you thinking at that time? (**B**)

Transition question (**E** and **F**)

- Was there a time when you felt something to be true but it turned out wrong?

Client statement

"Wherever I go, I always feel like I am at the mercy of others."

Cognitive distortion

- control fallacy

Sequential questioning

- Was there a circumstance that made you feel helpless? (A)
- What were you thinking during that time? (B)
- How do you feel when you think this way? (C)
- How did you react when that happened? (D)

Transition question (**E** and **F**)

- Were you literally and figuratively being controlled by others to the point that you could not move?

In closing, when implementing cognitive behavioral therapy, you want to be able to apply the various techniques that you have learned in this section. This is a very basic understanding of the model that will hopefully help you feel more confident in implementing this with the client you work with.

PSYCHODYNAMIC THERAPY

Psychodynamic therapy focuses on the unconscious processes that are manifested in the client's everyday problems. This is on the other end of the spectrum in relation to brief therapy and cognitive behavioral therapy, which are present-focused and not past-based. The premise is defining how the client's unresolved past conflicts are continually infiltrating the present time. The goal of therapy is to provide self-awareness to the client by identifying the unresolved conflicts and symptoms, bringing that awareness to the client which is consciousness, and separating the needs of the past versus the present. The process requires deep exploration of the client's pathology and the ability of the practitioner to adapt to tying together common themes of behavior that are dysfunctional to the client. The theory comes from four schools of psychotherapy which are:

- Freudian psychology
- Ego psychology
- Object relations
- Self-psychology

Freudian psychology which comes from Freud himself is based off of drive theory. The concept is that sexual and assertive energies are seeking to be fulfilled which comes from the id, guided by the ego. However, given the external environment one is born in, the ego must balance fitting appropriate norms of society, and at the same time try to find ways of fulfilling sexual drives and desires. If these energies become stunted or held back due to societal norms, defense mechanisms become constructed in order to try to deal with the balancing act that the ego is trying to engage in.

Ego psychology, which stems from the work of Freud, addresses the issue of ego functioning in relation to the world that the client lives in. The concept addresses the client's ability to adapt, to be resilient in relation to ego functioning and to be clear in their own reality. Object relations focuses on the way one is shaped by the relationships that are surrounding them. Based on this premise, suffering and pain comes from the inability to maintain healthy relationships with others. Object relations seeks to find that balance of being a part of the objects or significant others in your life, while at the same time being different enough to be your own person. Lastly, self-psychology focuses on the development of one's own self-esteem. In this construct, self-esteem is defined by an individual's concept of self based upon the established rules and regulations of one's surroundings, along with the ability to differentiate oneself from those around you. Each of these four schools of psychology have contributed to the formation of the therapy model that is psychodynamic theory.

Freud (Langa, 2016) believes that the unconscious mind is the primary source of human behavior. In relation to psychodynamic theory, he believes:

- Childhood experiences become the template and foundation of who you become as an adult.

- Most psychological pain in everyday life stems from unresolved past issues that occurred in childhood.
- Most dysfunctional behavior comes from unconscious drives.

From this premise, most behaviors can be defined by looking into the past and not the present. Different from present-oriented therapy models, psychodynamic theory believes that if you do not address the core problems which come from the past, then present-oriented solutions become only a Band-Aid to problems. Therefore in treatment, it is a matter of tying in the past behavior and consciously connecting the pattern that the client is continuously engaging in. This is what forms the personality of an individual. Langa (2016), in her work using psycho-dynamics theory with South African teens and masculinity, found that much of what each participant perceived to be masculine came more from their early years as a child growing up. Often these male teens' struggle with defining masculinity was their core perception of masculinity as children versus the direct conflict with their current beliefs as teens. This inner struggle or unconscious drive, could only be solved by consciously bringing past views on masculinity to awareness and to change it at present time. The South African teens were then more able to come to terms with their own personality. Freud defined three parts of the personality which is the id, ego, and superego. The *id* is the drive component and comes from the primitive parts of being a human being. The id consists of the *Eros* which is the libido, and *Thanatos* which are the survival instincts. The second part of our personality is the *ego*, which is the mediator between trying to satisfy the id's desires and fitting into one's own existing society. The last component of the personality is the *superego*, which is the internalized moral standards learned from the existing society one lives in, including the influence of the parents. Freud believes that ultimately, it is a matter of addressing and balancing the various drives and the components of personality to achieve a sense of peace within oneself.

FREUD'S PSYCHOSEXUAL DEVELOPMENT

Freud's belief in the concept of drive theory is the source of how he views human development. Freud believes that there are five stages that an individual must go through, and if a person becomes stunted in any stage, the forming of a pathology becomes developed. Each psychosexual stage is viewed as a conflict, and in each stage, a resolution to each drive state must be resolved. Freud describes the concept of *conflict resolution*, which means that each psychosexual stage is a battle, and the particular drive associated in each stage needs to be satisfied, meaning the battle must be won. Therefore, the libido needs to overcome and win in five successive battles for successful coping to emerge. Below are the five psychosexual stages:

- **oral stage** (birth–1)—the mouth is the source of fixation and unresolved issues at this stage can lead to oral fixation that can come out in the form of smoking
- **anal stage** (1–3 years)—The anus is the source of fixation and this is the time of toilet training. If unresolved, issues can come out in the form of being stingy, anal, and being obsessive.
- **phallic stage** (3–6 years)—The genitals are the source of fixation. This is where the oedipal complex occurs and if unresolved, can lead to being sexually exploitative later on in life.
- **latency stage** (6–12 years)—The source of fixation is on sexual gratification and identifying with the libido
- **genital stage** (12+ years)—The source of fixation is on the genitals and the goal is to establish sexual satisfaction and satisfying relationships.

As stated earlier, each successive stage or battle needs to be completed or else psychopathology will emerge. Below is the pathology that can take place if each stage is unresolved:

ORAL STAGE PATHOLOGY

As an adult, unresolved conflict can lead to a person developing an oral fixation. This can come in the form of smoking, sucking on their thumbs, or even biting their nails. Freud believed that these actions would occur under stress.

ANAL STAGE PATHOLOGY

Unresolved conflict during this stage could come in the form of shame and negative experiences with the anus when being toilet trained. As an adult, this can come out in the form of being rigid, punishing to others, being selfish, and obsessed with orderliness. On the flip side, a healthy individual during this stage would be the opposite and would be more giving and sharing with others.

PHALLIC STAGE PATHOLOGY

This is the stage where the Oedipal and Electra complex is developed for males and females, respectively. The oedipal conflict for the boy is having sexual desires for the mother, but fearing that the father may take her away because of the fixation on the penis. Conversely, the Electra complex is the desire of the female to possess the father and struggling with the fact that she does not have a penis. For both the male and female to resolve this conflict, one must identify with the same sex parent and learn the characteristics related to that sex. If it goes unresolved, Freud believed that this would lead to romantic relationship failures in the future.

LATENCY STAGE PATHOLOGY

Freud during this stage believed that no sexual development takes place. He believed that the energy becomes repressed and becomes channeled in outward activities that include engaging in school activities and friendships. This is the stage where human relationships become. Unresolved conflicts in this stage can lead to isolation and the inability to make and sustain meaningful relationships.

GENITAL STAGE PATHOLOGY

The genital stage is where puberty begins, and it is the time of sexual exploration and experimentation. Freud believed that this is where intercourse becomes a focus and if unresolved, can lead to an adult suffering from performance anxiety and not engaging in sexual intercourse. Most sexual actions will then be concentrated on kissing and oral sex versus intercourse of any kind.

The pathology that can develop from unresolved conflicts or lost battles will come out in the form of defense mechanisms in the future. It is by addressing these unresolved drive states that healthier coping skills can emerge.

DEFENSE MECHANISMS

Defense mechanisms are psychological strategies that are unconsciously used to protect a person from anxiety arising from unacceptable thoughts or feelings. Freud noted a number of ego defenses which he referenced throughout his written work. Defense mechanisms include:

- **dichotomous thinking**—all-or-nothing thinking going from one extreme to the other

- **displacement**—pitting issue onto another person when he/she is upset at someone else
- **idealizing**—trying to see perfection in everything
- **reaction formation**—doing the opposite of how the client is really feeling
- **projection**—issues of the self are being projected on to the others
- **isolation**—withdrawing from undesired symptoms
- **regression**—going back to a previous level of functioning
- **denial**—withdrawing and suppressing what has taken place
- **passive/aggressive behaviors**—withdrawing and being overly accommodating to becoming extremely volatile within moments
- **splitting**—using others in your environment to diffuse your emotions to more manageable levels

The use of defense mechanisms are utilized to protect oneself from feelings of anxiety or guilt, which arise because one feels threatened, or because the id or superego is becoming too demanding (Freud, 1937). Ego defense mechanisms are natural and normal, and need to be worked through. If defense mechanisms get out of control through constant frequency, a neurosis will develop that includes states of intense anxiety, phobias, and obsessions (Ziegler, 2016).

It is important during the therapeutic process to identify defense mechanisms and to help consciously create healthier outcomes for the client in present time.

SUMMARIZING PSYCHODYNAMIC THERAPY

In summary, the id's libido (sexual energy) centers on the different parts of the body during each psychosexual stage of development and personality results from that dynamic. Failure to resolve conflict at each psychosexual stage leads to insufficient gratification and cognitive distortions in the form of defense mechanisms. *Personality theory* states that structural and developmental processes are based off of the needs to satisfy drives.

Structural theory has 3 structures which are the *Id*, *Ego*, and *Superego*.

- Id—life and death instincts, source of psychic energy. Operates on the pleasure principle and seeks immediate gratification to avoid tension
- Ego—develops at 6 months of age in response to the Id's inability to gratify all of its needs. Defers id's gratification through rational thinking

- Superego—emerges at 4–5 years old and represents the internalization of society's values and standards conveyed by the parents through rewards and punishments

The maladaptive behavior based on this theory stems from an unconscious and unresolved conflict that occurred during childhood. It is the goal of therapy to have the client experience a cathartic, emotional release that will recall the unconscious material and allow the client to heal. Therapy goals and techniques that will need to be enacted will be:

- confrontation
- clarification
- interpretation
- working through

The analogy of understanding all of this is that the id is the horse, the ego is the rider of the horse, and the superego is the land in which the id and ego navigate. One's conscience that stems from the superego are the handles that allow the horse and rider to navigate throughout society, and ideal self is the direction the horse is constantly being guided, even though this self does not exist and the destination cannot be reached.

THE CLIENT-THERAPIST DYNAMIC

During the therapeutic process of using psychoanalysis, the client will be involved in the process of *transference*, which is the redirection of the client's feelings from their significant relationships on to the therapist. The focus in therapy in large part is for the therapist to help the client recognize the transference of feelings from their past relationships, and exploring the meaning of those relationships. Because the transference between patient and therapist happens on an unconscious level, the therapist must be largely concerned with a client's unconscious material, and use the transference to reveal unresolved conflicts that the client needs to work through (clinpsy.org, 2018). Conversely, during the process of transference, there will be the development of *countertransference*. Countertransference is defined as redirection of a therapist's feelings toward a client, based on their own emotional entanglements towards the client (clinpsy.org, 2018). For example, a client who in the past experienced domestic abuse and is currently treating a client who is going a similar circumstance, may become overly emotional and involved in the client's life. A therapist's understanding of one's own countertransference is nearly as critical as the understanding of the transference of the client. It is important for the therapist to understand their own emotional processes so that it will not thwart the therapeutic process for the client. If the therapist is able to regulate their own emotions in the therapeutic relationship, the therapeutic dynamic can give the therapist valuable insight into what the client is attempting to elicit from their own unconscious.

UTILIZING HEALTHY COPING SKILLS

In assisting the client to help process their unconscious processes, and to help them understand how it is currently affecting their life now, the following process needs to occur:

- introjection—looking within to find out how you are contributing to the problem (identify unhealthy coping skill[s])
- identification—identifying and acknowledge the problem(s)
- anticipation—preparing for the discomfort in a healthy way once the problem has been identified
- sublimation—taking the unhealthy emotions and using it in a positive way
- altruism—using the difficulty to help others

Introjection is the process of being able to identify how the client is contributing to their own problems. This process involves identifying defense mechanisms of the client and taking that information to trace back unconscious patterns. The next process is identification. Identification is clearly stating the problem to the client and linking how unresolved past issues are contributing to the client now. Usually if there is an unresolved conflict, the problem will continuously occur in the client's life over and over. Anticipation involves understanding that once the problem has been identified, that the uncomfortable unconscious feelings will emerge in present time, and the client needs to understand and prepare for that. Sublimation is the next step and that involves the client then taking the insight that they have and using it in a healthy way at present time. No person can go back to their past, but one can come to terms with it by living their best life now. Finally, there is altruism, which is using the difficulty that the client has experienced, and using it to help others who are going through similar circumstances. During the therapeutic process, your job is explore with the client what is taking place in their life, help the client to come to terms with their unresolved conflicts, and have them live their best life now.

IMPLEMENTING THE THERAPEUTIC MODEL

Below is a vignette about the client, John:

VIGNETTE

John, a 30–year-old male, comes in to the clinic to see you. He states, "I have been having thoughts of suicide and it has happened ever since I had this situation at work." He shares, "I have been picked on by coworkers and even the supervisor there makes fun of me and puts me down." John adds, "I try to stand up for myself but in the end I just end up folding. I am even getting heart palpitations from it." John states that this has been going on for over a year and that he began seeing a therapist as well as working with human resources. John continues, "When it was time for me to stick up for myself and have the meeting with my boss, supervisor, and my human resources representative, I ended up just quitting." John states, "After I quit, I ended up drinking every day and isolating myself from everyone."

THE FIRST SESSION

The first aspect of treating John would be to establish an initial treatment plan for him. The treatment plan would include:

- assessing for possible suicide and providing crisis intervention
- making a referral to his primary physician to address his heart palpitations
- referral for a psychiatrist for a medication evaluation
- providing individual counseling services to the client
- providing a referral to alcohol treatment program to address his drinking
- providing a referral to legal services who can possibly provide a consultation to him regarding his workplace situation

THE THIRD SESSION

John ends up coming back for several weeks and this is what comes up during the third session:

> John, during this session tells you, "What happened at work is the worst thing to ever happen to me and it has totally ruined the rest of my life." John adds, "I am always wishing that there could be a place where I can

just be me. A place where there is no suffering and everyone can just be happy." John shares, "This has been happening my whole life and when I was in high school, I was always picked on and made fun of. I have never had any friends and I have always just been isolated my whole life." John states, "I have one friend but I try not to hang out with him because he is weird and he just doesn't get stuff. What a loser!"

Given the information that we have about John from both the initial session as well as the third session, we can begin to implement psychodynamic therapy using the healthy coping skills for the client:

Introjection—looking within to find out how you are contributing to the problem (identify unhealthy coping skill[s])

The unhealthy coping skills that John is engaging in are:

Regression

Client Statement: "This has been happening my whole life and when I was in high school, I was always picked on and made fun of. I have never had any friends and I have always just been isolated my whole life."

John is regressing back to when he was in high school and engaging in the same behaviors that contributed to him being picked on then, and that is now happening to him at work.

Dichotomous thinking

Client Statement: "What happened at work is the worst thing to ever happen to me and it has totally ruined the rest of my life."

John is using all-or-nothing thinking going from one extreme to the other sharing how his whole life is totally over, even though he can learn from this and still has many options in front of him.

Idealizing

Client Statement: "I am always wishing that there could be a place where I can just be me. A place where there is no suffering and everyone can just be happy."

John here, instead of addressing the problem, in reality is hoping and imagining a world where there is no suffering so that he does not have to deal with his pain and discomfort anymore.

Projection

> *Client Statement: "I have one friend but I try not to hang out with him because he is weird and he just doesn't get stuff. What a loser!"*

John here is taking his problems and instead of seeing it in himself is projecting his own feelings of being a loser onto his close friend. If John were more conscious, he would see that he is actually talking about himself.

Identification—identifying and acknowledge the problem(s)

Stating the Problem:

John does not know how to stand up for himself and this is a pattern that can be traced back to high school.

John has had this problem his whole life and it seems to be repeating itself over and over again. John had difficulty in high school and since that went unresolved, he is experiencing it still as an adult in his workplace

Anticipation—preparing for the discomfort in a healthy way once the problem has been identified

What John needs to prepare for:

John needs to prepare for the uncomfortable feelings that he feels and accept that if he does not work on healing his past and building skills in the present, that this will continue to occur.

John needs to acknowledge a pattern of relationships that correlate between high school and now and prepare for the fact that this may continue to occur until he can resolve this dynamic.

Sublimation—taking the unhealthy emotions and using it in a positive way

Making this a positive for John:

John can learn from this situation and be able to handle himself around difficult people, as well as develop meaningful relationships in the future.

John through this therapeutic process can come to terms with his unresolved conflict, as well as become the strong and resilient person that he deeply desires to be. He also has the chance through this process to not be so isolated and develop relationships moving forward.

Altruism—using the difficulty to help others

How John can benefit society:

John can use this experience to help others like his friend.

It appears that John's friend is also suffering from the same struggles that John is currently going through, and he can use this experience to help his friend overcome as well.

THE NINTH SESSION

As John is making progress, the following takes place during the ninth session:

> *John during the eighth session tells you, "When I was a kid, my mom and dad would always put me down and tell me not to talk. Whenever I did assert myself, I would get punished and just feel really helpless." John adds, "I always wanted a family like the Cosby show where everyone would just treat each other nicely. I still dream of having my own family now." John also shares, "My one friend that I have, I have been yelling at him whenever I talk about what happened to me at work because he just doesn't get it."*

Introjection—looking within to find out how you are contributing to the problem (identify unhealthy coping skill[s])

The unhealthy coping skills that John is engaging in are:

Displacement

> *Client Statement: "My one friend that I have, I have been yelling at him whenever I talk about what happened to me at work because he just doesn't get it."*

John is taking out his frustrations on his friend where it is safe for him to act out his anger, instead of directing it and addressing it towards his workplace, which is where the real problem lies.

Regression

> *Client Statement "When I was a kid, my mom and dad would always put me down and tell me not to talk. Whenever I did assert myself, I would get punished and just feel really helpless."*

John was not only experiencing this inability to stand up for himself in high school, but it was learned by the way his parents treated him. Whenever John would be assertive, it would be met with anger and hostility, and so John learned that it was not okay to stand up for yourself ever.

Idealizing

> *Client Statement "I always wanted a family like the Cosby show where everyone would just treat each other nicely. I still dream of having my own family now."*

John is dreaming of having a family like the television show where everything is scripted and perfect. Instead of dealing with the reality of how painful his childhood was, he would often escape by dreaming of having what he saw on television.

Identification—identifying and acknowledge the problem(s)

Stating the problem:

John does not know how to stand up for himself and this is a pattern that can be traced back to high school as well as his upbringing with his parents.

In the third session, the problem was traced back to high school, but as the sessions progressed, John was able to see that it started with his relationship with his own parents. John has had this problem his whole life and it seems to be repeating itself over and over again. John had difficulty with his relationship with his parents, which then extended into high school and he is experiencing it still as an adult in his workplace since it has gone unresolved.

Anticipation—preparing for the discomfort in a healthy way once the problem has been identified

What John needs to prepare for:

John needs to prepare for the uncomfortable feelings that he feels which has been traced back to his relationship with his parents, and accept that if he does not work on healing his past and building skills in the present, that this will continue to occur.

John needs to acknowledge a pattern of relationships that correlate from his relationship with his parents, which then continued on to high school and is continuing to occur now. John needs to prepare for the fact that this may continue to occur until he can resolve this dynamic.

Sublimation—taking the unhealthy emotions and using it in a positive way

Making this a positive for John:

John can learn from this situation and be able to handle himself around difficult people, as well as develop meaningful relationships in the future. John specifically mentioned his own desire to have a family. He can use this as motivation to begin the process to do so.

John through this therapeutic process can come to terms with his unresolved conflict, as well as become the strong and resilient person that he deeply desires to be. He also has the chance through this process to not be so isolated and develop relationships moving forward which includes having his own family.

Altruism—using the difficulty to help others

How John can benefit society:

John can use this experience to help others like his friend but also his future children when he has his own family.

It appears that John's friend is also suffering from the same struggles that John is currently going through, and he can use this experience to help his friend overcome as well. Also, when he has his own family in the future, he can teach his children to be strong and independent adults who can live the life that they want to live.

This is a brief outline of how to use psychodynamic theory, which can often be confusing and difficult to implement. It often takes time to help clients process their feelings and identify patterns that are taking place in their life. It is also important to note that this therapy model does not suit every client that you treat and that you should always base the model of therapy that you use to cater to the client's needs.

ATTACHMENT THEORY

Attachment theory is focused on the bonds that are formed with other people throughout a lifetime. Similar to psychodynamic therapy, the model looks at the relationship between child and caregiver, and how that template affects the outcomes of future relationships that extend to adulthood. The model comes from John Bowlby and he believed that attachment was an evolutionarily process. He emphasized the importance of how a child bonds with the attachment figure, and based upon how that attachment is formed, either positive traits or pathology can occur. Krampe (2013) found that in her study with father attachments and children, that an innate symbol and structure is developed in the psyche of those children studied. It is through that subjective realm, that creates that foundation to how that child will interact to the outside world.

ATTACHMENT PHASES

Researchers Schaffer and Emerson (1964) conducted a longitudinal study with 60 infants, and based on their observations, they were able to identify four phases of attachment:

Pre-Attachment Phase—this takes place from birth to about 3 months and during this time, the baby shows no preference to any caregiver that is assigned.

Indiscriminate Attachment Phase—this takes place from one and a half months to two months, and the baby begins to discriminate between caregivers and seeks out the primary attachment of the mother.

Discriminate Attachment Phase—this occurs from seven to eleven months and the infant begins to form a strong bond with the primary caregiver. This is where separation anxiety from the caregiver begins to occur.

Multiple Attachment Phase—this takes place at about nine months and strong bonds begin to form with other attachment figures outside of the primary caregiver. This usually includes other family members.

It is emphasized the importance of attachment and how that shapes the foundation for the child moving forward. It is a straightforward process that defines the various levels of emotional bonding.

AINSWORTH'S EXPERIMENT

Attachment by definition is the emotional bond to another person. Bowlby emphasized the importance of early attachment and the importance it has for the lifetime of an individual. Mary Ainsworth expanded on the work of Bowlby and conducted what was known as the "strange situation experiment." She did research by observing children from twelve to eighteen months old. The research focused upon how children responded when separated from their caregiver during a specified period of time, and how they responded when the caregiver returned. Through this experimental research, Ainsworth was able to identify different attachment styles based upon the behaviors exhibited by each child. The research also gave a glimpse of how the child may turn out into adulthood. Ainsworth identified four attachments styles:

- secure
- anxious ambivalent
- anxious avoidant
- disorganized

PATTERNS OF ATTACHMENT

SECURE ATTACHMENT

Based on Ainsworth's study, children who were securely attached generally became visibly upset when their caregiver left, and appeared to be happy when their parent returned. Children with secure attachments will seek out their caregiver whenever they feel any anxiety or fear, and will be greeted with warmth and acceptance from the caregiver. Characteristics of a securely attached child are:

- able to separate from parents
- seek comfort from parents when frightened

- return of parents is met with positive emotions
- prefers parents to strangers

If this secure attachment becomes the template for the child, then as adults, they will tend to have:

- healthy and long-term relationships
- a positive view of oneself
- ability to effectively communicate and connect with others
- ability to ask for help and support when needed

Adults with a secure attachment are believed to have meaningful relationships throughout their lives, and live a life that is connected and not isolated from others.

ANXIOUS-AMBIVALENT ATTACHMENT

This attachment style during the experiment would reflect the child being suspicious of strangers while feeling greatly distressed when the caregiver left the room; however, the return of the caregiver did not bring support or comfort to the child, and the child would display dichotomous behavior of avoidance and anger towards the caregiver.

Based on this attachment, children:

- are wary of strangers
- become greatly distressed when the parents leave
- do not appear to be comforted by the return of the parent
- experience a mothering style which is engaged but on the mother's own terms

In this attachment style, the child's needs are ignored unless the focus of activity is dedicated to the needs of the parents. Children in this attachment style learn that their needs are not important, and that they must perform and please others in order to receive a positive response.

As an adult, an anxious-ambivalent type will:

- have difficulty maintaining close relationships
- often be overly insecure and needy with their intimate partners
- experience excessive long-term grief when relationships do not succeed

As adults, this attachment style will often have difficulty establishing and maintaining close and intimate relationships. This will often lead to over-dependence on their partner, unrealistic expectations, and suffering through constant feelings of guilt and anxiety.

ANXIOUS-AVOIDANT ATTACHMENT

Children with an anxious-avoidant attachment style often avoided their caregiver during observation. This avoidance became especially pronounced after a period of absence when the caregiver left the room. These children did not the reject the attention from their parent, but neither did they seek out comfort or contact from them. Even when the parent left and the stranger entered the room, these children showed little preference between the parent and the complete stranger.

A child with this attachment style will:

- often avoid their parents
- not seek out much comfort or support from their parents
- show little or no preference between strangers and parents

This style of attachment develops from a mothering style which is more disengaged. The child's needs are frequently not met and the child comes to believe that communication of needs has no influence on the mother. The child in this attachment style will become detached and not place much emphasis on their own emotions.

As adults, this attachment style will:

- have problems with intimacy in relationships
- invest little emotion in social or romantic relationships
- be unable or unwilling to share thoughts or feelings with others

As adults, this attachment style will invest little into intimate and close relationships. They will usually experience multiple relationships and will feel very little distress when they end. It is difficult for this attachment style to display empathy to those they are close to, and they can come across as aloof and callous.

DISORGANIZED ATTACHMENT

Children with this attachment style tend to have a chaotic relationship with their caregiver. These children often displayed dazed and aimless behavior, sometimes seeming confused or apprehensive in the presence of their caregiver.

A child with this attachment style will show:

- a mixture of avoidant and resistant behaviors towards the caregiver
- dazed, confused, and apprehensive gestures
- appearing frightened

Caregivers who provide this style of attachment are considered both frightened and frightening to the child. Interactions with a caregiver are often erratic and unstable, which will create the inability to form a coherent and interactive bond. Oftentimes the child will develop a sense of learned helplessness because of the lack of security and attachment with the caregiver.

As adults, those with this attachment style:

- may take on a parental role with others in their life
- will often act as the caregiver towards their own parents
- will be overly involved in helping those around them

Based on the confusion that takes place with this style of attachment, they will often become disorganized and their own personal life is often chaotic. On the flip side, they will often be very responsible and dedicated to helping others solve their problems, but will not use that focus and attention to solve their own.

The four attachment styles reflect the inner world of the child and how that template becomes the foundation for future attachments with others as adults. The model is useful and functional in its ability to help an individual understand the nature and foundation for relationship struggles, that include with family, friends, and intimate relationships.

IMPLEMENTING ATTACHMENT THEORY

Attachment theory is an effective way of exploring a client's template by looking at how an individual was raised, the attachment style that was formed because of their upbringing, and then tying in the patterns of maladaptive behaviors that the client is engaging in due to unresolved pathology. This takes a psychodynamic approach in the sense of focusing on the past and childhood experiences, but it also takes into account present relationship problems. From a practical point of view, when an individual can identify their own maladaptive patterns, this can help them be more proactive in relation to the relationship choices that are being made in present time. It also allows for a good foundation to look at relationship dynamics that are in place, and it helps both practitioner and client to go in a healthy direction. Attachment theory is a great tool when implementing couples therapy because each partner can explore both their attachment style and their present beliefs regarding their relationship.

COUPLES THERAPY

There was research performed that spanned 40 years on couples therapy in which they synthesized the approaches of the most successful methods of intervention. Providing couples therapy as a practitioner requires specialized training and skills as you navigate the nuance of identifying each person's individuality in conjunction with their identity as a couple. Practitioners who go into couples work take years of rigorous coursework and supervision, as well as continuing to receive education throughout their careers to learn about the field's newest developments. In terms of the study, there were five basic principles that were identified in providing effective couples therapy (Benson et al., 2012):

CHANGING THE VIEW OF THE RELATIONSHIP DYNAMIC

In the couples session, the practitioner must attempt to help both individuals to see their relationship in a more realistic manner. It is important to help the couple to see their dynamic in a healthier context and this is where the use of attachment theory can come into play. One way of looking at couples therapy is to have each individual see more of their similarities in the relationship than differences. This allows for each individual to see how this will be a team process, and an experience for individual healing to occur.

MODIFYING DYSFUNCTIONAL BEHAVIORS

Unhealthy coping skills that include blaming the other partner, or completely stonewalling and not talking to the partner needs to be understood as being unproductive. It is important for the practitioner to observe the interaction between the partners, in order to identify what each individual is truly trying to convey. Practitioners need to help problem solve and help to provide insight oriented techniques to help the couple come up with healthier strategies of communication. Effective couples therapy will help alleviate the negative ways the partners behave with each other, and will address immediately any harm that is being done to each partner physically, economically, and psychologically. In order to do this, social workers must be thorough in their assessment and rule out any immediate red flags. Healthy levels of communication include the use of "I" statements and using timeouts as a technique to help avoid unhealthy conflicts.

INCREASING EMOTIONAL CONNECTEDNESS

As a practitioner it is important to identify the attachment styles of the couple being seen, and if possible, identify if any unresolved past issues are being projected onto the partner. It would be important to separate unmet past needs versus present-day adult relationship issues. Oftentimes, this can be intermixed and it can be confusing for partners. For example, someone with an anxious-ambivalent attachment may be putting too much pressure on their partner and it may have little to do with what the partner is actually doing. In identifying attachments, it outlines deficit needs of each partner, and this can lead to a healthy discussion about how as a couple, each person can be more supportive to one another.

IMPROVING THE COUPLE'S COMMUNICATION

Communication needs to be healthy and the social worker needs to make sure that any form of communication that is abusive or harmful be addressed immediately. Couples should not insult or put down their partner in any way, shape, or form, and rules of healthy communication need to be established during the therapeutic process. It is the job of the social worker to coach the couple to communicate in healthier ways when speaking to one another, as well as learning how to be better listeners.

PROMOTING THE STRENGTH OF THE COUPLE, INCLUDING THEIR INDIVIDUAL STRENGTHS

Effective couples therapy not only addresses the problem areas in the relationship, but it also addresses the positives of their relationship dynamic. In promoting the strengths of the couple, it helps to provide more objectivity and will help make this whole process feel less like a chore. Also in defining the couple's strengths, it is important to note the individual strengths and characteristics that each person brings to each other. It is the job of the social worker to make sure that objectivity is kept throughout the process.

PUTTING IT ALL TOGETHER

Below is a vignette of a couple who are coming to see you for therapy:

John and Tina come into therapy as they state that they are having marital problems. John states, "I do not feel like my wife is there for me and I feel really uncomfortable around her." Tina on the other hand responds and shares, "I just want space and I think that John is too needy. He needs to be more of a man." John and Tina share that they have been married for less than a year, but that they lived together previously for five years. They share that after they were married, "This was when we started to have serious problems." During the initial assessment, you find out that John grew up where his mother was very controlling. He shares that she never really listened to him and that he "had to follow her rules or else she would punish me."

John shares that he never really dated that much and that he had one relationship that lasted about two years. He shares, "I want this marriage to work." Conversely, Tina shares that both her mother and father were very distant as "they would do their own things." Tina adds, "My father left us when I was seven, and my mother was only concerned about him anyway." She adds, "My mom would go out with her friends and I would just do my own thing." Tina shares that she had many relationships and adds, "many were very casual and I did not think too much about it." John shares that he was instantly attracted to Tina and appreciated how she was so strong, and Tina shared how "I knew that I wanted something more, and so when I met John, I knew that he was a good man." They both seem committed to making the relationship work but they both share, "I feel like I am falling out of love."

CHANGING THE VIEW OF THE RELATIONSHIP DYNAMIC

One of the best ways to change the relationship dynamic is to focus on what is working in their relationship. They both are committed to making the relationship work, and before the marriage, they shared that their relationship was working. It would be finding out what they did before the marriage that was helping their relationship, and what changed after the marriage occurred. Also, it was shared that John really respects the strength of Tina and how Tina when she met John knew that she wanted something more knowing that he could offer that to her. From what is being shared, this highlights the positive aspects of their relationship. In assessing this relationship dynamic, it would be worth exploring their attachment style and how that may be contributing to their relationship issues.

MODIFYING DYSFUNCTIONAL BEHAVIORS

It is important to address the immediate red flag of John's statement in defining what Tina punishing him means. Also, Tina not calling him a man and any sort of demeaning behaviors that she is directing towards him need to be stopped immediately. Conversely, it seems like John is becoming too dependent in the relationship and it appears that he does need to develop more of his individuality and from there identify his needs in the relationship.

INCREASING EMOTIONAL CONNECTEDNESS

In defining their emotional attachment, John appears to be anxious-ambivalent and Tina anxious-avoidant. For John, that would explain why he is so needy in the relationship, because the parenting that he received was on the mother's terms, and he really did not get to develop his own individuality. Conversely, Tina's attachment explains why she can be so aloof and detached from the emotional aspect of the relationship because the parenting that she received was uninvolved. It appears that through this relationship dynamic, they have the ability to heal from their past and grow with each person being their best now.

IMPROVING THE COUPLE'S COMMUNICATION

This is where the use of "I" statements would be important for the clients to use to take ownership of their feelings. Also, in relation to their attachments, each individual would need the space to share about their childhood experiences and how that is being brought into the relationship now. This allows not only healing from the past, but it also allows for each individual to grow as a person, and possibly as a couple throughout this process. John needs the space to work out that unmet part of himself which leads to his needy behaviors, and similarly for Tina, her aloofness and lack of emotional awareness stems from her needing to address that unmet need as well.

PROMOTING THE STRENGTH OF THE COUPLE, INCLUDING THEIR INDIVIDUAL STRENGTHS

What seems very clear is that Tina and John really do want to be together and that they are committed to making this relationship work. They also can learn from each other as John can learn to be more independent from Tina and conversely through this dynamic, Tina can learn to be more emotionally connected to her own feelings. Also, if John were manlier, Tina would need to be aware of the fact that there would probably be more fights between the two, and that John's personality allows for Tina to be the strong woman that she is. Also with John, if Tina were just as emotional as he is, everyday tasks would become difficult and everyday duties would probably be difficult to get done. John should appreciate that since she is less emotional, it provides him the space to accentuate the sensitive traits that he has. In this context, this is an ideal relationship for both to grow as adults now.

FAMILY THERAPY

Family therapy can be a revolutionary tool that can help families move forward from dysfunction to healing. It's an important part of the healing process, both for the person in therapy, and for the entire family as a whole. The goals of family therapy can vary based on the intervention strategy used, but common goals include:

- improving overall family communication
- increasing understanding of each family member and the family dynamic as a whole
- the building of stronger and healthier relationships based on understanding
- improving overall support of each family member

Where an individual practitioner for mental illness or addiction might strive to help that person, a family practitioner tries to help everyone involved improve and feel better. Family therapy can also be helpful in cases of substance abuse and addiction. Families impacted by addiction may respond with confusion, anger, guilt and the family may find it extremely difficult to trust and work together. Family therapy can break through these barriers and help the group to function in a healthier manner.

An analogy of a family is to see the unit as an organism, with the behavior of one person affecting the behavior of all the other members. If one person in the family becomes angry and upset, the rest of the family will become affected and will respond accordingly whether the outcome is positive or not. It is therefore key to establish a healthy family dynamic where stress and difficulty can be dealt with in a healthy manner. As a social worker providing family therapy, it is important to have the family strive toward common goals, while incorporating individual needs. It is a complex process as family members have deep connections involving individual life stages, external factors outside the family, and the family issues themselves.

It is important to have all of those needs communicated and incorporated during the therapy and this is where skills training comes into play. Some examples of skills training include:

- learning effective communication
- proper delegation of duties based on family roles
- developing proactive listening skills
- the healthy managing of anger

In relation to family therapy, we will be covering three family therapy models:

- extended family systems therapy
- strategic family therapy
- structural family therapy

EXTENDED SYSTEMS FAMILY THERAPY

Bowen family systems theory is a theory of human behavior that views the family as an emotional unit and uses systems theory to describe the complex interactions within that unit (Your Mindful Compass, 2018). Bowen saw the family as an emotional system which governed human relationships going through the life cycle stages (Carter and McGoldrick, 1988). He believed that differentiation, or the individual level of emotional maturity to break unhealthy family cycles among family members produced variation. This would either create healthier family dynamics for future family generations or if differentiation is low, will continue the unhealthy family cycles, often becoming worse and exacerbated with each generation. This concept is known as a multi-generational transmission. The goal of extended family systems therapy is to increase individual family members' level of differentiation. In doing so, it is important to identify those with high differentiation, because they will be key in helping to create a healthier family dynamic. Emotional issues, biological and environmental influences are considered as each individual family member learns to adapt within the family unit, which will extend over the generations. There are four premises in relation to this model:

PAIN EXTENDS TO EVERYONE

Unhealthy behaviors extend and matriculate to every single family member inducing anxiety and depression

TOGETHER VS. SEPARATE

Understanding your relation to your family and seeking a greater good versus individual gain

THE FEELING GUIDANCE SYSTEM VS. THE INTELLECTUAL GUIDANCE SYSTEM

Being totally consumed by your emotions and having no insight over being able to see family dynamics and to focus on solutions

TRIANGULATION

Utilizing others in your problems thus creating bigger problems for the family system

There are seven basic concepts of Bowen's family systems theory that we will be going over. Each of the concepts was developed to help describe patterns in families in order to help defuse anxiety. The cause of anxiety in families is the perception of either too much closeness or distance in the family relationship. The degree of anxiety in any one family will be determined by current levels of stress and the generational family pattern that is being transmitted from generation to generation. If family members do not have the capacity to think through their responses to relationship issues, and instead are reactive through perceived emotional demands, a state of chronic anxiety and reactivity becomes the behavior keeping one in a state of low differentiation. The main goal of Bowenian therapy is to reduce chronic anxiety by (FSI, 2018):

- facilitating awareness of how the emotional system functions
- increasing levels of differentiation, where the focus is on making changes for the self rather than on trying to change others. (p. 2)

DIFFERENTIATION

Once again, *differentiation* is the individual level of emotional maturity to break unhealthy family cycles. Levels of differentiation take place not only in families but in social groups, and they affect how people think, feel, and act. Those with low levels of differentiation will be involved in what is known as groupthink, meaning conforming to what the group wants and sacrificing one's own individuality. The less developed a person's self is, the more impact others will have on the functioning and behaviors of that person. Bowen (Your Mindful Compass, 2018) developed a scale to measure differentiation of self. Bowen wrote it as a way to see the enormous variety in functioning but there is no scale to measure the level of differentiation. The scale goes from 0 to 100, going over four quadrants:

0–25 This quadrant represents having no differentiation. In this stage emotional maturity is lacking and as a result, many generational family processes are absorbed and lived out without much conscious thought. There is very little to no ability to stand up for oneself and this person is living in constant anxiety and completely reacting to the family or group dynamic. At this stage, almost all decisions are made reactively to follow along or oppose others based on trying to eliminate uncomfortable feelings.

25–50 This quadrant represents low differentiation. One can know the difference between facts and feelings, but intense reactive feelings dominate the individual, along with high levels of anxiety that impede healthy functioning. In this stage, decisions are solely made in order to feel better. People in this stage lose sight of important principles in their life when confronted with difficulty, and simply react. In this stage, when times are calm is the only time principled and logical thinking can be executed. Principles can enable people to withstand the pressure to give in to relationship demands and this is the stage where living by those principles is a struggle.

50–60 This quadrant represents moderate differentiation where individuals are more aware of the difference between feelings and thinking, and are clear about the principles that they have defined as important. Decisions are more thoughtful and relationships are calmer, even in times of turmoil (Your Mindful Compass, 2018). During this stage, there are still symptoms of family pain, but there is a development of skills in recovering well and not staying caught in the negative cycles. People operate being more on open with others and when opposition of views, do not get highly emotional. In this area, differentiation is gaining strength and there is consideration of long-term implications when making decisions.

60–75 People in this quadrant have high differentiation and are free of the controlling emotional system of groups or family dynamics. There is more freedom to be yourself, to let others be, and the lack of desire to control others. Decisions are clarified and are connected to basic principles on having proper boundaries. They can express beliefs without being reactive to others and find satisfaction in both emotional closeness and in goal directed activities.

75–100 This quadrant represents an individual having the highest level of differentiation. The individual is functional at exceptional levels in emotional, cellular, and physiological functioning.

There are ways to raise one's level of maturity but it takes sustained effort to decrease reactivity and be guided more by thought than just emotions. Learning to separate oneself from the entanglements of others is the main discipline and skill that will help a person find balance between being their own person, and still finding a way to belong to a group dynamic. The scale uses numbers to indicate the variation and the general markers for emotional maturity as to how people are able to handle anxiety and be more mature and principle based (Your Mindful Compass, 2018). Bowen emphasized that during times of trouble and emotional turmoil, it is crucial to increase differentiation. This process involves becoming better defined individuals, being able to separate out from the pressure in the surrounding emotional systems, and living out one's own moral code. As one continues to grow in differentiation, one gradually moves up the scale.

NUCLEAR FAMILY

The *nuclear family* is the core family unit, and there are four patterns of relationships within that unit to address. This concept describes the four relationship patterns within a family to manage anxiety and stress:

MARITAL CONFLICT

The tension and conflict between the partners

DYSFUNCTION IN ONE SPOUSE

The overcompensating of one spouse due to the lack of responsibility in the other

IMPAIRMENT OF ONE OR MORE CHILDREN

This can be due to the child being scapegoated and blamed for the family problems

EMOTIONAL DISTANCE

This can lead to family members cutting off emotionally from one another to not deal with the family dysfunction

In relation to differentiation, families that function at higher levels of it will pass on the healthy levels of behavior to the next generation. Conversely, families that have lower levels of differentiation will pass on the continued pathology to their generation. With low differentiation, the passing on of pathology gets worse from generation to generation if no intervention takes place.

FAMILY PROJECTION PROCESS

This concept describes the way in which parents pass down their emotional issues on to their own children. The way a parent decides to raise their children, based on this premise, is determined by the existing pathology of that parent. For example if a parent is too disengaged from their child because of the difficulty of handling their own emotions, this will then translate into their own child developing similar coping skills of being withdrawn and unable to deal with their emotions. Conversely, if a parent becomes too enmeshed with their child because of their own fears and anxieties, this will then get passed on to the child who will then develop similar, anxious coping skills. Bowen believed that particular child behaviors were indicators of maladaptive behaviors being passed down. Behaviors include:

- an excessive need for attention or approval
- taking on perfectionistic behaviors because of the need to meet expectations
- constant criticism of self or others
- constant acting out when expressing emotions to relieve anxiety

Bowen believes that children are symptom carriers of the parents, and ultimately this leads to a decline in differentiation for the child. Parents with low differentiation will often use the child as an excuse for problems. They will scapegoat the child and not take any responsibly for their own actions. This leads to couples fighting and if a parent is ill, the problems exacerbate. Bowen focuses on the impact of low differentiation on the emotional functioning of a single generation family, and asserts that relationship fusion needs to be eliminated.

MULTIGENERATIONAL TRANSMISSION

This concept describes how levels of differentiation between parents and their offspring are passed on. If an unhealthy family transmission is passed on unresolved, the next generation will incur even greater pathology and lower differentiation. The way people relate to one another in one generation may create intense sensitivities, which are transmitted across generational offspring. An example of this is alcoholism and how that family problem gets passed on from generation to generation. An offspring in an alcoholic family will receive the transmission of this problem mentally, emotionally, and biologically. Similarly, parents with more anxiety and less maturity can pressure their children because of their unresolved generational past, and in doing so will make their children more vulnerable and symptomatic, leading to another generational offspring being even more symptomatic. Oftentimes individual problems are not just the problems of the moment, but a history of pain and unhealthiness that has gone unaddressed. It is the job of the social worker to increase differentiation of family members to break unhealthy generational cycles and to increase differentiation.

SIBLING POSITION

Bowen's theory incorporates psychologist Walter Toman's work relating to *sibling position*. Sibling position is simply the birth order of the family offspring. Toman believes that the oldest child is more likely to take on leadership roles and be more independent, while the youngest sibling would engage in more dependent behaviors allowing decisions to be made on their behalf. The middle child by Toman is seen as the more open-minded one and will be a middle ground between independence and dependence. Toman's (1961) research showed that spouses' sibling positions when mismatched often affected the chance of divorcing. It is important to note that Bowen's work does not discuss the impact of gender and ethnicity on sibling position and family roles.

EMOTIONAL TRIANGLE

Bowen described triangles as the smallest stable relationship unit (Kerr & Bowen, 1988). An emotional triangle is when conflict between two individuals with at least one person having low differentiation, recruits a third person to the conflict to help reduce tension and anxiety. Individuals with low differentiation will problem-solve by recruiting more people than are needed to solve problems. This can often occur by one individual forcing the third party to choose sides and trying to get that person to blame the other individual. In the family dynamic, tensions between the parents can lead to the recruiting of one of their children by scapegoating them, and blaming all of their relationship problems on that child. In general, triangles allow the two individuals who are having conflict to reduce their feelings of tension, because of the recruitment of the third individual. If unhealthy, this will cause the recruited party to choose sides, and an increased escalation of the two-person problem now becomes a three-person issue. Therapy therefore is a form of de-triangling, as a couple with conflict can come see a therapist, and the third party here would not take sides but rather fuse the two to address the conflict in a healthier manner. The ultimate goal would be to eliminate the triangle, and increase the differentiation of both individuals who came in. What would look like a three-person issue would eventually be directed back to the two individual parties involved with the assistance of the practitioner.

EMOTIONAL CUT-OFF

An emotional cut-off is when a family member will make the decision to completely cut off contact with other family members to address the unhealthy family dynamic. An example of a cut-off is moving out, or leaving the country to get away from the family. Cut-offs carry forward unresolved emotional issues in one's family of origin, and passes that forward into future nuclear families and new relationships. Bowen acknowledges that emotionally cutting off shows traits of differentiation, but it also reflects the desire to escape and run away from the problem. In family therapy, there is the fine line between being a part of the family dynamic, and yet still having the differentiation to be your own individual. This dynamic becomes difficult to balance in really unhealthy family systems. Cutting off for the short term can hold benefits, but eventually the internalized pathology needs to be addressed.

IMPLEMENTING THE MODEL

Bowen's use of this model is to assist each family member to have greater differentiation. He believes that if there is greater differentiation, there will be greater accountability, and the transmission of pathology can stop being passed on. This will in turn prevent future generations from experiencing the pain that generations before have experienced and felt. To accomplish this goal, Bowen believed in three stages:

- **Stage one** is providing psycho-education regarding the therapy model and how it is going to be implemented. The goal here is to reduce the anxiety that is being felt by each family member, and to educate them on the process.
- **Stage two** is increasing differentiation of the adult family members by teaching them to separate from the unhealthy family dynamics that are in play. This would include hearing personal statements from the adult members and identifying what individuality would look like to each person.
- **Stage three** is to get the parents to take responsibility for what they have learned from previous generations, and how they have passed it on to their own kids. It is also having the parents acknowledge the ways the children have been symptom bearers and the children to share how that has affected them. This stage would attempt to get buy-in from all family members to break the family cycle all together.

VIGNETTE

VIGNETTE

A client named Jennifer comes in to see you and shares, "I am having a lot of problems at home and it is affecting me a lot right now." The Ct shares, "I am one hundred pounds overweight and the doctor told me that if I do not clean up, I may lose my leg due to my diabetes getting worse." The Ct added that she is having problems at home as she lives with her parents and younger brother, and the whole family is overweight. She added, "There is a long history of obesity and diabetes in my family and my dad and mom both have had their feet amputated." She adds, "My parents are also very critical of me because I am in school to get my masters in social work and they guilt me into not moving away from them." Jennifer also adds that she is the go-between when her parents fight and her mom will often seek her support. At the same time, Jennifer shares that she is emotionally and financially dependent on them as well, and that it is her desire to move out and build a healthier life on her own. Jennifer shares that it is putting a strain on her mentally, emotionally, and physically. She originally wanted to do family therapy but her family refuses to go and feel like it is not needed. Jennifer closes with "I want to have a really healthy family in the future of my own where we share and support one another and promote a healthy lifestyle."

STAGE ONE

Aim to reduce Jennifer's anxiety by encouraging her to learn how the symptom is part of her own behavioral pattern of relating.

Problem

The client has low differentiation and is emotionally dependent on her parents, as well as needing their financial support. The client is also 100 pounds overweight and wants to become healthier as she is diabetic and may lose one of her legs. Jennifer and her mother have a relationship that is too enmeshed (no boundaries) as well as having the same issue with her whole family. There is a multigenerational transmission of mental, physical, and emotional illness and Jennifer can break that cycle for herself and her future children.

Intervention

Individual therapy because the parents refuse to come to therapy. The client will work on increasing differentiation and reaching out to those in her family who also would want to promote a healthy lifestyle. Jennifer will need to have firm boundaries in keeping a healthy relationship dynamic with her family, as she increases her level of differentiation.

Goals

- Obtain her MSW degree as she has one more year left
- After graduating, get a full-time job and after six months, move out and get an apartment on her own
- Lose 50 pounds in one year and not have her leg amputated
- Develop a healthier support system outside of her new family to promote her healthier lifestyle
- Eliminate the unhealthy triangle with her parents and develop a healthier relationship

STAGE TWO

Focus Jennifer on adult issues of the self by seeking to increase her level of differentiation. Clients are helped to resist the pull of unhealthy family dynamics and creating a new process for oneself.

Using process questions

Process questions are questions that induce and cause the individual to focus on their behavior in relation to the family unit. In doing so, the hope is that the client will feel more empowered and be able to see that they alone can change their life even with the negative behaviors within the family. In Jennifer's case, she is not only dealing with her family, but also the generational cycle of unhealthiness as well. Some of the questions to ask might be:

- How much differentiation do you have from your own family?
- How do your family members influence you negatively, and what do you need to do to change it?
- What are the self-sabotaging behaviors that you engage in?
- Provide an example of a triangle with your family and describe what happened. Also, describe how that situation could have been different if you were more differentiated.

Writing a letter to the family using "I" statements

This is a powerful and safe way for Jennifer to express her feelings to her family. Jennifer can decide at the end whether she would want to share that letter with her family or not; however, the purpose is for Jennifer to emotionally become less reactive, gain more insight into her family dynamic, and increase her level of differentiation.

STAGE THREE

Jennifer is coached in differentiating herself from her family of origin. She has broken away from the unhealthy projection process, is highly differentiated, and the result is her having decreased anxiety and greater self-responsibility within the nuclear family system.

Outcome

The client has high differentiation and is no longer emotionally dependent on her parents, nor does she need their financial support. The client has lost 35 of the 50 pounds and is living a healthier lifestyle. She is controlling her diabetic symptoms and does not need to have her leg amputated. Jennifer and her mother have a relationship that is no longer enmeshed and Jennifer has overall better boundaries with her whole family. The multigenerational transmission of mental, physical, and emotional illness that Jennifer has suffered from has been broken and she is on her way to having the future family that she desires.

Intervention

Individual therapy was done because the rest of the family refused to come to therapy. The client increased differentiation and she is living a healthier lifestyle regardless of the family continuing to live the same way. Jennifer established firm boundaries by using interventions that included process questions and letter writing using "I" statements. Jennifer is open to helping her own family members if they are willing to change their own lifestyles. Currently, she communicates with them, but will not engage when the family process becomes unhealthy.

Goals achieved by Jennifer:

- Jennifer obtained her MSW degree

After graduating, Jennifer was able to get a full-time job and after six months, she moved out and has an apartment of her own.

Jennifer has lost 35 of the 50 pounds in one year and her leg does not need to be amputated. She has the rest of the year to reach the target weight loss goal.

Jennifer joined a gym as well as a weight-loss support program and has developed close friendships through that process. She also has friends that she made during her MSW program.

Jennifer has eliminated the unhealthy triangle with her parents and she shares that now her parents seek her advice and guidance. She shared that her family is more open to changing.

STRUCTURAL FAMILY THERAPY

Salvador Minuchin, who founded structural family therapy, uses as a foundation systems theory in his approach to address family dynamics. Instead of just looking at the individual members and their symptoms, he likes to take a macro perspective in seeing how the family environment is creating the maladaptive behaviors for each member. Minuchin believes that as the practitioner, it is important to look at the communication that takes place between members, as he defines them as transactions that signify the various components of the family system. It is a circular approach in assessing the family structure and he believes that all dynamics on the various levels need to be examined. He breaks aspects of the family down to the spousal subsystem, the parental subsystem, and the sibling subsystem. He wants to look at each component separately and then piece together the family structure as a whole. For example, a mother who is overly engaged with her daughter is completely disengaged from her son. Because of this dynamic, the sister and brother do not talk to each other very much, and they all spend very little time together at all. In this dynamic the parental subsystem by the mother is inconsistent and it appears to be directly influencing the sibling relationship. Minuchin would address each subsystem and completely restructure the boundaries of the mother to each child, and with siblings in their dynamic.

Minuchin believes that dysfunction in the family stems from rigid structures within the family dynamic. The goal therefore is to modify the family structure and have a more open dynamic. It is important to define the unsaid family dynamics when assessing a family. *Homeostasis* is the equilibrium state by which a family is able to solve problems. Homeostasis by itself is neither good nor bad, however it is the indicator by which the family functions. An example is a family who has a domineering father who sets all the rules, and therefore the homeostasis of the family is to do whatever the father wants. Although this is not the ideal way for a family to function, that would be the current way in which the family addresses family problems. Arguing with and challenging the father in this example would be inefficient due to the unequal power dynamic, and the futility of the situation. Ultimately, the situation would most likely go back to the father making the decision and the family accommodating because of the efficiency of it.

Nichols and Minuchin (1999) believe that the structural family approach is an aggressive form of treatment. Vetere (2001) found that this form of family therapy was effective in treating incarcerated youth and their family members. The practitioner quickly takes on an authoritarian role and challenges the family dynamic. The process can become quite emotional, but it is important as the practitioner to continue to challenge the family. Friesen (1995) highlights five goals of structural family therapy:

- Establish a strong family hierarchy dynamic.
- Establish a healthy parental subsystem where they act as one team and split against one another.
- Create a healthy sibling subsystem dynamic.
- Enhance the differentiation of all family members.

FAMILY BOUNDARIES

According to Minuchin, understanding a family requires identifying the processes and boundaries that operate the subsystems and coalitions in that family. Minuchin defined three types of interpersonal boundaries (clear, rigid, or diffuse) that determine the overall ability of the family to adapt successfully to change.

Clear boundaries—boundaries formed around a generic subsystem where they are firm yet flexible, permitting maximum adaptation to change.

Clear boundaries would be allowing the child to share their thoughts and feelings about a situation, allowing them to be their own individual, and at the same time enforcing rules regarding what can and cannot be done. This over time allows the family to grow and adapt as life continues to change. The child is able to develop their own individuality while still following and respecting the rules of the household.

Rigid boundaries—imply disengagement between family members or subsystems. The prevailing non-communicative pattern hinders support and limits effective adaptation.

An example of rigid boundaries would be parents who would not even listen to the child and would only care if the child is following their rules or not. Oftentimes there is a lot of verbal abuse and punishment for not following the rules and because of that, a lack of individuality develops in the child, who is solely focused on consequences of actions. This type of boundary reduces the deviation to change and focuses on conformity.

Diffuse boundaries—imply enmeshment where everyone is into everyone else's business. In this case, no one and everyone is taking charge and effective guidance during times of change is impossible.

An example of a diffuse boundary would be a mother who talks to her teenage daughter like they are best friends, and is hanging out with her daughter's friends. She is sharing personal issues with her and not acting like a mother to her. Over time this creates emotional chaos and a lack of firm boundaries within the family dynamic.

It is important to know that boundaries are reciprocal. For example, if a mother is too enmeshed with her husband, only focusing on his needs, the mother is then disengaged from her children who are being neglected. Another example is if the father is too enmeshed with his son, he is disengaged from his daughter who is not getting her needs met by her father. According to Minuchin, it is through observing patterns of interaction repeated across time and situations that an understanding of roles, subsystems, coalitions, hierarchy, and rules can be achieved. This in total will define what the family structure is.

FAMILY SUBSYSTEMS

Within the family are subsystems that Minuchin believes need to be addressed. Subsystems are the smaller units within the family system that comprise the unit as a whole. Minuchin describes the three subsystems:

spouse subsystem—This defines the relationship dynamic that husband and wife or partners have with one another. This is important because any friction in this dynamic can spill over to the other subsystems.

parental subsystem—This looks at the way the parents collectively and individually address their children. This looks into communication and the enforcing of family rules. This also addresses how the children view the parents, who are the authority figures.

sibling subsystem—This looks into how the children get along with one another. Minuchin (1981) stresses the importance of this dynamic because they are of the same generation, and this dynamic is a strong foundation for how the children will interact outside of their home.

The family may be comprised of these subsystems and operate either according to a generic or an idiosyncratic hierarchy.

generic hierarchy—a typical and expected hierarchy where the parents are the authority figures and the children will follow their rules.

idiosyncratic hierachy—an irregular and unexpected hierarchy where the parents are not the authority figures but the children are.

It is important to be able to identify and understand each subsystem within the family dynamic.

THREE CHRONIC BOUNDARY PROBLEMS OR RIGID TRIADS

Unhealthy family dynamics lead to chronic boundaries or rigid triads. The reason for this is in family members trying to establish power. Power is defined by how much influence one has within the family dynamic. Often family members will align together forming a **coalition**. A coalition is when two individual family members will form a union and go against another family member. This is known as a rigid boundary and it seeks to force conformity of the third individual. This is a smaller dynamic of groupthink and the goal is to isolate the other member from the rest of the family. Other examples include of chronic boundaries are:

detouring—when the parents focus on the child either by overprotecting or blaming (scapegoating) the child for the family's problems.

stable coalition—when a parent and child form a cross generational coalition and consistently gang up against the other parent.

triangulation—(aka unstable coalition) occurs when each parent demands that the child side with him or her against the other parent. In this situation the child is being pulled in two directions.

IMPLEMENTING THE MODEL

In implementing structural family therapy, it is important to note that the model views maladaptive family behavior as the dysfunction resulting from an inflexible family structure that prohibits the family from adapting to maturational and situational stressors in a healthy way. It is necessary to develop an open family system that is open and adaptable to change, and for that to be achieved, a restructuring of the family dynamic needs to take place. The following therapeutic techniques need to be utilized by the social worker:

Joining—The social worker's first task is to develop a therapeutic system by joining the family in a position of leadership.

Evaluating the family structure—Once the social worker has joined the family, he or she is in a position to evaluate the family's structure, including its transactional patterns, power hierarchies, and boundaries. The evaluation may include a family map, which enables for a structural diagnosis where enmeshments and disengagements are taking place.

Restructuring the family—The social worker will use a number of techniques, many of which are designed to deliberately unbalance the family's homeostasis, in order to facilitate transformation of the family structure. Techniques include enactment which family members role play their relationship patterns.

JOINING

In joining the family as the practitioner, it is important to identify the many aspects that will need to be addressed by you. First of all, it is establishing an empathic approach and really listening to what the family is sharing. Respect must be given for the fact that they are the experts of their dynamic and it is your job as the outside observer to provide constructive and helpful feedback. Second, it is understanding that there will be resistance from the family as you take on the authority role. The transference of resistance from the family is normal as a new presence is joining, and it is learning to be okay with that. As the practitioner, it is important to use that resistant energy to get buy-in from the family and to establish healthy rapport. A third component is to be able to identify the strengths of the family. In identifying the positives, it will allow the family to see what they are actually doing well, and it will also show how as the practitioner, you are taking an objective approach. The final component is to be aware of your own countertransference. This is vital, because since this is a very aggressive approach that often challenges what is taking place, emotional struggles that may emerge from the practitioner will hinder the therapeutic process.

EVALUATING THE FAMILY STRUCTURE

As the practitioner has fully joined the family structure, it is important to look into and define the family structure as a whole. One way to do that is to perform *enactments*. An enactment is when the practitioner will ask family members to replay a scenario that has taken place within their family. As the practitioner, you want the family members to enact scenarios that the family is really struggling with. By doing that, you are able to see not only the system as a whole, but you are also able to see each subsystem and how they are responding to each enactment. When conducting enactments, it would be beneficial to identify situations that affect the family as a whole, as well as identifying situations within each subsystem. By having the family play out each type of enactment, it allows for the practitioner to properly diagnose the structure of the family. Some questions to ask yourself during the enactments are:

- Who are the members that are disengaged?
- Who are the members that are overly enmeshed?
- Is there a generic or idiosyncratic dynamic taking place?
- Which subsystem is filtering out to other subsystems?

Enactments are a great way to assess the family dynamic in a more efficient manner.

RESTRUCTURING THE FAMILY

In restructuring the family, it is important to use the enactments that were performed, and from there systematically break down everything that was seen. Using the example mentioned before about the mother who is overly involved with the daughter but completely disengaged from the son, the practitioner can break down the system dynamics by subsystems.

parental subsystem

- The mother is too enmeshed with the daughter.
- The mother is too disengaged from the son.

sibling subsystem

- The brother and sister are not communicating because the mother's dynamic with the daughter has no boundaries.

Questions that would be important for the practitioner to ask would be:
Mother

- How would you describe your parenting style with your daughter?
- How would you describe your parenting style with your son?
- What inconsistencies do you see?

Daughter

- How would you describe your relationship with your mother?
- What are some of the struggles that you are having with her?
- Has this dynamic with your mother affected your relationship with your brother? If so, please explain.

Son

- How would you describe your relationship with your mother?
- What are some of the struggles that you are having with her?
- Has the relationship that your mother and sister have, affected your relationship with your sister? If so, please explain.

This is just a small example of taking a family issue and breaking it down into its subsystems, as well as looking at the family dynamic as a whole. There are clearly two different parenting styles taking place from the mother, and the dynamic is filtering to the sibling subsystem. Also, in this example, it would be important to get the feedback of the other parent and to look at the spouse system as well. Enactments open the door for dynamics to emerge from each subsystem, which opens the door for the whole family dynamic to be seen.

Another component that is important when restructuring is to use *reframing*. Reframing is simply looking at a situation from a new perspective or point of view. Reframing allows for the removal of all-or-nothing thinking to situations and allows for complimentary and healthy behaviors to take place. In putting together a plan for the example used, use of reframing would be:

parental subsystem

- The mother who is too enmeshed with the daughter will establish healthy boundaries by being more a mother than a friend.
- The mother who is too disengaged from her son will work on building a healthy mother-son relationship by engaging in activities that he enjoys.

sibling subsystem

- The brother and sister who are not communicating because of the mother's dynamic with the daughter will work on establishing better communication with each other away from the mother.

Here is an example of the dynamic being restructured, but also the mother can reframe this situation by realizing that she can have meaningful relationships with both her children. This in turn can allow the siblings to establish a more meaningful relationship with one another. All of these interventions then open the door for a more open family system.

STRATEGIC FAMILY THERAPY

According to Haley, strategic therapy takes place when a practitioner defines a goal of work for the family, and the group strives to achieve that goal. The goal should be achievable and accepted by the family and should be focused on the short term. After achieving the goal, the work may be terminated or another goal can be set for the family. Strategic therapy is seen as an orientation and activity of a therapist who takes responsibility for building the strategy of change for the family. According to Haley, a family is a social group with a shared history and a shared future. Interpersonal events within a family are perceived and described by a circular model rather than a cause/effect perspective. The recurring sequences of behavior between the family members belonging to the system are significant and the sequences of behaviors are controlled by the rules that can be identified by the therapist. This identification then in turn can result in the changing of the dysfunctional family process. The symptom is a part of the communication sequence of events between family members. It results from a current social situation within the given family, as the past is seen with minimal importance.

FUNCTIONAL AND DYSFUNCTIONAL FAMILIES

In describing family pathology, Haley used the terms *functional* and *dysfunctional* family to assess the way members communicate with one another. In this approach, a functional family is a family that keeps the balance between stability and the opportunity of change. A functional family has a clear hierarchical organization where parents manage and take responsibility for the family. Similar to Minuchin, he believes in a generic hierarchy versus an idiosyncratic dynamic. Another similarity is the identification of subsystems as listed below:

spouse subsystem—This defines the relationship dynamic that husband and wife or partners have with one another. This is important because any friction in this dynamic can spill over to the other subsystems.

parental subsystem—This looks at the way the parents collectively and individually address their children. This looks into communication and the enforcing of family rules. This also addresses how the children view the parents who are the authority figures.

sibling subsystem—This looks into how the children get along with one another. Minuchin (1981) stresses the importance of this dynamic because they are of the same generation, and this dynamic is a strong foundation for how the children will interact outside of their home.

Haley believed that the bonds of the same generation level are stronger than the trans-generational bonds. This means that the bonds between parents are stronger than the bonds between any parent and their child. Similarly, he believed that the bonds between siblings were stronger than the bond between a child and one of the parents.

In a dysfunctional family the functioning is unstable and focused on previous behaviors that do not allow for adaptability for change. Dysfunctional families will often ignore the time passing by and continue engaging in consequential behavior that becomes repetitive. Age regression prevails in terms of the phenomena of trance. This means that individual's actual emotional age will manifest itself. For example a 45-year-old father who is really not emotionally ready to be a father, regresses into his actual emotional age of 23 by constantly going out and partying with his friends versus being responsible at home. In dysfunctional families, the hierarchy is not clear and is mostly reversed. Parents avoid responsibility; they tend to give over the control while children try to take it over. Haley believed that boundaries should be clear and not rigid or enmeshed. Haley also used the concept of family boundaries to diagnose family structure.

- **clear boundaries**—boundaries formed around a generic subsystem where they are firm yet flexible, permitting maximum adaptation to change.
- **rigid boundaries**—imply disengagement between family members or subsystems. The prevailing non-communicative pattern hinders support and limits effective adaptation.
- **diffuse boundaries**—imply enmeshment where everyone is into everyone else's business. In this case, no one and everyone is taking charge and effective guidance during times of change is impossible.

In dysfunctional families, the trans-generational bonds are stronger than the bonds of the same generation level, which creates the diagnosis category called a perverse triangle (Haley, 1990). This type of bond mostly lasts for the next generations and creates a trans-generational sequence of perverse triangles. It is characterized by the following:

- One family member within the coalition is from a different generation than the other one. (e.g., mom and sister are closer than sister and brother)
- The coalition is directed against another person within the family. (e.g., mom and sister are ganging up against the brother)
- The coalition is built and maintained unconsciously. (e.g., mom has low differentiation and is teaching her daughter to have failed marriage as well)

PARADOXICAL DIRECTIVES

One of the frequently applied techniques is paradoxical intervention. This is often used when an individual is resistive and their natural response is to avoid taking an action. A *paradoxical directive* uses the client's resistance in a constructive way by having the symptoms redefined and assigned a positive function that serves the family. They can be used during the family therapy session but are used more outside of the therapy session as outside assignments. There are two basic types of paradoxical directives. The first one is playing up the symptoms, when a therapist recommends all family members to do intentionally what they have already been doing to maintain the family problem. Examples of these types of directives include:

- prescribing the symptom—instructing a family member to deliberately engage in the symptom
- positioning—exaggerating the severity of the symptoms

An example of prescribing the symptoms would be a family member who begins to yell during conversations and so the directive would be for the individual to "Continue to yell even though I cannot hear anything that you are saying." The hope is that the permission will allow the individual to rebel and actually not engage in the behavior. An example of positioning would be an individual who suffers from panic attacks and fears having a heart attack, by allowing that person permission to have a heart attack at that very moment. Once again the intention is to expect that the individual will actually have his symptoms diminish because permission was granted. Another reason to engage in these directives is to get family buy-in and cooperation of the assigned goals of therapy.

The second type of paradoxical interventions is the directive of delaying improvement and recovery of the family. The goal is to build motivation to make a change by promoting the idea of not changing. If it is effective, the family itself will start to urge the social worker that they cannot wait and will fight the desire to not change. Examples of these directives include:

- restraining—encouraging the family not to change.
- ordeal—an unpleasant task that the client must perform whenever a symptom occurs.

In restraining, you can directly tell the family that you believe that the family is not ready to move on and just say, "I do not think you guys are ready and we need to slow things down." An ordeal could be used when an argumentative father dislikes his grandmother and must buy an expensive gift every time he gets into an argument with her. Here the continued unhealthy behavior of yelling rewards the person that he does not want to show kindness to. Both directive and non-directive methods can be applied. The social worker tests the readiness of the family to cooperate as well as its willingness to engage in the therapy process. When the family is ready to accept direct suggestions, then paradoxical directives will no longer need to be used.

IMPLEMENTING THE MODEL

In strategic family therapy, you the social worker are the problem-solver and solution-finder. The practitioner is the referee and coach and is actively involved in the game versus acting like a spectator passively observing the action playing out. Once again, the goal is not to focus on where or how the problems started, but rather just address the issue at the present time. The practitioner needs to be actively involved and responsible in helping the family to turn their lives around by helping them strategically plan, execute, and measure outcomes. Haley outlined five integral stages that all strategic therapists implement:

- identify solvable problems
- set goals
- design interventions to achieve those goals
- examine the responses
- examine the outcome of the therapy

The work is planned and divided into consecutive stages and moving from one stage to another is only possible after the goal from the previous stage is achieved.

HAVING CONTACT WITH THE FAMILY

Strategic family therapy starts when the contact with the family is established. The practitioner will focus on each person present during the session, and one by one hear what each individual sees as the problem regarding the family. Also the question will be asked to each person present, "What is the goal of therapy in your opinion?" and the social worker can use that information to try to understand each individual perspective to the problem. It is important during this time to build a supportive atmosphere as well as make sure that full cooperation among all family members is taking place. If there are any disputes during the processing, it allows permission for the dynamic to play out because the therapist will be able to see the unhealthy family dynamic as a whole. This process is building the balance between engaging and being part of the family, as well as establishing your authority as the therapist.

DIAGNOSING THE FAMILY

Diagnosing refers to understanding and presenting the problem in relation to a system versus addressing each individual. It involves describing dysfunctional interaction sequences within a family and determining the rules responsible for such sequences. At this point, you would look at the different subsystems that include the spouse, parent, and sibling systems. At the same time it would be important to identify if the family is running under a generic or idiosyncratic hierarchy and look at the overall boundaries in the family, identifying if they are clear, diffuse, or enmeshed. From here, a hypothesis is formed, defining the systemic function of the symptom and the overall problem. Here both the problem and the goal of the therapy are defined in detail. The goals need to be precise, described in simple language so the family can understand, and most importantly, achievable. It is recommended to make a quick diagnosis which will cover the initial and then usually after the second meeting with the family professional jargon is avoided and the social worker neither interprets nor educates parents on how they should behave in their roles. The social worker should formulate the diagnosis in cooperation with a therapeutic team and in the very least with supervision. Supervision is the key element here, in particular if the therapist works with a family individually. In larger therapeutic teams, it is possible to work while consulting with other staff who are either able to observe or get information during the consultation.

PRESENTING THE STRATEGIC FAMILY THERAPY PLAN

At this point, your job as the social worker is to present the plan to the family. Directives refer to new behaviors and those behaviors need to be understood by each family member. The social worker should clearly explain all directives to the family, so the transition of cooperation and implementation becomes easier. A good rule of thumb is to address the overall family hierarchy first, then address the family subsystems next, and then address boundaries. Addressing family hierarchy first helps in making sure that the parents are respected as the parental figures and a generic system is in place. From there, the social worker then plans to fix each family subsystem and then the boundaries between individual relationships. Also, if there is great resistance, the use of paradoxical directives can be assigned to address any family pathology. It is vital that the social worker is creating and practicing the strategy of behavior change within the family during the therapy sessions. The practitioner encourages undertaking new activities during therapeutic sessions and, in particular, practicing the recommended tasks between consecutive sessions. It is vital that the social worker observes the changes or the lack thereof and provides adequate modifications of directives in order to build cooperation aimed at achieving the previously set goals. It is important to note that any lack of changes within the family is not considered a resistance or failure, but rather as feedback for the therapist to modify the strategy and find a way to enhance the family's motivation.

VIGNETTE

The Johnson family comes in to see you for family therapy services. There is the father Michael, the wife Sue, their oldest daughter Lisa, and their younger son, Russell. When each person was asked what is bringing everyone to therapy, Michael responds first, "My daughter Lisa has a mouth and complains about everything and she causes so many problems in our family." The wife, Sue, then chimes in, "Oh Michael, you don't mean that, and Lisa, you and I will be meeting your friends for coffee, right? I can come?" At that point Lisa shares, "My mom wants to be best friends with me and my father goes out and drinks all night and wants us to respect him at home. I just want a normal family." Russell then adds, "Lisa, you always stir the pot. Dad is doing his best and everything is not as bad as you make it seem." Sue jumps in and says, "You two are both right, and Russell, you are going to do your homework after this, right?" Russell responds, "Shut up, mom! I will do what I want." Sue looks to Michael and he begins laughing saying, "Russell is just being Russell and that was funny."

ASSESSMENT

We will be combining both components of structural and strategic family therapy models to address this situation with the Johnson family.

When looking at their dynamic during the conversation in therapy, Michael appears to have a drinking problem, appears to be the authority figure in the family but is not really engaged in parenting his children nor being a spouse to his wife. The wife Sue seems to enable Michael and his lack of responsibilities as well as enabling his drinking, and tries to be best friends with both her kids. Russell appears to have a close relationship with his father and has respect for him, but clearly has no respect for his mother Sue. The way that he talked back to her was unacceptable and shows the lack of authority Sue has over her kids. And finally Lisa appears to have very high differentiation and has great insight into the family problems. She would be a good resource in the therapy process because her insights appear to be spot on.

FAMILY SYSTEM

In relation to the family system, the family is not running under a generic hierarchy but under an idiosyncratic system. The children, Lisa and Russell, have little respect for the parental authority in the house, and it is evident by the fact that Sue is acting like she is afraid of her children and trying to be friends with them, and Michael is enabling the children when she is being insulted by them. During the family therapy session, it will be important to work with both Michael and Sue to help establish a generic hierarchy in their home.

FAMILY SUBSYSTEM

In looking at each subsystem, it will be important to address the problems in each:

spouse subsystem—The relationship between Michael and Sue appears to need work. Michael has a drinking problem and there is a lot of enabling by the wife, Sue. It would be important to have Sue become more differentiated and really get her opinion and thoughts about their dynamic as husband and wife.

parental subsystem—As parents, Sue is trying to be best friends with her kids, and Michael appears to not be that involved. Michael even laughed when their son talked back to Sue and did not show her any support as a parental figure. It would be important to explore each parent relationship and address the boundary issues that are involved in each relationship.

sibling subsystem—The relationship between Lisa and Russell appears strained and it would be important to strengthen that bond. Lisa has issues with both her father and mother, and Russell appears very close to the dad but not to the mother. It would be important to allow Lisa's perspective to be shared as well as to get down to what Russell is feeling versus just trying to please his father.

FAMILY BOUNDARIES

In looking at the boundaries, it would be important to look at each relationship dynamic:

Michael and Sue—There appears to be no clear boundaries between the two and just with the given information, they seem to be too enmeshed. They will need to work on having clearer boundaries both in their marriage and their role as parents.

Michael and Lisa—In this father-daughter dynamic, the relationship is disengaged. Lisa does not really engage with her father and the same goes for Michael, who uses her as the scapegoat to the family problems.

It would be important to establish clear boundaries by Michael being more of a parent to Lisa and through that process, Lisa having a voice and establishing respect for her dad.

Sue and Lisa—Here Sue is too enmeshed with her daughter Lisa. She is treating her like she is her best friend versus being her mother. There are no boundaries as Sue is trying to hang out with Lisa's friends and Lisa is the one dictating the terms of their relationship. It would be important to establish clear boundaries in this relationship dynamic

Michael and Russell—In this father-son dynamic, they appear to be too enmeshed. Russell seems to have great respect for his father but Michael appears to not be doing his job parenting his kids and showing support to his wife when she is trying to enforce rules. The enmeshed relationship is leading to the disengaged relationship with Lisa. Clearer boundaries here can assist Michael in improving both relationships.

Sue and Russell—In this mother-son dynamic, there is a definite disengagement. Russell has no respect for his mother. Sue is overly involved and enmeshed with Lisa and she is completely disengaged from Russell, which may be the reason why he is acting out and treating her with disrespect. If Sue can establish clearer boundaries in both dynamics, and Russell can show more respect to his mother, the dynamic can improve.

Lisa and Russell—This brother-sister dynamic appears to be disengaged, and as Haley pointed out, same-generational relationships are vital to the success of the family. Both siblings are involved in trans-generational relationships with their parents that should be taking place with each other. As each subsystem is addressed and there is a restoring of the generic hierarchy, as well as improvement in the family subsystems, a healthier relationship can be formed between the sister and brother.

REFERENCES

Ainsworth, M. D. S., Blehar, M. C., Waters, E., & Wall, S. Patterns of attachment: A psychological study of the strange situation. Hillsdale, NJ: Erlbaum; 1978.

Aponte, H. J., & VanDeusen, J. M. (1981). Structural family therapy. In A. S. Gurman & D. P. Kniskern (Eds.), *Handbook of family therapy* (pp. 310–360). New York: BrunnerIMazel, Inc.

Beck, A. T. (2005). The current state of cognitive therapy: a 40-year retrospective. *Archives of General Psychiatry, 62,* 953–959.

Beck, J. S. (2005). Cognitive therapy for challenging problems: What to do when the basics don't work. New York: Guilford Press.

Beck, J. S. (2011). *Cognitive behavioral therapy basics and beyond.* New York: The Guilford Press.

Benson, L. A., McGinn, M. M., & Christensen, A. (2012). Common principles of couple therapy. Behavior Therapy, 43(1), 25–35.

Berg, I. K., & Dolan, Y. (2001). Tales of solutions: A collection of hope-inspiring stories. New York: Norton.

Bowlby, J. (1969). Attachment. Attachment and loss: Vol. 1. Loss. New York: Basic Books; 1969.

Clinpsy Organization (2018). Transference and countertransference. Retrieved from: https://www.clinpsy.org.uk/forum/viewtopic.php?t=1979

Colapinto, J. (1982). Structural family therapy. In A. M. Horne & M. M. Ohlsen (Eds.), *Family counseling and therapy* (pp. 112–140). Illinois: F. E. Peacock Publishers, Inc.

Corey, G. (2001). *Theory and practice of counseling and psychotherapy* (6th ed.). Pacific Grove, CA: Brooks/Cole Publishing Co.

Carter, E. & McGoldrick, M., (Eds.) (1988). *The changing family life cycle* (2nd ed.). NY: Gardner Press.

Davidson, R. (1994). Can psychology make sense of change? In G. Edwards & M. Lader, M. (Eds.) *Addiction: processes of change (Society for the Study of Addiction Monograph No. 3)*. New York: Oxford University Press.

Family System Institute (2018). Bowen family systems theory and practice: illustration and critique. Retrieved from: http://www.thefsi.com.au/wp-content/uploads/2014/01/Bowen-Family-Systems-Theory-and-Practice_Illustration-and-Critique.pdf

Friesen, J. D. (1995). Theories and approaches to family counseling. *International Journal for the Advancement of Counseling*, 18, 3–10.

Freud, A. (1937). *The Ego and the mechanisms of defense*, London: Hogarth Press and Institute of Psycho-Analysis.

Freud, S. (1909). Notes upon a case of obsessional neurosis. In Standard edition (Vol. 10, pp. 153–249).

Freud, S. (1915). The unconscious. SE, 14: 159–204.

Gladding, S. T. (1998b). Working with single-parent families. In S.T.

Gladding, S. T. *Family therapy: history, theory and practice* (pp. 209–228). New York: Prentice-Hall Inc.

Haley, J. (1990). Why not long-term therapy? In J. K Zeig & S. G. Gilligan (Eds), *Brief therapy: myths, methods and metaphors* (pp. 3–17). N.Y: Brunner/Mazel, Inc.

Heather, N. (1994). Brief interventions on the world map. *Addiction, 89*(6),665–667.

Heather, N. (1995). Interpreting the evidence on brief interventions for excessive drinkers: the need for caution. *Alcohol and Alcoholism, 30*(3), 287–296.

Kerr, M., & Bowen, M. (1988). family evaluation: an approach based on Bowen theory. NY: Norton.

Krampe, E. M. (2003). The inner father. *Fathering, 1*(2), 131.

Langa, M. (2016). The value of using a psychodynamic theory in researching black masculinities of adolescent boys in Alexandra Township, South Africa. *Men and Masculinities, 19*(3), 260–288.

Lester, D. (1997). Toward a system theory of the mind. *Journal of the Royal Anthropological Institute*, 3, 1392–1394.

Linehan, M. M. (2014). *DBT skills training manual, second edition*. New York: Guilford Press.

Miller, W. R., & Rollnick, S. (1991). *Motivational interviewing: preparing people to change addictive behavior*. New York: Guilford Press.

Minuchin, S. (1974). *Families and family therapy*. Cambridge, MA: Harvard University Press.

Minuchin, S., & Fishman, H. C. (1981). *Family therapy techniques*. Cambridge, MA: Harvard University Press.

Minuchin, S., & Nichols, M. P. (1993). *Family healings: tales of hope and renewal from family therapy*. New York: The Free Press.

Nichols, M. P., & Minuchin, S. (1999). Short-term structural family therapy with couples. In J. M. Donovan (Ed.), *Short-term couple therapy* (pp. 124–143). New York: Guilford Press.

Rollnick, S., & Miller, W. R. (1995). What is motivational interviewing? *Behavioral and cognitive psychotherapy*, 23, 325–334.

Schaffer, H. R., & Emerson, P. E. (1964). The development of social attachments in infancy. *Monographs of the Society for Research in Child Development*, 29, 94.

Toman, W. (1976). *Family constellation* (3rd rev. ed.). NY: Springer. (Original work published 1961).

Trepper, T. S., McCollum, E. E., De Jong, P., Korman, H., Gingerich, W. J., & Franklin, C. (2012). Solution-focused brief therapy treatment manual. In C. Franklin, T. S. Trepper, W. J. Gingerich, & E. E. McCollum (Eds.), *Solution-focused brief therapy: A handbook of evidence-based practice* (pp. 20–36). New York, NY: Oxford University Press.

Vetere, A. (2001). Structural family therapy. *Child and Adolescent Mental Health, 6*(3), 133—139.

Wilson, T. D. (2004). *Strangers to ourselves*. Harvard University Press.

Your Mindful Compass (2018). Murray Bowen, M.D. and the nine concepts in family systems theory. Retrieved from: https://yourmindfulcompass.com/about/dr-bowen/

Ziegler, D. (2016). Defense mechanisms in rational emotive cognitive behavior therapy personality theory. *Journal of Rational-Emotive & Cognitive-Behavior Therapy, 34*(2), 135–148.

CHAPTER 10

The End-Stage of Treatment

THE LATE STAGE

The *late stage* follows the middle stage and represents the transition stage into the termination phase or end stage of treatment. There are four important aspects in this stage which need to be consolidated to ensure positive therapeutic results. The aspects are:

- The reduction or elimination of the symptoms for which the client came into treatment
- The grief process of mourning and acknowledging the mixed emotions of positive and negative emotions as the therapeutic process is coming to an end
- The identification and acknowledgment of how old negative patterns of behavior have been replaced with positive behaviors and discussing how the client has been able to achieve and maintain these behaviors
- The discussion of creating an action plan to ensure that the client will continue to maintain and sustain these positive behaviors

There is a definite overlap in relation to the goals of the late stage and termination stage, however the late stage prepares the client for termination, while the termination stage hands over responsibility completely for the client to continue on to maintain. The distinction will be more clear as the chapter moves on.

THE THREE TYPES OF TERMINATION

Termination simply means that the therapeutic relationship has come to an end. Ideally, it would be that the client has successfully completed treatment but oftentimes that is not the case. There are basically three types of termination that can take place when working with a client:

- termination by mutual agreement

- social worker-initiated termination
- client-initiated termination

TERMINATION BY MUTUAL AGREEMENT

Termination reflects in the best scenario the end of treatment because the client has accomplished the said goals outlined during the therapeutic process, and is ready to move on without the assistance of the therapist. The termination stage by mutual agreement implies that the social worker and the client recognize the maturity and autonomous nature of the client at this stage. This is the stage where there is a positive transference of emotions elicited from the client, a dominance of positive behaviors are formed through the client's own independence, and overall unhealthy coping skills are no longer being enacted to help the client deal with their life. If successful and mutually agreed upon, the client becomes aware of their own strengths and realizes that they are able to deal with their own life independent from the social worker.

SOCIAL WORKER-INITIATED TERMINATION

The social worker may initiate termination because the needs of the client may be out of the scope of practice, or the overall level of competence to implement treatment is not available. If a social worker continues to implement treatment under these circumstances, this can lead to greater stress on the practitioner, and could possibly cause severe harm to the client during the course of continued treatment. Even if the client feels like progress is taking place under these circumstances, the practitioner still has the right to terminate treatment. There may also be other range of issues that may result in the social worker initiating treatment termination such as:

- a planned retirement from practice
- a leave of absence for personal reasons
- Being trainee or intern and the therapeutic relationship is coming to an end
- If the social worker is in eminent danger for example being stalked or assaulted due to the therapeutic relationship

It is important that if you are terminating services with your client, to make sure that the client does not feel abandoned and that continuity of care is ensured to make the transition as smooth as possible.

CLIENT-INITIATED TERMINATION

There may be many reasons why the client may initiate termination with a social worker. The client may have *fiduciary* issues and lose the ability to continue paying for treatment due to:

- loss of employment and no longer being able to pay
- loss of health insurance coverage
- changes in the client's financial situation due to other personal issues

There may be also life issues that take place with the client such as:

- moving to another area due to a job transfer
- going to retire
- employment opportunity in another area

There may be a multitude of reasons why a client may initiate termination with you. One very important reason to explore is that the client may not be satisfied with the progress that is taking place during the therapeutic process. There may be a discourse in relation to the client's needs and the therapy model that is being used by the practitioner. In this case, the client may want to seek out other services and may just drop out of treatment all together without any follow-up. Regardless of how termination takes place, it is important to make sure to handle this process ethically making sure that you are advocating and seeking out the best interest of the client.

NASW AND THE TERMINATION STAGE

In the NASW Code of Ethics (2017), 1.17 Termination of Services states[*]:

> (a) Social workers should terminate services to clients and professional relationships with them when such services and relationships are no longer required or no longer serve the clients' needs or interests.

> (b) Social workers should take reasonable steps to avoid abandoning clients who are still in need of services. Social workers should withdraw services precipitously only under unusual circumstances, giving careful consideration to all factors in the situation and taking care to minimize possible adverse effects. Social workers should assist in making

[*]   National Association of Social Workers, Code of Ethics. Copyright © 2017 by National Association of Social Workers, Inc. Reprinted with permission.

appropriate arrangements for continuation of services when necessary.

As stated in section (b) regarding termination, *abandonment* can occur when treatment ends prematurely for any number of reasons. For example, the client may no longer be able to afford services, or simply because the client's treatment goals are not being met, the client decides to abandon treatment all together. It would be beneficial to take the necessary precautions to avoid abandonment from occurring by planning and working through a comprehensive termination process with the client. This would include identifying and combining the positive outcomes and lessons that were learned during therapy, and helping the client to utilize those skills moving forward. During a successful termination process, a client should be able to:

- identify the positive outcomes that have taken place during treatment
- have discussions about the therapeutic relationship itself and how that has translated and affected their relationships in the outside world
- discuss how the client is going to use what was learned in therapy on his/her own

A successful termination will prepare the client to venture out without the assistance of the practitioner and continue to thrive. There should be positive feelings from both the social worker and the client as the treatment comes successfully to a close. Conversely, abandonment can lead to feelings of anxiety, confusion, and sadness from both parties, because the desired effects of treatment did not take place. Abandonment does not lead to a sense of closure, and often leaves the client in a state of limbo, because it is unclear what the client needs to do moving forward. As a social worker, ensure that abandonment does not take place for the client, and that continuity of care is maintained as much as possible.

MEETING THE CLINICAL, ETHICAL, AND LEGAL OBLIGATIONS OF TERMINATION

As social workers and practitioners, it is important to know that you are not obligated to provide continued treatment to a client if you feel that in your clinical judgment, it is not to the client's benefit. This does not fit under the category of abandonment because you are not just leaving the client high and dry, but rather you are ethically and legally advocating for your client. In the landmark rulings of *Capps v. Valk* (1962) and *Collins v. Meeker* (1967), the rulings made clear that health professionals do not have an obligation to continue treating a client if professionally it is deemed that doing so is not in the best interest of the client. Even if the client feels that the therapeutic process has been beneficial, it does not supersede the judgment of the practitioner. It is important to understand the legal and ethical guidelines regarding termination, especially when making decisions that can be difficult such as making the decision to end treatment. As is stated in the ruling of *Capps v. Valk*:

> If a [health professional] abandons a case without giving his patient such notice and opportunity to procure the services of another [health professional], his conduct may subject him to the consequences and liability resulting from abandonment of the case. (p. 290)

RECOMMENDATIONS FOR ETHICAL PRACTICE

It is important to provide ethical practice when you are terminating with a client. As far as maintaining ethical standards during this process, it is suggested to:

HAVE DISCUSSIONS ABOUT THE TERMINATION PROCESS WITH YOUR CLIENT

The discussions should begin early in the initial session as you are going through informed consent, and continue on throughout the therapeutic process. It would be important to make sure that the client does not feel like you are trying to end the relationship quickly, but rather, you are approaching this topic in an ethical manner and for their benefit. It would also be important to discuss when treatment could be interrupted such as in case of emergencies or when taking a vacation.

GO OVER PRACTICE AND POLICY PROCEDURES RELATED TO YOUR WORKPLACE

Ideally, there would be a brochure that would provide all policies and procedures that could be handed to the client so that it is readily accessible to the client when needed. Regardless, it is important to discuss all pertinent issues that could directly affect the client, which could include what would happen if you decided to leave your current place of work.

DOCUMENT IN YOUR NOTES TREATMENT GOALS AND OUTCOMES

This allows you to chart and monitor the progress of the client and it also creates a direct focus in relation to treatment. This is also important regarding the termination process, because if it ever comes up where you feel that ethically your service is not benefiting the client, you have the documentation to justify your decision to end treatment.

CONSULT

It is vital for you to consult with your colleagues, supervisor, or anyone who can offer you assistance when needed. Especially when it comes to the termination process, getting feedback and having as much information as possible from trusted sources, will only help you in your decision-making process.

HAVE APPROPRIATE REFERRALS AVAILABLE THAT MEET CLIENT NEEDS

If treatment needs to be terminated early with the client still having ongoing needs, it would be important to discuss this openly with the client and offer appropriate referrals to the client. It would also be important to provide a reasonable time period for the client to make contact with and arrange for treatment with another therapist. It would be important to document all of these discussions and actions throughout this whole process.

ATTEMPT TO CONTACT THE CLIENT IF A DROPOUT OF TREATMENT OCCURS

If a client drops out of treatment, it is important to just accept the decision, especially if you feel that ongoing treatment is still needed for the client. It would be beneficial to make an attempt to reach the client and if possible, have a discussion about why the client has stopped coming to treatment. If contact cannot be made, a letter should be mailed out discussing the fact that the client has not been coming to treatment, and offering other referrals that the client can also seek out. Termination should be something that is planned and hopefully mutual, but regardless of how treatment ends, it is important for the practitioner to address the situation ethically. Although the word suggests an ending, termination really is the start of a new beginning for the client. It addresses that the client is once again in charge of their own world without the weekly check-in with the social worker. And though this may feel scary or sad to the client, it marks another stage or transition in the client's life.

IMPLEMENTING THE TERMINATION PHASE OF TREATMENT

As the client transitions from the late stage to the termination stage, it is important to make sure that all areas are addressed so that proper closure for the client can take place. The three interventions of the therapist during this stage are:

- the transferring of the client role and responsibility of utilizing the teachings and methods learned in the therapeutic relationship
- the handing over of permission for the patient to develop their own life and to act upon what was learned throughout the therapy process
- the acknowledgment of the client's autonomy, and the freedom to pursue the life that he/she wants to live

During this transfer of responsibility, it is important to make sure that the client is as prepared as possible, so use these sessions to cover the potential troubles and pitfalls that may occur.

FOCUSING ON WHAT WORKED FOR THE CLIENT

When you are focusing on what worked for the client throughout therapy, it is important to just simply ask, "How did this work out for you?" More specifically, it can be broken down into the following questions:

- What were the cognitive skills you learned?
- What were the behavioral skills you learned?
- What were the interpersonal skills you learned?

In asking these specific questions, you are specifically focusing on the cognitive structures where success took place, the specific behaviors that were effective, and the client's own understanding of self. This is a comprehensive review and understanding of what it took for the client to have reached their personal level of success.

ADDRESSING FUTURE STRESSFUL SITUATIONS

In addressing potential pitfalls for the client, it is helpful to have the client think about and make a list of the situations that are likely to arise in the future that may exacerbate symptoms and result in the client possibly falling back. You can ask the client the following questions:

- What kinds of potential stressful situations might you experience that would send your thoughts and emotions into a deep spiral?
- How will future stressful situations be handled if it goes bad?
- Knowing what works for you, how can you address these situations in a healthy way?

In going through this list and going through how things can go bad or good, the client is practicing and preparing in advance, and is taking full responsibility for their ability to handle stressful events in the future.

CREATING AN EMERGENCY PLAN WHEN THE CLIENT HITS A LOW

It is important to encourage your client to talk about potential dangers meaning when the client hits a low. This can often happen even if the client is giving their best effort—still, a diminishing of overall functioning and mood occurs. It is important here to work out a plan of what to do and who to call, to help deal with that possibility. This may occur even though the client is implementing all of the right strategies learned in therapy, but still the client is overcome with intense distress. That sometimes happens, despite our best efforts. For example, people may become overwhelmed by one very big negative event like the death of a loved one, or by a series of negative events all happening at once and making it difficult to cope. This can happen to anyone.

It can also be due to events out of one's control, as I had a client who suffered from bipolar disorder, and just because of the cycles of her mood, she would hit a low regardless of what was taking place in her life. When she sensed that her mood was shifting to a depressed state, we created an emergency plan for her that included having her favorite comedies and movies that she would watch immediately, as well as having comfort food like ice cream available to her. She also had her best friend, who knew to come over and help her process, as well as set up an immediate follow-up session with me. And even though she did not feel like it during those times, she would also hit the gym with her best friend, and in doing so over the few days when the symptoms came, it greatly reduced her depressive episodes. It is important that clients think back to their most recent bouts of struggle and try to remember what their triggers were when the symptoms come. Helping your client make a list of the symptoms that they would consider to be their signal that they are going to hit a low is helpful. This way they can notice them right away and make immediate plans for constructive action.

DEVELOPING THE FINAL PLAN

The final aspect is to develop a comprehensive plan that will help the client make the transition as the therapeutic relationship comes to an end. In using the late and termination stages of treatment, the client should feel confident about how to handle the difficulties that they will need to face moving forward. It is also recommended that therapy ends in a gradual and systematic way. The final few sessions could be spaced out biweekly or possibly monthly in order for the client to begin to disengage from the therapeutic relationship. This can help the client to establish greater independence and use the tools learned in therapy to combat any uncomfortable feelings that emerge. Also when having your last session, it is good to set up a future session so that the client can check in and discuss the progress and the transition that they are making.

The follow-up session can be set up about one to two months after the final therapy session has ended. During the final sessions, it is encouraged by the social worker to discuss with the client:

- what the ending of therapy means to that person
- their ideas about what was more helpful and what was less helpful during treatment
- their feelings about the therapist as a person

Talking directly about these issues helps to create a more positive ending, and will give the client a sense of closure that is very important. Another topic that may come up at this point in time is whether or not the client should continue with another professional therapist or perhaps join a self-help group or a support group as the termination process reaches its end. In the least, during the termination stage, client contacts that include friends and family members should be addressed in relation to who the client can reach out to. These are all important issues that should be addressed honestly and thoroughly throughout this phase of treatment. There are no general guidelines that are appropriate for all clients; however, individual needs should be addressed.

VIGNETTE

Below is a vignette from Chapter 9 and it will be used to implement the late and termination stage with the client over the next seven sessions.

> **VIGNETTE**
>
> Paul, age 40, comes in and shares,"I suffer from a lot of anxiety and I always feel on edge." The Ct states that he has come in because "recently I interviewed for a job that I really wanted and I was not offered the job." He adds, "I always fail and things never really work out for me." The Ct adds,"other people do not really understand me and because I am so different, I cannot really relate to people." The Ct currently lives in an apartment by himself, but he shares, "I need to find a job fast because my savings is dwindling down." He adds that "I am good for about four more months, and after that I will be on the street." Paul states that he has two good friends and "I have a pretty good relationship with my family" but "like I said, I am so different from others that I cannot really be understood. I can tell that people do not really like me. I am very intuitive and I can feel things a lot of times." Paul adds that "Wherever I go, I always feel like I am at the mercy of others." He adds that he drinks about three times a week having about 4–6 beers when he goes out.

THE LATE STAGE

SESSION 1

In the first session with the client we are going to cover two of the four aspects that are related to the late stage of treatment. In doing so, we are covering the beginning stage of treatment and the initial treatment plan that was provided. The aspects that are to be covered will be:

- the reduction or elimination of the symptoms for which the client came into treatment
- the grief process of mourning and acknowledging the mixed positive and negative emotions as the therapeutic process is coming to an end

In addressing the reduction or elimination of the symptoms for which the client came into treatment, we would look at the diagnosis and treatment plan for the client. For Paul he was diagnosed with Generalized Anxiety Disorder and his initial treatment plan during the beginning stage was:

- refer for crisis intervention services if needed
- provide a referral for medical check-up
- provide a referral to a psychiatrist for a medication evaluation
- referral for alcohol treatment centers as well as AA
- provide individual counseling to the client on a weekly basis
- provide a referral for employment services as well as to the employment benefit services

In looking at Paul's progress up to this point:

Dx Generalized Anxiety Disorder

The client initially scaled his anxiety from 0–10 being a 9, to now currently being a 2 or 3.

Treatment Plan

Refer for crisis intervention services if needed

The client did not need crisis intervention services throughout the therapy process.

Provide a referral for medical check-up

The client has improved his overall health, being more physically active and reducing his alcohol intake.

Provide a referral to a psychiatrist for a medication evaluation

The client was provided the referral but decided to try without medications and he shares that he is doing fine.

Referral for alcohol treatment centers as well as AA

The client is continuing to attend AA meetings and shares that it is helping stay clean and sober.

Provide individual counseling to the client on a weekly basis

The client has been compliant throughout treatment and has had success during the therapeutic process.

Provide a referral for employment services as well as to the employment benefit services

The client was able to find a new job and states that he is enjoying his new place of work.

The second part of the session would be addressing the grief process of mourning and acknowledging the mixed positive and negative emotions as the therapeutic process is coming to an end. After reviewing the success of the beginning stage of treatment and how the client has succeeded, it would be allowing the client to process and mourn as the therapy transitions towards the end. The client Paul shared:

"I am really happy that I have come so far and I am very proud of myself, but at the same time, I am so sad because it feels like this chapter of my life is coming to a close. I am scared and excited as I move forward on my own."

SESSION 2

In the second session with Paul, we would cover the last two components of the late stage, which will also help the transition into the termination stage of treatment. The last two late-stage goals are:

- the identification and acknowledgment of how old negative patterns of behavior have been replaced with positive behaviors and discussing how the client has been able to achieve and maintain these behaviors

- the discussion of creating an action plan to ensure that the client will continue to maintain and sustain these positive behaviors

In the identification and acknowledgment of how old negative patterns of behavior have been replaced with positive behaviors and discussing how the client has been able to achieve and maintain these behaviors, it would be important to look at what took place during the middle stage of treatment. Here were three examples of statements made by the client when implementing CBT:

Client statement

"I suffer from a lot of anxiety and I always feel on edge."

Cognitive distortion

- all-or-nothing thinking

Client statement

"I always fail and things never really work out for me."

Cognitive distortions

- all-or-nothing thinking
- catastrophizing
- overgeneralizing

Client statement

"Other people do not really understand me and because I am so different, I cannot really relate to people."

Cognitive distortions

- blaming
- labeling
- mental filtering

In reviewing the cognitive distortions that the client has engaged in, it would be important to review what effect that had on the client's overall well-being, and how the client was able to reframe and rationally make sense of what he was doing. The client in examining his irrational state-ments was able to develop healthier coping skills that included:

- being more rational and knowing that all situations are not all-or-nothing where his self-worth is always on the line
- recognizing that even though he feels like he is not successful, he has accomplished a lot in his life and many aspects of his life have worked out for him
- acknowledging his similarities to other people in that he wants to be understood and wants to connect with other people
- being more open-minded by recognizing that focusing just on the negatives is not a realistic way of looking at his life

The next stage in the session would then address the discussion of cre-ating an action plan to ensure that the client will continue to maintain and sustain these positive behaviors. It is important to note that the discussion takes place here and that the specifics of how to maintain will be addressed in the termination stage. In the late stages, the social worker here is estab-lishing the dialogue as the review of all of the successes the client has made is being done from the beginning and middle stages of treatment.

THE TERMINATION STAGE

SESSION 3

In the third session, here you would address the first portion of the termi-nation stage which is the transferring of the client role and responsibility of utilizing the teachings and methods learned in the therapeutic relation-ship. More specifically we would address focusing on what worked for the client. The following questions can be asked:

How did this work out for you?

> *The client shared that he learned all of his irrational thoughts, and how they lead to his feelings and his behaviors of inaction*

What were the cognitive skills you have learned?

> *The client learned to challenge all irrational thoughts and to use rational questioning whenever he feels anxiety or feels overwhelmed in general. The client uses the cognitive reframe of anxiety of "What I resist will persist and what I embrace will erase."*

What were the behavioral skills you have learned?

The client substituted avoiding situations and not engaging in anxiety-provoking activities with pre-planning his anxiety and reframing anxiety to mean action. The client now engages in a behavior whenever he feels anxiety.

What were the interpersonal skills you have learned?

The client, instead of avoiding and isolating himself whenever he feels anxiety, now seeks out support by reaching out to his friends and engaging in healthier coping skills that include exercise. The client is also not using alcohol as a crutch to reduce his anxiety symptoms.

SESSION 4

In this session, the social worker would address the next intervention, which is the handing over of permission for the patient to develop their own life and to act upon what was learned throughout the therapy process. Here the focus would be on addressing future stressful situations that may occur for the client. You can ask the client the following questions:

What kinds of potential stressful situations might you experience that would send your thoughts and emotions into a deep spiral?

The clients shared that his list of possible concerns are:

- dating
- issues involving his family
- interviewing for his desired job
- taking a public speaking class to address his desire to be a presenter in relation to his job

How will future stressful situations be handled if it goes bad?

The client acknowledges that he will avoid situations and then go into all of his unhealthy coping skills that include:

- all-or-nothing thinking
- overgeneralizing
- a negative mental filter
- blaming

Knowing that you know what works for you, how can you address these situations in a healthy way?

The client shared that even though things may not turn out the way that he want, it is not the end of the world and that life still moves forward. The client also shared that instead of not admitting his fears, that he will be open about them and deal with them in a healthy way. His greatest anxiety is dating and going after his desired career path.

SESSION 5

The fifth session would focus on the intervention of the acknowledgment of the client's autonomy, and the freedom to pursue the life that he wants to live. As the client takes the responsibility of moving forward, discuss creating an emergency plan when the client hits a low. The client described what hitting a low means:

The client shared that he would begin isolating himself, avoid all anxiety-provoking situations, act out towards his good friends, and then begin drinking in excess because he feels overwhelmed.

The client acknowledged that this low can happen and that signs include spending excessive time alone in his apartment. His immediate plan will be:

To seek out his friends and talk about what is going on his life. The client will also contact his sponsor in AA and not resort to drinking, and if necessary, the client will reach out and set up an appointment with the social worker.

SESSION 6

In this session the focus would be on developing the finalized plan for the client. As stated before, the final aspect is to develop a comprehensive plan that will help the client make the transition as the therapeutic relationship comes to an end. At this point a review of what has been summarized from the previous session can all be combined and put together.

PAUL'S FINALIZED TREATMENT PLAN

COGNITIVE SKILLS LEARNED

The client learned to challenge all irrational thoughts and to use rational questioning whenever he feels anxiety or feels overwhelmed in general. The client uses the cognitive reframe of anxiety of "What I resist will persist and what I embrace will erase."

BEHAVIORAL SKILLS LEARNED

The client substituted avoiding situations and not engaging in anxiety-provoking activities to pre-planning his anxiety and reframing anxiety to mean action. The client now engages in a behavior whenever he feels anxiety.

INTERPERSONAL SKILLS LEARNED

The client, instead of avoiding and isolating himself whenever he feels anxiety, now seeks out support by reaching out to his friends and engaging in healthier coping skills that include exercise. The client is also not using alcohol as a crutch to reduce his anxiety symptoms.

Potential stressful situations

The clients shared that his list of possible concerns are:

- Dating
- Issues involving his family
- Interviewing for his desired job
- Taking a public speaking class to address his desire to be a presenter in relation to his job

Negative coping skills to avoid

The client acknowledges that he will avoid situations and then go into all of his unhealthy coping skills that include:

- all-or-nothing thinking
- overgeneralizing
- a negative mental filter
- blaming

Healthy coping skills

- Use the cognitive reframe "What I resist will persist and what I embrace will erase."
- His self-worth is not defined by situations but by who he is as a person
- The client will embrace his fears and engage in action whenever he feels any anxiety
- The client will pursue his greatest fears of dating and pursing his dream job

Emergency plan

The client shared that instead of isolating himself by avoiding all anxiety-provoking situations, acting out towards his good friends, and then begin drinking in excess because he feels overwhelmed, he will instead engage in the following behaviors:

> To seek out his friends and talk about what is going on his life. The client will also contact his sponsor in AA and not resort to drinking, and if necessary, the client will reach out and set up an appointment with the social worker.

All of this would be reviewed and discussed before the close of this next to last session.

SESSION 7

This the final session would focus on the closure of the therapeutic process and allowing the client to mentally and emotionally come to terms that this is the last session. The focus on this session would be addressing:

- what the ending of therapy means to that person
- their ideas about what was more helpful and what was less helpful during treatment
- their feelings about the therapist as a person

In working with Paul, the following would be addressed in the final session:

WHAT THE ENDING OF THERAPY MEANS TO PAUL

The client shared that he is proud of all of the work that he had done, and that this is a sign of success that he no longer will be coming to treatment. The client shared that there is sadness because therapy was a stable aspect of his life, but that he fully accepts the responsibility of his well-being moving forward.

PAUL'S IDEA ABOUT WHAT WAS MORE HELPFUL AND WHAT WAS LESS HELPFUL DURING TREATMENT

The client shared that what helped him the most was redefining anxiety into an action response versus an avoiding response. The client added that he was thankful to be able to identify his negative coping skills and what he struggled with the most was trying to get out of his head. He defined that process as "paralysis through analysis."

PAUL'S FEELINGS ABOUT THE SOCIAL WORKER AS A PERSON

The client shared that he had positive feelings towards the social worker and that he was very appreciative of all of the work that has been done to improve his life. The client added that he felt very close to the therapist, similar to a friend, and that this experience has translated to him having better relationships outside of therapy.

This vignette is an overview of how to implement the late and termination stage of treatment when working with a client.

REFERENCES

Capps v. Valk, 369 P.2d 238 (Kan. 1962).

Collins v. Meeker, 424 P.2d 488 (1967).

NASW (2017) Code of Ethics of the National Association of Social Workers. Retrieved from: https://www.socialworkers.org/About/Ethics/Code-of-Ethics/Code-of-Ethics-English

Penn, L. S. (1990). When the therapist must leave: Forced termination of psychodynamic psychotherapy. *Professional Psychology: Research and Practice*, 21, 379–384.

Index

CPSIA information can be obtained
at www.ICGtesting.com
Printed in the USA
FSHW010548190122
87748FS